IGN�TE™
YOUR
WISDOM

Other international best-selling compilation books
by IGNITE for you to enjoy

———————

Ignite Your Life for Women

Ignite Your Female Leadership

Ignite Your Parenting

Ignite Your Life for Men

Ignite Your Life for Conscious Leaders

Ignite Your Adventurous Spirit

Ignite Your Health and Wellness

Ignite Female Change Makers

Ignite the Modern Goddess

Ignite Love

Ignite Happiness

Ignite Your Inner Spirit

Ignite The Entrepreneur

Ignite Possibilities

Ignite The Hunger In You

IGNITE™
YOUR
WISDOM

INTRODUCTION BY

JB Owen
Founder of Ignite and JBO Global Inc.

PROJECT LEADERS

Sarah Cross   Steph Elliott

Diana Lockett   Jo Dee Baer

ADDITIONAL FEATURED AUTHORS

ALESSANDRA C.L. PASUT • ALY INCARDONA • BARB LILLEY
CINDY TANK-MURPHY • DAVID SMALL • DR. ERIN SEPIC • DR. KERRY A. EGAN
JAMEECE PINCKNEY • JANE KILPATRICK • JANINE MAREK • JENNA HAJI
KATHERINE DAVIDSON • KATIE SMETHERMAN • LOREE J. KIM, PHD, ESQ.
MALISSIA WOODALL • MARLA FORD BALLARD • MARY STREETER • MARYANN SWAN
MELANIE SUMMERS • MICHELLE NORLIN • MIKA HEINONEN • NICOLE MIXDORF
PETER GIESIN • ROSEMARY FRENCH • SHARON EISTETTER • STACIE SHIFFLETT
STEPHANIE FABELA • TISH MEEHAN • VICTORIA RADER

PUBLISHED BY IGNITE AND PRINTED BY JBO GLOBAL INC.

Published and printed by JBO Global Inc.
5569-47ᵗʰ Street Red Deer, AB
Canada, T4N1S1 1-877-677-6115

Editor-in-Chief by JB Owen
Book and Cover design by Dania Zafar
Edited by Alex Blake, Michiko Couchman, Mimi Safiyah, and Sarah Clark
Designed in Canada, Printed in China
ISBN 978-1-7923-8763-0

First edition: April 2022

Ordering Information: Quantity sales. Special discounts are available on quantity purchases by corporations, associations, and others. For details, contact the publisher at the above address. Programs, products, or services provided by the authors are found by contacting them directly.

Dedications from our Project Leaders

This book is dedicated to our 90-year-old selves. To the stories, we create in our lives and the lessons we take from them. To the wisdom we hold in the journey. To the people who sprinkle our lives with joy and meaning. To the 90-year-old sitting in the rocking chair on the porch, who is saying, "Thanks for the dance, the courage, the awe, and wonder. Now is your time to create new stories, play with the miracle of life, and dream big, so I can sit in peace and savor the memories. Thank you for the light you brought to the world and the ripple you created."

Sarah Cross, Project Leader.

This book is dedicated to all the beautiful versions of YOU. To the parts of you that flowed through life with ease and grace and the parts of you that were called to embrace the uncertainty of life with profound love, courage, and the knowing that there is divine wisdom in it all. May you bask in the tender truth of each chapter and the wisdom of these writings that transcend time, experiences, and generations.

Diana Lockett, Chief Communications Officer, Ignite Publishing.

This book is dedicated to YOU. Wherever you may be in the world, may you take a piece of this book with you. May you learn from its knowledge and live in wisdom. May you Ignite your life, empower yourself, and pour love and light into humanity.

Steph Elliott, Project Coordinator

This book is dedicated to all our authors who were courageous enough to unearth their personal journeys and share their wisdom with the world. I thereby honor every reader who will benefit from this wisdom, will proceed to heal themselves, and pass this newfound wisdom on to others. A life well-lived is one where you immerse yourself in your personal journey and learn from the lessons along the way.

Dr. Jo Dee Baer, Project Leader

TESTIMONIALS FROM AUTHORS

This experience has been amazing. The quality of editors and the abundance of support has made this process truly one of a kind.

David Small

Working with the Ignite team to share my story has been transformational. It's a beautiful process on my healing journey. Thank you to the Ignite team and all the authors!

Steph Elliott

My Ignite experience has helped me to build my confidence as a writer. The support I received from JB and the editing team allowed me to bring my story to life while being held and guided by this amazing team. I am so grateful.

Mary Streeter

This is my second book with Ignite, and I loved every moment of the experience. The care and attention Ignite gives to both your story and you is unique and unforgettable. Ignite are masters in creating safe spaces and world-class mentoring. Each book is a collection of inspiring and touching stories and *Ignite Your Wisdom* will create a ripple effect of its own. Thank you to all the wonderful souls who made this possible.

Sarah Cross

I am glad I embraced the dark cavern of my past to entice this story to come to fruition. I would have never had the audacity to share it if not for the support and encouragement of the amazing Ignite team and process! I feel elated to share my wisdom and inspire others with a story whose time has come.

Malissia Woodall

Writing my story in the *Ignite Your Wisdom* book has been an enriching process. The talented publisher JB Owen and her very skilled team helped all the authors every step of the way to make our stories shine!

Sharon Eistetter

This experience was exciting and freeing. Thank you, Ignite, for giving me a platform to help inspire others!

Aly Incardona

This was my first time writing for Ignite Publishing, and I found it an informative and uplifting experience. The entire team was eager to see each of us succeed and constantly showered us with support, encouragement, and validation throughout the process. I'm excited to have learned so much and am grateful to have had the opportunity to participate in *Ignite Your Wisdom*. Thank you, Ignite! I appreciate you!

Janine Marek

The dynamic Ignite team is one of a kind. Their wisdom, support, high vibrations, and incredible resources are all part of an enlightening experience. I have no idea where this road leads, and I am so excited to embrace the unexpected doors that will open.

Jane Kilpatrick

I am a new author, and I did not know what to expect when I decided to move forward with the Ignite process. The Ignite team made us feel comfortable, welcomed, and empowered from day one! The process provoked me to engage during our sessions and go deep within myself to unlock thoughts I had tucked away since childhood to bring my chapter to life. I'm extremely grateful for the experience and thankful for the incredible opportunity to share my story in *Ignite Your Wisdom*. I'm ready to keep honing my writing skills and move on to Ignite book #2!

Jameece D. Pinckney, JD, M.Ed

My experience with Ignite Publishing has been inspiring. Without JB Owen and her team's support, guidance, and encouragement, I'd still be trying to figure out how to become an author. The team is nothing short of amazing! If you're contemplating becoming an author, wait no more. Ignite will give you all the tools you need to be successful.

Cindy Tank-Murphy

Writing my story and being supported through it has been transformative. The writing program delivered a solid structure to guide my clarity and to improve as a writer. However, their care is the special ingredient that made this process so exceptional.. Ignite specializes in providing caring mentorship and providing a community that gave me a cocoon for my personal metamorphosis. I started this journey scared, insecure, and plagued with shame. I'm leaving this journey feeling proud and in touch with a compassionate self-acceptance that has forever changed my life.

Stephanie Fabela

Thank you to JB and the Ignite team for allowing me to participate in this wonderful experience. It has given me the push that I needed to start my journey to become a writer.

Barb Lilley

Writing with Ignite has been a transformational journey that has allowed me to translate emotions and experiences into words that do my story justice. I have had the incredible opportunity to work alongside talented editors who helped to shape the vision of my story so it can resonate with the reader. The writing process Ignited in me a sense of creativity and has helped me integrate my life experience in a brand new way.

Jenna Haji

Having the opportunity to write for Ignite has been pivotal in supporting me through a transformative time in my life. In having the opportunity for my story to be seen and received, I was able to find meaning in all chapters of my life and write with an honesty and artistry that feels purifying. I am so grateful to Ignite for everything it has brought into my life.

Alessandra C. L. Pasut

By sharing the challenging journeys in our life with others, we are able to see the valuable lessons in them that we can grow from and use to transform ourselves to reach a profound wisdom. I believe the reader will also be strengthened and encouraged to do so. Ignite has done this for me, and I know they will do it for all that read their amazing transformational books. Blessings!

Michelle Norlin

There is something so healing about writing your story. I began this journey with so much fear. The team at Ignite are amazing, professional, and the process is a step-by-step journey. They walk this journey with you; you don't do it alone. If you have a story that can help someone heal, definitely write it with Ignite Publishing.

Rosemary French

This was indeed a transformative process. I didn't think I would be pushed as hard as I was (from the inside) to remember how to write for OTHERS and not just myself. It felt like I hatched myself all over again, and now I am ready to start a blog and start writing for other publications. Such a beautiful, supportive process!

Dr. Erin Sepic

I'm thrilled to be a part of the Ignite compilation book and share the pages with so many talented and inspiring co-authors. As a first-time author, I felt supported, guided, and empowered by the skillful and encouraging Ignite team. The step-by-step process was never overwhelming and was instrumental in helping me unlock the wisdom buried in my story. I'm deeply thankful for this wonderful opportunity to take my journey down a new trajectory that I previously hadn't imagined for myself. Thank you, JB, for believing in me, believing in the power of our stories to help others heal, and for providing the perfect vehicle for that journey.

MaryAnn Swan

JB Owen and her entire heart-centered collective are truly Igniting the planet! Their sharing and caring system allowed both my story and the Wisdom experience to birth another personal life revelation. Now, as a second-time Ignite author, I am so thankful to build on my life's library.

Dr. Jo Dee Baer

Working with JB Owen and her team is amazing! They walk each of the authors through the process of writing in a supportive and professional manner. Telling our stories is a cathartic experience. It cleanses our souls from remaining stored emotions and offers others in similar situations hope.

Stacie Shifflett

What an amazing experience it has been working with Ignite to become a published author! They have a top-notch team which make the process so easy and fun. I truly enjoyed diving into the writing and editing experience and have learned so much insightful knowledge in regards to book publishing. It has been wonderful building connections in the Ignite authors online community that will bring new opportunities. I highly recommend working with Ignite!

Nicole Mixdorf

I have always wanted to write and be published, but I didn't have a direction to go in or a formula to achieve my desire. One thing led to another, until life happened and I buried that dream... that was until I met JB Owen and all the gifted and talented people at Ignite Publishing who gave me back my dream. I felt comfortable and at ease throughout the entire process. .I am so grateful to all of them and the hard work they do.

Melanie Summers

I highly recommend working with the Ignite team. The editors were on point with their suggestions, and the process was completely guided for beginners who might be just starting their writing career. I loved their writing portal, which is personalized, gorgeously branded, and organized impeccably, so that it was easy to find everything I needed in a convenient dashboard. We could communicate with co-authors in many formats and at multiple opportunities. I connected with many soul sisters in this community of empowered women, leaders, and business owners. We shared a special journey of growth. The Universe brought us together for a reason: to manifest this timelessly inspiring book, *Ignite Your Wisdom*. I have zero hesitations about recommending Ignite Publishing to beginners and experienced authors. You know that you've enjoyed the process when you feel confident and inspired to write more books!

Loree J. Kim, PhD, Esq

I loved the Ignite process because I learned so much about storytelling during it. The team is very supportive, and the editors that help you polish your story are amazing, very flexible, and compassionate. If you have ever wondered if you can write, this is the perfect platform to being an empowered and empowering author.

Mika Heinonen

The experience of writing my chapter in *Ignite Your Wisdom* has completely transformed my life on so many levels. I am finally able to find the wisdom in the traumas and challenges that I have encountered in my life. I have found peace.

The entire Ignite team has been so supportive during this process and helped me to finish my chapter when I wanted to give up. I found my courage and resilience with their guidance and support. If you are considering joining the Ignite family and sharing your story with the world, all I can say is DO IT! Jump in, and trust that you will be supported the entire way through.

Tish Meehan

Working with Ignite has been a great experience. The support, training, and guidance that have been available throughout the writing and publishing process have been extraordinary.

Marla Ford Ballard

After working with Ignite for many years, I finally dove into writing my first Ignite chapter, and I could not be happier about the journey. I ask myself: *What took me so long?*

JB Owen and the entire Ignite team guide you through the process seamlessly and ensure that you will complete your chapter proudly. The editors were phenomenal in providing comfort to my story and provided great feedback that made me feel more empowered as a writer. To everyone who is unsure if they want to write a book, just do it! You won't regret it.

Katie Smetherman

The desire to write my story and connect to women in similar situations has been with me for years, and this program has led me through a process that has helped me to actualize that dream. With the support of excellent editors I have refined my writing, and I am excited to reach women in need of courage to overcome the heartbreak of betrayal.

Katherine Davidson

Contents

WHAT IS AN IGNITE BOOK?

BY JB OWEN

Inside the pages of this book, you will find a part of your story, your thoughts, your worries, wishes, ideas, and dreams. Somewhere within these pages will be a reflection of *your* story in the memories shared by our authors. We know this will happen because Ignite stories represent the stories in all of us. They are Universal. It doesn't matter where you live, the color of your skin, your gender, or how much money you have in your pocket… Ignite stories reflect every one of us. They are the stories of all the human conditions, and they touch the very essence of what makes us human; in our magical human experience.

The very word *Ignite* signifies the intention of our books and describes the goal behind the stories that are shared inside. We see our books as gifts to the world. Every book we publish is created with the desire to inspire, uplift, and Ignite the reader towards something greater within themselves. We believe that that our books and stories bridge the gap and foster deep connections; each story that is shared can become a beacon for what is possible for every person on our planet.

As you begin reading the upcoming pages, you will find that every story starts with a *Power Quote*. It is a self-affirming, self-empowering statement designed to uplift and awaken you. It is written to make you ponder, push you forward, and encourage you to break outside your comfort zone. Power Quotes are phrases that offer encouragement, insight, and hope. They are meaningful statements intended to provoke thought, Ignite ideas, spark action, and evoke change. Every power quote is written to Ignite something in you, so you can be all that you desire to be.

Below the power quote, you will find each author's personal *Intention*. These are the individual insights and genuine wishes the author wants to share with you. They are the reasons they have written their story, filled with both purpose and meaning. Each author desires to IGNITE something powerful in you, and they share that lovingly in their intention. From the beginning of their chapter, they want you to know they want you to know what they wish their story will do for you.

After the intention, you will read the author's transformational Ignite *Story*. It is a genuine account of how the author went through their journey to emerge a greater expression of themselves. Through their unique experiences and circumstances, the authors explain how their "Ignite Moments" transformed them, awakened them, and set them on a new trajectory in life. They reveal their honest feelings and share their personal discoveries. They give you an insightful account into the moment that resulted in magnificent change and elevated their consciousness.

We all have *Ignite* Moments that change us, define us, and set us forth on a wonderful new journey of inner exploration. These stories are derived from those moments and told in the most endearing and heartfelt way. They show that *life-altering* situations are designed to impact us in a way that ultimately inspires us to step into the person we were born to become.

Once you have read the story and discovered the author's gems of wisdom, you will find their exciting *Ignite Action Steps*. Each author shares a powerful, doable action that you can enact/apply/use to move you toward greater ful-fillment and set new habits that will benefit you. Each action step is an idea, process, and practice that has been successful in the author's life. The goal is for you to implement that step into your life and manifest positive change. Each Ignite Action Step is different and unique, just like you are, and each has proven to have amazing results when done diligently and consistently.

As you sit down to read this book, know that it is not required you read it in the traditional way; by starting at the beginning and reading through to the end. Many readers flip to a page at random and read from there, trusting that the page they landed on holds the exact story they need to read. Others glance over the table of contents, searching for the title that resonates with them. Some readers will go directly to a story recommended by a friend. However you decide to read this book, we trust it will be right for you. We know that you may read it from cover to cover in one single sitting or pick it up and put it down a dozen times. The way you read an Ignite book is as personal as every story in it, and we give you complete permission to enjoy it in whatever way fits you.

What we do ask is, if a story touches you in some way or inspires your heart, that you reach out and tell the author. Your words will mean the world to them. Since our book is all about Igniting humanity, we want to foster more of that among all of us. Feel free to share your sentiments with the authors by using their contact information at the end of each chapter. There isn't an Ignite author who wouldn't love to hear from you and know how their story impacted your life.

We know that the phrase "Ignite Moments" will now become a part of your vocabulary. You'll begin to think about your own impactful moments and the times in your life that Ignited you in a new way. If sharing your story feels important or the idea of writing your Ignite Moment is percolating to the surface, please reach out to us. We believe every person has a story, and everyone deserves to be seen, heard, and acknowledged for that story. If your words are longing to come forth, we want to be there for you to make it happen. Our desire is to Ignite a billion lives through a billion words and share share seven billion Ignite Moments. We can only do that by publishing publishing Ignite Moments from people like you!

As you turn the page, we want to welcome you to the Ignite family. We are excited for what is about to happen; because we know the stories in this book will will provide wisdom and Ignite you from within. As you dive into the upcoming pages, a million different emotions will fill your heart, and a kindred spirit with our authors will be established. We know that this will be a book that both awakens and inspires, transforms and motivates. May you be loved and supported from this page forward, and may all your Ignite Moments be filled with exceptional blessings.

INTRODUCTION

BY JB OWEN

Welcome to a beautiful book about wisdom. A compilation book designed to instill new ideas, heartfelt support, and nuggets of wisdom derived from individuals just like you. This book has come together in record time as each of the authors happily shared their special knowledge knowing that it was destined to arrive, right here, in your hands. All the maneuvering, deciding, actions, information, and an internal "yes" had to transpire for you to be holding it as you are. It is a wonderful thought to behold. Imagine all the steps that were taken, from gathering these authors to writing, editing, printing, marketing, managing, and making sure that whatever needed to happen, occurred so that you could be reading it now. That shows just how marvelous and magical "everything" is to support wisdom to unfold in this way. As you open the pages and read the stories, we know that the right and perfect story, written just for you, will stand out and impact your life. We are sure of it, and we are excited for you. Excited that the wisdom you seek has arrived, wrapped in a book, perfectly designed for you, ready to propel you forward, as it touches your heart and fills your mind with glorious new ideas and insight.

After you read it, what you do with this knowledge is yet to be discovered. How you take the wisdom from here and go forward will be the journey you decide. The journey of discovery, transformation, and change is often filled with the most extraordinary life lessons and profound awakenings. We hope one of our stories will be the catalyst for precisely that. Where you take yourself after you finish this book will be a gift to the world that we are excited to witness. May your wisdom be deep and vast, epic and grand, gregarious and filled with glee.

*Wisdom illuminates the path and can bring inspiration on one's journey!
On our journey to IGNITE Wisdom, we found truths, uncovered myster-
ies, and discovered intimate details about ourselves. We share our wisdom
moments with the hope that our light brings inspiration to you and many
new discoveries along your path.*
~ *Ignite Author, Jameece Pinckney*

They often say wisdom comes from hindsight. The ability to look back
and see something from a different perspective and gain valuable information
from it. While writing this book, all of the authors took the time to look back
and find the wisdom within their personal journeys. Then they put them here,
within these pages, ladened with insights and oozing with knowledge, hoping
to pass that on to you.

For me, wisdom seems to have been the word of the year. Many things have
happened to bring wisdom to the forefront. Changes, adaptations, growth, and
life's endless wonders have filled me with a plethora of wanted and warranted
wisdom. I have learned wisdom is a unique thing. It can come in waves like
a bashing ocean, relentless in its delivery. It can sneak up on you like a baby
fawn, quietly meandering through the forest. It can come in a raging fire or
show up like a thundering storm. Wisdom takes all shapes, sizes, and forms;
formidable when it arrives, impactful when it takes hold. It can yank your
breath away in an instant and then leave you reeling for years, all designed to
awaken you and make you pay attention.

Part of my journey has been accessing, dissecting, and trying to capture
the essence of wisdom. What is it exactly? When does it arrive? How does
one obtain it? I have asked myself if it is age, circumstance, or luck? Do you
call it to you, welcome it in, or just deal with it when it arrives? Many have
spoken about wisdom. Since the beginning of time, the elders and the "wise"
have shared wisdom and knowledge in the hopes that it educates and supports

future generations. But does it? Do we gain wisdom and then act differently? Do we have wisdom and prevail? Is one's life any more fulfilling when it is filled with wisdom?

These questions all begged to be answered, and what I have learned is that wisdom is for the individual to discover. Each and every person must chart the way to wisdom on their own map. No two adventures will be the same, and the treasure will not be found in the same spot by two different individuals. This quest is a solo one, marked with findings, clues, and arrows along the path to uncovering the true wisdom we seek.

In my desire to obtain more wisdom, I ventured out on a journey of epic self-discovery. Along the way, unexpectedly, I gained more wisdom than I could have ever imagined. I was struck daily by wisdom and information that awakened my heart and opened up my mind in ways that I did not think possible. I was in awe, transfixed and humbled by the wisdom flooding into me each and every day. That experience was so profound, life-changing, and rewarding that I sat down and began writing a book about it called *Wisdom From the Back of a Bike.*

And yet... along the way, this book, *Ignite Your Wisdom,* began unfolding and took precedence. My other book was put on hold until this one was completed. But it struck me while working on this project how parallel it was to that project. Wisdom was all around me, in my work, at home, with my clients, and in the topic of my new personal manuscript. Of course, that could not be a coincidence.

To convey just how aligned the message of wisdom has been, allow me to share chapter one of my solo book. I felt it was a perfect fit for this book and an example of how the cosmic message of wisdom is in us, with us, and around us, at all times. It is like a web of tree roots, fanning outward, seeking new soil to plant in, intertwining with others, getting stronger with each inch it traverses. I have realized that wisdom is endless, limitless, and infinite. It speaks all languages, touches all hearts, and is always present. I could not deny its presence in so many different ways, and I wanted to share the impact it has made in my life through both of these books.

Here is chapter one from; *Wisdom From The Back Of A Bike.* I share it just to give you some wisdom into how wisdom unfolds. Enjoy.

The desirable, illustrious, and sought-after notion of having great wisdom has been written into every fairy tale and told at every campfire since the beginning of time. From wise men to wise old trees, to every wise creature imaginable, wisdom has filled the minds and been passed down through the ages since man could first communicate. Wisdom has existed in every culture, and country, forming the cornerstone for all the great philosophies and the backbone of psychology, sociology, and human development. Wisdom has been the granddaddy of all virtues. It is something all humans appreciate, aspire for, attempt to gain, and intrinsically desire.

Yet, how do we truly pinpoint the process of acquiring the wisdom we need?

The Webster dictionary says wisdom is, "The quality of being wise; knowledgeable, and the capacity to make due use of it." The Oxford dictionary states it as "The quality of having experience, knowledge, and good judgment." Some Indigenous cultures have described wisdom as "the state of being wise, discerning, and insightful." Buddhism translates "Wisdom" as "Intelligence" or "Understanding." The sacred meaning of wisdom is the ability to think and act using knowledge, experience, understanding, common sense, and insight.

Defined in these ways, it seems wisdom is something you both obtain and use. It is to be acquired first, then executed, and then shared. It has the inward quality of coming into one's life and, at the same time, an outward momentum of instilling it in others. You must learn it first before you can pass it on. Over time, true wisdom becomes like a trusted friend and a discerning teacher wrapped together with the ability to cite expert advice and offer in-depth opinions at a moment's notice.

Folklore tells us that wisdom can be found in the patience of a warrior, the calmness of a sage, or the stillness of a monk. Native Indians believe It comes in many forms, to all people, at every age if they desire to use it purely. From all of my research, wisdom appears to have no limits and is given freely to those that seek it.

In the Bible, James 1:5 tells us, "If you ask for wisdom, God will give it generously without finding fault." In the Sanskrit teachings of Sravana, hearing, seeing, and feeling are used to receive wisdom. A Google search states, "That any person who is interested in trying new things and then reflects inward on the experience has the ability to gain wisdom." Confucius said, "By three methods we may learn wisdom: First, by reflection, which is noblest; second, by imitation, which is easiest; and third by experience, which is the bitterest."

That all leads to the consensus that we can only truly know wisdom by first experiencing it. It doesn't arrive from a desire to have it. Seeking to have wisdom does not make it magically appear. Nor does wishing for it ensure you will one day be deemed enlightened and therefore wise.

On the site wikihow.com, it states, "Wisdom is a virtue that can only be acquired through experience. Anyone who is interested in trying new things and reflecting on the process has the ability to gain wisdom. By learning as much as you can, analyzing your experiences, and putting your knowledge to the test, you can become a wiser person."

This very notion of needing to 'experience' something in order to have wisdom was in contrast to the images of my childhood where wise men were created amongst a tower of books, or scholars were formed from endless hours of mental contemplation. I had always thought that study, thinking, and astute silence produced the wisest of the wise. Instead, I found out I was deeply wrong.

Wisdom, as I have learned, is born from experience, birthed from the very act of taking action. It isn't given as a reward to only the diligent who sit patiently waiting. Nor is it doled out according to age, gender, or a certain religious inclination. Wisdom, in fact, is a gift that is found on the edge of a cliff the moment before diving, at the top of a mountain after a long uphill climb, or amidst the completion of a daunting expedition. Wisdom can also be found in the parting of two sets of lips after a long-awaited kiss, from a trembling hand that reaches out, or in the whisper of a goodbye that should have never been said. Wisdom is what comes from giving it your all, going full out, and overcoming all apprehension. It could be in a business you know you have to pursue, going to a new city with only a pocketful of coins, pounding a stake into the ground, stepping on a stage, saying yes to a ring, or while pushing the gas pedal right to the floor. The greatest forms of wisdom come directly from the sweating of the palms, the knocking of knees, and the intake of breath that expands your lungs because it is filled with both fear and exhilaration all at the same time.

I myself didn't know that wisdom was earned by doing things outright until I felt it forming ever so slowly in every fiber of my being as I got up off my couch and began cycling 5000km across Canada. I was tired of listening to others talk about wisdom like it was a commodity one could purchase for a discounted price or could find through a two-for-one offer online through a scrolling app. I knew wisdom wasn't going to show up from devouring a workbook or sink into my psyche just because I had watched a great video clip. Instead, I found out its presence was revealed day after day as I sat peddling continually on the back of my bike. Yes, the back of an 8 and a half foot long, carbon fiber mammoth of a bike designed for two that my husband and I took the task of riding to the other side of the continent.

That tandem, a specialty bike I bought a few summers before, had been sitting in our garage throughout the winter and had only been out half a dozen times in the previous two years. It is a beautiful piece of engineering and a *delight to ride, but the long Canadian winters left only a few short months to enjoy it. The outdoor conditions on the prairies meant squeezing it in during the summer months, and with travel and work, the times I got to use it were minimal at best.*

Aching to up-level my life and in search of learning more, something told me to get on that bike and ride. Not a little joyriding about town, but an epic long-haul adventure that would truly Ignite something inside of me. Everything was pushing me to put a pin in my life so I could actually experience a life-altering transformation via that bike. Of course, I didn't know all of that at the time. I am writing this now utilizing the gift of hindsight, the ability to look back and see what I couldn't see when it was still unfolding. I am using what I know now to retrospectively see what I didn't know when I started, and that has been the powerful catalyst for this book.

It was the process of doing it, living in the moment, and taking those big deep inhales of breath that showed me how to develop the wisdom I was searching for. I discovered there was no way to simply learn wisdom; instead, I found out it was doing the work and making the effort that allowed the wisdom to unfold.

And not just little bits of wisdom. Galactic inner self-wisdom on a personal and spiritual level all percolated to the surface on that magnificent journey across 5 provinces, during 56 days of travel while spending 44 days on the back of a bike. It soon became the kind of wisdom that I felt must be shared. Because for decades, I, like everyone else, had been idly waiting for wisdom to grace me as I aged. And, I maneuvered away from anything too painful so as not to force wisdom to arrive too harshly. I tried faithfully at times, thinking wisdom would come from training courses and listening to 'the teachers' of the time. I bought into the idea that wise, insightful wisdom would be derived from sitting at my altar meditating for hours on end. I went to retreats and listened to the 'wisdom sharers,' believing that somehow the wisdom I needed would seep into me. I was misguidedly searching for the wisdom I wanted in all the ways that were outside of me.

In fact, not realizing it, I was like many, just waiting for wisdom to show up one day like a distant relative ringing the doorbell for a surprise visit. I felt wisdom would just appear, and I would have it. I thought that once enough time had passed, I would have earned my stripes, and wisdom would be bestowed upon me. Then I would evolve, and my next level of growth would be achieved. Yet, I didn't even know what exact wisdom I was seeking. The age-old beliefs of my elders? Or maybe the practical understanding of my ancestors? Without really thinking about it, I was content just to let wisdom mosey into my life whenever it wanted without going out and getting it. Until that day, I clipped onto my bike and said to my husband, " I am ready; let's ride. "

I have learned, and I desire to share with you, that going out and gaining wisdom is the most beautiful thing you can do for yourself. Not learning about wisdom or the many theories one might recite, but instead, gaining wisdom through living life's lessons. I am not talking about trying to implement ancient ideals because you've read them; no, I'm referring to the deep-rooted feeling that you fundamentally feel because you have gone out and done what you needed to do to reach that next evolution in your life.

Some have refuted that wisdom is all learned, simply transferred information associated with common situations. Others have quipped that it is from watching, processing, and having the intelligence to do the right things based on the information gathered that perpetuates greater wisdom. I boldly say that wisdom is the knowledge of 'knowing thyself.' And that comes from doing what it takes to find the deep, inner awareness that awakens you to exactly who you are. In essence, discovering one's self.

One can't learn that kind of deep wisdom from an infomercial, webinar, or podcast. It has to be experienced to fully be known. It has to be felt to be understood. So many people sit idly listening to others speak and try to absorb the wisdom they share, only to find it lost or forgotten the very next day. The mind does not remember it because the body did not experience it. The feelings were not cemented into learning because the process wasn't actually felt from within. We learn from doing, and it is in the doing that we learn.

My 56 days on a bike, pedaling tandem, revealed a plethora of moments that led to great wisdom and magical learning. It brought forth powerful feelings and rich awakenings that tapped into the innate wisdom inside of me. Some days it arrived after cresting the top of a hill; other days it formed blinded in a rainstorm. Each day as I became more aware, and tuned in, I heard the many lessons the Universe was trying to tell me and felt the great emotions I was ready to receive. The wisdom arrived as I listened, watched, and surrendered to exactly what was before me.

I can tell you wisdom has no shortcuts. It comes when we do the work and go the full distance to find it; in our own unique way. There is no exact path for us to follow like a GPS map, with a big red dot marking the spot. Each person is required to make the journey themselves and exert their own personal effort. Yes, you can read a lot of stuff and sound as though you are wise, but a quote from everydayhealth.com says, "When it comes to acquiring wisdom, the truth is while many of us may desire it, there are probably few who know what it *truly is. Wisdom is not the same thing as knowledge. You can very easily be acquainted with facts, truths, or principles, but if you don't apply this information to your life, you are actually the opposite of wise. Wisdom, especially spiritual wisdom, is not just about knowing what's good for you, but applying that knowledge to your everyday life. When you do that, this is when you know that you are truly wise."*

As Lao Tzu said, "At the center of your being, you have the answer; you know who you are, and you know what you want."

Winnie the Pooh said, "You're braver than you believe, stronger than you seem, and smarter than you think."

Marcus Aurelius said, "Very little is needed to make a happy life; it is all within yourself."

I'll admit I am still on the life-long journey of seeking wisdom. All that has been given to me is just a drop in the bucket of what is available; I know that now. Yet, what I have learned is wisdom is a journey each and every person must take on their own accord. You must walk your path, slay your dragon, and traverse your mountains, rivers, and valleys; at your own pace. All that is out there for you is there just waiting for you to find it. It is eager for you to arrive by boat, automobile or train. It could be after a race, during birth, or standing in the rain. It could be when you most need it or when you least expect it. But it has to be lived, experienced, and felt. You have to be in it, feeling it, a part of every aspect of it, to be known. Wisdom comes when you are hanging on by a fingernail and pushing through with all your strength. It is as much an awakening as it is a trial of personal will and sheer determination. People can tell you, but you will have to live it to feel it.

The stories in this book are from those that have lived it and lived it full out. Their courageous stories are told to remind you of the journey you have walked. In their stories, you will see your story. Something they will share will remind you, speak to you, and awaken the wisdom inside you that is longing to come out. These stories are like keys to a lockbox filled with wonders, insights, and inspirations. As you read them, the locks will be opened, and new ideas will blossom. You will remember those moments in your life where wisdom was standing right there, waiting for you to take it for a spin, put it in your pocket, and welcome it in. Then you will be touched and transformed. You will remember that wisdom and feel it with all your heart. You'll see how your adventures have created wisdom, and you will gain from it in return.

When you desire wisdom, it arrives. When you seek it out, it shows up. When you need it, go look for it. Wisdom is not elusive; it is earned. It is something that you receive when you step into it, and since you are here, taking action and eager to learn, it shall be yours. The wisdom you seek is seeking you.

Have fun.

Be open.

Listen within.

And live full out in your wisdom.

Manly P. Hall quotes, *"It is said that wisdom lies not in seeing things, but seeing through things."*

You get to experience life and gain wisdom in your own way. It is not for anyone to decide or to dictate. The work you are about to embark on is the work of doing life and living it your way. Wisdom is not a passive sport. It is a lifelong, life-filled, life-enduring gift you've got to go after. No one will give wisdom to you, and you wouldn't want them to. You are here because your wisdom is excited to come forth. Let it grace you, fill you and teach you just how amazing you truly are.

"The wisdom you seek is also seeking you." ~ *JB Owen*

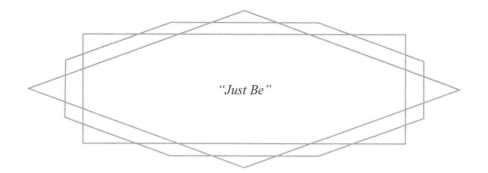

"Just Be"

NOTHING WAS SACRED

BY JB OWEN

It is my intention that you find the peace, harmony, and love that resides within you. As we walk this journey of life, we take on many hardships at pit stops and weigh stations filled with doubt and fear. Resentments, anger, loss, and failures weigh heavy upon us until, one day, the load is so heavy we feel as if we can not breathe. There is a journey required to emerge from such a place. A road must be traveled; things must unfold, awakenings have to happen to emerge anew. There is only one road sign when this happens: *Start*. The rest is one step in front of the other, one moment after the next. One revelation, one ah-ha, one epiphany, all unfolding in perfect harmony to help you get to the next, and the next, and the next. Your road to self-love, self-worth, and self-actualization is never-ending. It goes on for a lifetime, but to experience it, you have to wake up one day and say, "Today is the day I am willing to say yes to me." And... *Start*.

I remember the time distinctly, 4:47 AM. I woke up with both the excruciating pain in my back and the blazing need to pee. I lay there immobile for a moment, staring at the neon green numbers on my bedside clock. I was reluctant to move, pausing in the moments before the agony would begin. Yet, within seconds, the urgency from my bladder insisted I do something. Trying desperately to move as little as possible, I gently extracted my arm from under the covers and reached up for the large red plastic cup that stood next to my alarm clock. Moving like an injured caterpillar, I inched my body closer to the edge of the bed. Holding my breath from the pain that reverberated in my spine, drilled into my hips, and sent screaming jolts of shooting fire down my leg, I wiggled in agony until I could roll on my side and reach the edge. Half breathing, half panting from the energy I had to exude to make it, those few inches caused me to stop and rest. I noticed the light from outside on the deck as it shone in through my patio window. My room was hollow and empty, exactly how my life felt. I was alone, by myself, with no one sleeping beside me to support me or help in any way. My two small children lay innocently sleeping in their rooms down the hall. I didn't have the heart to wake them despite the fact my son, only eight years old, had helped Mommy out of bed hundreds of times before.

Like the dew shimmering off the grass in the backyard, a layer of sweat formed on my brow as I used every ounce of my strength to pull my right leg over and use its weight to draw me out of bed. With part of my body still leaning on the bed and part of it dangling over the side, I whimpered internally as my spine raged with violent, anguishing spasms. Thousands of paralyzing pain-arrows shot outward from my back, hitting my brain like a million razor blades. I cried out like a dying animal as I yanked down my pajama bottoms and shoved the plastic cup between my legs to quickly catch the urine that was escaping my body.

Panting in anguish, teetering on just a few toes touching the floor, my hands trembled as I placed the warm liquid on my night table and took a deep breath before returning to bed. I had to wipe the tears from my face — they came with little provocation and seemed to be always staining my cheeks. I didn't feel that flash of sadness that often precludes crying; tears just streamed constantly and continually; that was my life these days.

With every part of my body reeling, I slid back under the covers, clenching my jaw and gritting my teeth. I made deep guttural sounds as I tried to lift my hips back up onto the bed. I could feel my heart racing, flooding endorphins into my body to counteract the pain radiating from the center of my back. Little reprieve came as I curled around a pillow and begged for sleep.

For years I had had back pain, and for years I had encountered bouts like this one that had me in bed for weeks, unable to function, take care of my kids, or live any kind of life. More than a decade before, I had fallen at work and endured eight months of rehabilitation and therapy. They did everything to heal me, needles, injections, traction, physiotherapy, acupuncture, swim therapy, and muscle restoration. Short of surgery, I had done it all, and since I wasn't willing to go under the knife, this had become my life. I had good days and bad days. Months would go by where I'd function close to normal, and then the stress would add up, the pressure would become insurmountable, and I'd be bedridden for weeks. There were times I couldn't drive due to the anguish in my leg. I couldn't pick up and cuddle my young children. I wasn't able to carry the groceries into the house or even stand up from a chair without the help of another person. I was helpless in many ways — insufficient as a person, wife, and mother. I felt every bit of that inability, and the fact that I was alone, just compounded the suffering I endured.

Watching the clock go from 4:47 to 4:48 to 4:49 seemed to be my life. Minute by minute, ticking away. Minute by minute, nothing happening, nothing changing, only the numbers on my bedside table could move; not me. I squeezed my eyes tight, hurting inside in ways I could not bear. My life, divorce, bankruptcy, failures, disappointment, and humiliation all racked within me. I was like a fox caught in a snare, howling to be freed, gnawing at its own leg, ripping apart its flesh in the hopes of escaping. But escape to what? To a blood-torn, gaping wound so massively irreparable that nothing could fix it. There was no return. The damage was too extensive; the horror had been done. It seemed there was no way out but to end the suffering.

As more tears came, I gasped for breath like a fish on a dock, taking its dying breaths. I tore at the bedsheets with my fingers and raged with anger, hatred, suffering, and sorrow. I clenched every muscle in my body to match my fury, only to be reduced to whimpering as the pain in my back delivered excruciating anguish to match my outrage. In the throngs of self-pity and seething sorrow, I begged to talk to God. I desperately needed him to hear me; to notice me. All I wanted was for Him to grant me a brief moment of reprieve; mere seconds to be released from my grief and desperation. I cried giant, hot tears fueled by the heat of my rage and the magnitude of my suffering. I longed for Him to be in the room with me so I could go to Him on my hand and knees, hunched over in humility, crying at His feet. I yearned for Him to allow me to rest my cheek against his dust-covered feet and wash them with my never-ending tears. In humble reverence and brokenness, pleading in desperation, I begged God to help me. To save me, to deliver me, please.

That was when, for the first time ever, I heard a voice. My voice, my soul's voice, God's voice, I wasn't sure, but it was a clear and definitive message that was impossible to ignore. It came from within me and yet filled the entire room. It was booming like a lightning storm overhead, and yet it pinged around in my skull like a pinball machine on full tilt. I thought it would wake up the children, and yet it was so personal that it felt like the most intimate whisper, the most personal message. It was the kind of sharing that only my heart could hear.

Without any doubt, I was told, "Go to Sedona. Go and heal."

Sedona? What is Sedona, I thought? With hands trembling, I reached for my phone that was sitting next to my pee cup. I immediately began googling Sedona and Healing. The very first thing that popped up was a retreat center, deep offroad, secluded, and built by a Korean Tao master. I was intrigued, so I continued reading…

Located on a stunning, 163-acre stretch of land in the high Arizonan desert, 4,500-feet above sea level, situated amidst the Coconino National Forest. Cradled by Sedona's renowned vortexes and healing red clay rocks, it's ideal for exploring nature, gazing at the stars, and re-connecting with everything that's important.

Everything that's important, I thought to myself. Everything in my life was a mess. I was a single mom, on her second divorce, living in one of my mother's rental properties, barely able to get out of bed. Getting the kids to school felt important. Having a clean kitchen felt important. Being able to pay my bills was definitely important, but none of that seemed to be what the ad was talking about. *Everything that's important* swirled around in my head as I kept reading.

The surrounding mountains with the beauty and energy of their natural vortex welcome the visitor "home" to the peace and tranquility of Mother Earth. The retreat offers endless places to walk and meditate. The flow-ering and fruiting trees, plants, birds, and wildlife produce Earth's blessings along with the care of atten-tive practitioners. The organic garden and the kitchen are splendid. The meals were absolutely delicious, and plentiful. Definitely, a place to heal.

"Definitely, a place to heal." Those words spoke to my heart and offered a faint glimmer, a possible lifeline that awakened in me something that had been sleeping for almost a decade: hope. Yet, in my skepticism, I found it odd that in under a minute I had found a place on the internet that was exactly what I was wishing for. It seemed too coincidental and freaky. I had asked — begged — for a sign, and there it was, on an ad, on my phone, at 5 AM. I wasn't sure a vortex was what I needed.

I set down my phone and grabbed the bottle of painkillers and muscle relaxants that were never far from my reach. I swallowed them whole and without any water; a practice I had mastered. Enduring another jolt of back pain, I curled into a ball, pulled up the covers, and waited for the pills to kick in. *A place to heal, a place to heal, a place to heal* played repeatedly in my mind as tears dripped onto my pillow. *Hold me, Lord,* I asked. *Help me, God, please. Help me get over this pain… help me get to Sedona.*

Not knowing how, why, or what I was actually doing, I boarded a plane within a week. I was wheeled onto the airplane in a wheelchair and given two seats so I could lie down and not have to sit. The attendants were helpful despite their concerned looks and fragile attitude toward my incremental movements, beads of sweat, and sharp squeals of pain. Just getting out of the wheelchair and into my seat required three of them to assist. I took the maximum allotted amount of my government-controlled painkillers to get me through the flight. It was excruciating, but I kept telling myself, *A place to heal, a place to heal, a place to heal.*

A gentle and caring driver met me at the Phoenix airport and allowed me all the time I needed to hoist myself up into the van that would make the four-hour drive to Sedona. For some reason, I felt safe in his presence. He was an extension of the retreat center, and I felt myself relax until we turned off the highway and headed into the desert. The drive was one of the hardest things I have ever done, next to being in labor. The back road to the secluded center was forty miles on a dirt road riddled with mud ruts and potholes. I moaned in pain as I dug my nails into the seat, enduring every bump, dip, and reverberation of the vehicle. Eventually, the pain was too much, and I passed out, exhausted.

I remember being gingerly lifted from the van by the most loving group of hands. It felt like angels had come to get me and deliver me to heaven. I was delirious from the pain and overmedication. I was as broken as a body could be. I couldn't walk, hold up my head, or even speak. It took every ounce of my strength to get there, and now that I had arrived, every fiber of my Being gave way like a string breaking under a weight. I was in a fog of pain, sadness, and surrender. Like a drowning victim, I clung to one of the arms that were holding me. I didn't see any faces, I just heard calm and soothing voices of comfort. I could smell sweet, red clay from the nearby rocks and hear the birds gaily chirping overhead. All I remember as I was laid down on the bed in my room was *a place to heal, a place to heal.* I was here finally, where I could heal.

When the alarm went off at five o'clock the next morning, I was eager to begin my restorative journey. It took me time to hobble to the meditation hall, but I found it by maneuvering through the dark with a flashlight in hand. I had no idea what I was going to do, but I was open, ready, and willing. I thought, *I will do whatever they tell me,* because I obviously did not know how to fix my life or heal myself. With zero resistance and one hundred percent participation, I welcomed the learning and committed to healing myself.

I started with prayer, up to five hours at a time, with my forehead on the ground. I couldn't sit with my spine injury, so on my knees, with my hands open in front of me, both in offering and receiving, I prayed in reverence to the God that helped me get here. At first, the pain was so overwhelming all I could do was lie there and cry. Every muscle hurt; every millimeter of my body wailed like a banshee in torment. At the end of a session, the healers had to help pick me up off the floor. I couldn't move; enduring such debilitating pain and crying in a pool of my tears, left me lifeless. Like a ragdoll, they'd pull me to my feet and wait patiently for my legs to find their strength. They never judged me or rushed me. They supported me fully, adding love toward my healing with the expectation I'd be back the next day for more.

Each day, I dug deeper into my recovery, searching for a waypoint toward a glimpse of relief. I learned how to talk to my pain, love it, and listen to its cries and needs. I did Chi Gong, breathing, chakra healing, sound meditation, visualization, and personal affirmations, all to understand why such anguish had taken residence in my body. I discovered new modalities of healing I didn't know existed and used the power of my mind to go into my spine and work on repairing what it needed.

Much of my trip was an existential journey to places I had never been; inside my body and out into the galactic Universe, connecting with a Higher Consciousness and awakening to every facet of my existence. I discovered my energy centers and my Chi, listened to my spirit, and heard the cries of my soul. These were not things I had been introduced to before. I didn't know they existed, and I surely had not been honoring or loving them as I should have.

It seemed I had a lot to learn: how to create a morning routine, spend time journaling each day, do my sun salutations, walk with my head tall looking forward, and feel my feet on Mother Earth. I even had to learn how to eat; slowly, chewing my food, respecting where the food came from, taking in the lifeforce it provided, and eating in quiet appreciation. Not just one thing had to change — everything had to change. My mind, beliefs, attitude, and gratitude all had to be rewired and renewed. I became a top student in learning how to relive my life.

Over time, I regained my strength, balance, equilibrium, and ability to function. I dove deeper into the practices, the focus, and meditation, and surrendered to All that was grander than me. I found peace on the walks into nature and awe in the birds overhead. I could feel the trees whispering and speaking; I could even see them breathing! A flower had a message of reliance and strength. A tiny caterpillar showed signs of curiosity and wonder. Clouds shaped dreams and desires, while the small stream on the property spoke of possibilities and opportunities as it flowed through the fountain and babbled ideas of joy and bliss. My gray world of sorrow and grief was transforming the same way Dorothy's life in Kansas changed into dazzling colors when she arrived in Oz. Everything had new meaning, and I felt truly awakened for the first time

As part of my training, I was asked by the healers to walk out into the desert and create a sacred circle. In it, I was instructed to add objects or tokens that represented what was sacred to me. I did as I was told, packed a lunch, and headed out alone. I walked for what seemed like hours until a spot called me to stop. I began gathering rocks then sat down to form a two-foot-wide circle with them. Then I sat there. Staring at the circle. Not sure of what to put inside. I just sat there, looking at this empty circle in the dirt that I had created, and had no clue what to do next. I sat there doing nothing till the low setting sun told me to head back.

The next day, I ventured out to my circle, walking in a beeline directly to it. I have no idea how I found it, other than it called to me. For another full day, I sat staring at that circle. Staring at the emptiness in the middle. Reminded how my life was empty, my heart empty, my future felt empty also. I didn't have anything sacred; I didn't know what was sacred to me. Was it my home, my hobbies, family, career? Nothing seemed sacred. I picked up a small nubbly stick near me and began drawing in the sand around my circle. I made swirls and loops in the dirt decorating the area around it but still couldn't put anything inside.

Walking back that night, I found a tiny brown rock that resembled a seed. It told me to pick it up and put it in my pocket, so I did. Later, I stopped to tie my shoe on my way to the dining hall. There right beside me, was a rock, broken into two. Inside the center was a swirl of color and sediment, making it a treasure to look at compared to the dirty outside. For some reason, I grabbed it. When I returned to my room, I spent some time on my patio, gazing up at the moon and the stars. Out in the desert, with no lights from the city, one can see trillions of stars, the Milky Way, and the vast solar system. Both its beauty and its unlimitedness touched me. It felt like all the cosmos was open and available to me. Before going to bed, I saw a rock on my railing tilted as if it was facing the moon. When I looked at it, it resembled the stars, with glimmers of tiny metal fragments embedded in it. Its shiny texture intrigued me. I added it to my pocket.

The next morning before my trek out to my circle, I visited the center's gift shop. There I found two beautiful polished rocks. One was a deep emerald-green gem filled with a kaleidoscope of swirls, and another was a pink, sparkly geostone cluster. They remind me of my kids, so I bought them and tucked them into my bag.

As I headed in the direction of my circle, I was disturbingly off track. A rainstorm in the middle of the night had caused huge craters on the desert floor. Known as the "wash," because the water can not seep into the hardened surface, it finds the lowest point possible to converge and wash away. Often it makes massive dents in the ground and takes vegetation with it. I carefully climbed down into the wash and found a large stone to sit on. With all the water gone, I noticed the damage and destruction it had done in one day compared to what was so perfect the day before. Yet the rainwater had caused new flowers to bloom and colors to form on the desert floor. It was apparent how things can change in an instant, how nature rules. I thought to myself, *Wouldn't it be nice if our past could all be washed away... if something could just come and remove all the old debris.*

As I exited the wash, I slipped slightly and fell against the cliff wall. Putting my hand out to keep my balance, I found myself cupping a rock that fit perfectly in the palm of my hand. It was slightly rounded like my palm, and when I pulled back my hand, I saw it was thin and perfectly round. It looked like a dark gray sand dollar shell in the middle of the desert. I was fascinated and intrigued; how did it get here? Blowing the dust off the top, it made its way into my pocket.

That was when I was startled by the piercing shriek of an eagle. Right over my head was the most pristine bird, of great portions, screeching and cawing out loud. It soared in the air right above me, swirling and gliding effortlessly. Its wingspan was enormous, stretching to touch the horizon. I was in awe of its majesty, grace, and power. One flap of its wings and it could coast for what seemed like forever. It was calling to me, urging me to get to my circle and do my work. To focus on me.

At the top of the wash, I saw the great bird in the distance, knowing that was the way to my circle. With the vast desert before me, I continued walking. I was aware I was alone, until I saw movement in the sand to my left. A small gecko scurrying around, jetting here and there until he saw me. Unafraid, he didn't retreat; instead, he came closer, closer, and right up onto a small piece of petrified wood that was sitting at my feet. He climbed up onto it like he was entering a stage. Then he sat there still and relaxed, allowing me to *see* him. It was a long moment of connection between two creatures from two different worlds. Then he winked one eye right at me, scurried off, and was gone. I was transfixed with appreciation and humor. From that tiny creature came such personality and zest. He was funny, energetic and when he winked at me, I knew in my heart what he was trying to tell me; be happy, have fun, you got this! I picked up the piece of driftwood he had stood on and carried it with me.

When I finally made it to my circle, the rain had washed away my drawings, so I took the stick out of my bag from the day before and began redrawing loops and swirls around it. Because of the rain, the desert floor was clean, flat, and less dusty. I widened my art and made my drawings even bigger. That's when I found a stone, black as black and almost the exact same shape as the eagle's wing I had seen earlier. The rock was heavy and solid despite those wings that could fly, soar and take the bird wherever it wanted to go. I held the rock as I walked back to the center of the circle. I sat down and stared at my circle as I had the last two days. It was still empty, still barren. Tears began to form as I realized I had nothing sacred in my life. *Nothing is sacred; I have nothing sacred in my life.*

They say Mother Nature feeds the desert with the amount of water it needs, and when it has had enough, it no longer has to keep raining. I sat there crying for what seemed like an eternity, as the desert absorbed my tears, and then it told me it had had enough; the drought was over. I stopped crying. I looked at my circle. It was empty, and not because I had nothing sacred to put it in; it was empty because I had made *nothing* sacred in my life. I had not honored my body, my time, or my needs. I had not made my feelings sacred, myself sacred. My dreams, desires, and passions were lost. I had forsaken everything that mattered to me on the hamster wheel of life. I had let others abuse and belittle me, and crush my zest for life. I had nothing sacred because I had given up and had made nothing sacred to me.

Within an instant, I was reaching into my bag to find the green and pink stones that I had bought for my kids. I lovingly placed them in the center of the circle. They were the most sacred things in my life. I humbly thanked God for them and committed to honor and care, cherish and adore them, as they were the most sacred pair ever. Then I took out the tiny rock that looked like a seed and put it in the circle. I was going to plant more love, laughter, and joy with them. I was going to nurture more special times and water our sadness with as much love as possible. I was going to plant seeds of happiness and fun. I was going to feed and water all the things in my life that I needed.

I then found the rock that had been split in two and promised myself that I would always make myself, my body, and my health sacred. I didn't need to break in half to care about my well-being. My life may be muddy on the outside, but like that rock with its beautifulness inside, I will make working on my beautiful self... *sacred.*

I reached inside my pocket and rubbed the last remnants of dust off the sand dollar rock I found in the wash and placed it into the circle. I was ready to let go of my past and wash away all the pain. I had had a wave of destruction in my life, but now it was over. Newness, a clean slate, a fresh new day — I was committed to that and making my future sacred.

Then came the piece of petrified wood, my gecko friend's stage. I put it in the circle, knowing it was time to step up in my life, stop hiding, go back to living, speaking, showing up, being on stage, and having fun while doing it. I had let so much go in my shirking; it was time to return to the living and make my talent, gifts, and abilities sacred.

Next was the black stone that reminded me of the eagle. I placed it in the circle, knowing it meant adventure, strength, and the infinite ability to soar into a greater version of me. I was strong, capable, and could do anything I put my mind to. I was like an eagle, ready to take off, excited to be free.

That reminded me of the stone with the metallic flecks in my pocket. I placed it in the circle. It symbolized possibilities. Everything and anything was available to me. All the Gods, in all the heavens, in all the galaxies were there for me, infinitely supporting me with no end in sight, for all eternity. My soul was sacred. My connection to God was sacred. My Infinite Power and Source Energy were sacred. My soul and the energy in me were the most sacred of all.

I stood up, joyful with my circle, elated that I had so much, grateful for the treasure in my life. I felt euphoric, alive, and abundant. I could see all that was sacred to me. Then I noticed my drawings, extending from the circumference of the circle out in wild loops and artistic patterns. I sat back down and placed my wiggly stick, the one I had used to draw with, inside the circle. I was an artist, painter, designer, sculptor, and I could sew magnificently. I had given up all that. I let go of my creative side, my imagination, my whimsicalness. That was now going to be sacred again. The real me was sacred. My delightfulness was sacred. That creative JB was definitely sacred.

My circle felt full; my life felt meaningful, my body was healed, I had walked miles in the last few days and climbed, stretched, reached, sat, and tracked in ways I hadn't in years. I had listened to God, came to Sedona, and I indeed felt healed.

When I finally left the retreat center, I was elated and excited to get home. I wanted to charge forward in life and bring my kids along on the journey. I had all the tools I needed, a new understanding of myself, and dozens of well-formed habits that would keep me grounded and focused. I was dialed into the heavens, connected to Spirit, and I could feel all that power coming with me. Although it was hard to say goodbye to the new friends I had made and the staff that had so lovingly cared for me, I knew I would return and come back to the place where I had found my sacred Me. As I jumped into the van, everyone smiled, for my body was strong, and I could do it by myself. I hoisted my bag on my lap, slightly heavier than when I had arrived; it was filled with my rocks and wood pieces. I was bringing my circle home with me.

There is always a journey to finding yourself, to discovering, awakening, and connecting to a deeper understanding of what becomes the portal to optimum life. Sometimes it's tragedy, loss, and grief. Sometimes it is something else. Whatever it is, it brings wisdom into your life. You see things differently, view life more clearly, and find the voice inside that truly matters. You have all the answers in you. They are just waiting to be heard. When you stop and listen, pay attention, and know what is sacred to you, the world opens up. The heavens sing and the angels walk with you. Your life becomes yours to live, and you get to decide what to bring into your circle. You get to live the happiest, most joyous life possible. You gain the wisdom you need.

Take care of your circle and all the things you put in it. Make sure that each and every thing is sacred to you. Then make YOU the most sacred thing in it, and live each day from that place of sacred gratitude.

Follow up: I returned to Sedona the next year on the anniversary of my healing with the same rocks and pieces of wood I had taken from Mother Nature the year before. I went out into the desert and made a new circle to recharge my items and revisit my sacred knowing. For the next three years, I went by myself and repeated the journey into the desert for a day sitting with my circle and sacred items. In the fourth year, I took my new husband, Peter. I had shared with him my experience and the specialness of Sedona.

At the airport, when we weighed our luggage, we were overweight. I had to leave my rocks behind, knowing they were too heavy to bring. I was sad but believed I was meant to have a different adventure this time with the new love of my life.

When we got to the retreat center, it was a joy and bliss to see the loving practitioners and introduce them to Peter. Everyone was happy I was there to make my pilgrimage out into the desert. I shared that I wouldn't be going this year as I had to leave my sacred items at home. That was until Peter opened his backpack and revealed he had been carrying my rocks on his back all the way to Sedona for me so that I could have my sacred time in the desert. He wanted me to keep my tradition, and he knew how important my sacred items were to me.

That year, Peter and I each made our own sacred circle; they were side by side, touching one another. We put our sacred tokens inside, and then we both stood in the middle, hugged one another, and kissed in the beauty and the majesty of the sacred life we had built together. We promised each other that our kids' and our lives would forever be sacred until eternity.

Ignite Action Steps

Make a sacred circle. Go to the beach, the forest, the mountains, or anywhere in nature and create a sacred circle of your own. Use rocks, sticks, or anything you want to form a circle.

Sit with your circle. Study it. Look at how you made it. How big is it? What items did you use? Ask yourself how you felt about it while making it. How do you feel about it once it is done? How you create your circle is a reflection of how you do life. If you are resistant to making it, then maybe that is how you do life. If you judge the shape and size, perhaps that is how you judge your life. If you are excited and free, know that is how you show up in life. How you create your circle is how you create and manifest in life.

Then take the time to put things in your sacred circle. Find items in nature that represent certain things to you. A flower might mean life, beauty, or growth. A twig could be pointing in a direction for the future or symbolize a paintbrush or magic wand. Find rocks, shells, bark, moss, sandglass, or even pine cones and seeds to fill your sacred circle with what is sacred to you.

Let go of the thinking part of you and seep into the feeling essence of you. Decide what is sacred to you in your life and make it important in your circle. Let all the symbolism of each item infuse into you and empower your life. Then take your items home with you as a reminder.

Special Note: Right before I left Sedona, I had a picture taken of me beside one of my favorite trees. I have included it here for you to see the amazing angel spirit that is hovering above my head. It is the most beautiful affirmation that I was surrounded by spirits, guides, and a loving pink entity of support and protection coming home with me. I have a few pictures of me in this same pose and the pink light is in different shapes, moving and shifting around me... fascinating, amazing, and a sacred moment caught on film for all to see. ;-)

JB Owen — Canada
Speaker, Author, Publisher, Founder and CEO of Ignite Publishing,
Ignite Moments Media,
JBO Global Inc. and Lotus Liners
www.jbowen.website | www.igniteyou.life | www.lotusliners.com
🅕 jbowen 🅞 thepinkbillionaire ✺ pinkbillionaire

Sarah Cross

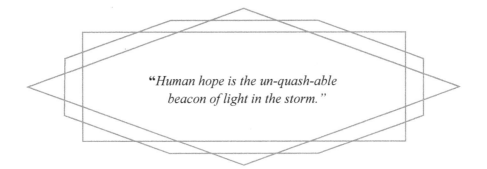

"Human hope is the un-quash-able
beacon of light in the storm."

Waves of Mercy

by Sarah Cross

Sometimes, life hands us unforeseen challenges. We can sit in the misery or find a path that leads to hope. My deepest desire is that no matter what life throws in your direction, you may draw on your inner resilience. When you offer support to others and embrace your strengths and gifts, you can unearth a path to purpose and fulfillment and become a beacon of un-*quash*-able light.

The smell of fresh fish lightly scented the heat of the open-air food market. Tongues chattered in a language I could not interpret. I pointed to the pile of large, vividly pink, fresh prawns; the size and appearance worthy of top gourmet restaurants. Fortunately, the locals understood me, and, prawns in hand, I crossed one more thing off my list. This was my fifth pitstop of the day. Normally, I would pause and savor the incredible array of local seafood that the market offered, but not today. Today I was on a mission.

The sun had been up for a few hours on the Malaysian island of Langkawi, and I had already visited many stores. It was Boxing Day and I was provisioning for the arrival of guests who had chartered the luxury yacht that I was working on. My next stop was a stark contrast to the exhausting heat of the outdoor market — a large refrigerated cold store with fresh imported fruits and vegetables. I shivered as I picked up the white polystyrene box sealing in the crispness of the bright, juicy berries. Such rare ingredients, flown in from Australia, were essential for the planned lavish feasts.

I received a call from our first mate. "Where are you? Are you nearly finished?" I responded that I was going as quickly as I could. A pang of frustration surfaced. Yesterday was Christmas Day, and I had deliberately restrained myself from drinking an extra glass of wine, or two. I was "chef onboard," so provisioning was my responsibility. I was up at least two hours before the rest of the crew this morning to get round to all the many shops. Progress was slow, and the car was starting to bulge with bags and boxes.

The second call came. "We need to leave ASAP; hurry up!" The pressure mounted and my pace quickened. At last, mission accomplished, I headed back to the marina. I pulled up right behind the aft deck and already the vessel's engines were fired up. Everyone was waiting for me. A team came out to greet me and scooped up the provisions to take them onboard, like hungry gorillas at feeding time. Soon the car had been emptied and I found myself in the galley, surrounded by stacked boxes, bursting with the finest ingredients, in the boat's normally spacious kitchen. Before I could even start unpacking, feet pounded down into the galley, alerting my senses. Usually, the crew on yachts have to walk like fairies; elephant steps are a habit that is drilled out of you. "Watch out!" The warning came. "There are some big waves coming."

"What waves?" I questioned. But the first mate had already disappeared. Confusion set in. How could we be rocked around? I mused. We were on a large one hundred foot, beautifully crafted, Italian-designed motorboat, securely tied up in our berth. I thought our marina, at the end of a long channel, with breakwaters beyond, was totally protected. I was wrong. The boat suddenly jerked and instinctively, I reached for the food. "Don't fall!" I prayed. Fortunately, nothing scattered across the room as the vessel lunged up and down.

My mind was bulging with questions, but I had my priorities. Finish stocking the cupboards, make the galley safe and then find out what was going on. At last, all packed away. I sped up the teak steps towards the bridge and stopped, utterly bewildered. I was expecting to see the marina with around forty small sailing and motorboats calmly floating side by side, a view that had remained static for the many months we had been based on Langkawi. But the picture had been destroyed in an instant. Right in front of me, where floating docks normally lay, were just poles. Twenty-foot boats collided with each other. Some lay stranded on the rocks, while others dragged each other, masts entangled, through the water. Yet, the biggest change was the noise. Like an orchestra of instruments without a composer, a deafening ensemble pained my ears; competing for attention, offbeat and angry. The ropes clanged and tinged like triangles against the masts, and fiberglass hulls boomed on the rocks like drums. Wooden docks crunched like cymbals as they ripped apart.

A whirlpool formed in front of us, slowly getting larger and larger, sucking everything into its path — a tornado in the sea. What my eyes were beholding was too much for my brain to navigate. A fear of personal safety and a loss of control consumed me. As I tried to comprehend what was happening, my breathing slowed, but my heart raced.

Before me were unfolding the effects of the 2004 Indonesian Tsunami, a wave of such magnitude that it killed over 227,000 people. It was fueled by an earthquake of a magnitude greater than nine points on the Richter scale. Waves had traveled at 500 mph — the speed of a jet plane — across the water. They landed like a brick wall upon coastal communities in over fourteen countries. It was the third-largest earthquake ever recorded globally and to date, the longest-lasting, at over ten minutes.

In the following moments, there was little to be done but watch and feel helpless. The strength of the water was too strong for even a small 250 horse-power motorboat. As the whirlpool grew, we questioned our safety and whether the multi-million dollar yacht we were aboard would become entangled in the maritime mess before us. But angels looked down upon us; the swirling carnage didn't scratch the pristine yacht. I was relieved we had been spared, yet found myself shaking uncontrollably.

As news began to trickle through of the devastation in surrounding countries and communities, it hit me how lucky we had been. Being based in Langkawi, we were in one of the closest foreign lands to Banda Aceh, the epicenter of the earthquake just 300 miles away. But because of the formation of the outlying islands, we had been saved from the full force of the impact and the wave had split just miles from our location. This meant places further south and north, even west across the Indian Ocean to Sri Lanka, had been absolutely decimated, while parts of Langkawi were only lightly touched.

Sitting on the shore, trying to take in the event, anxiety flooded my body as plans were made to head to higher ground. Uncertainties filled the air. My thoughts cast themselves back to my morning. I mused, what if I had arrived back five minutes later and was standing on the dock? What if our yacht had left the marina five minutes earlier and was pushed into the rocks? What if our lines were not slackened in readiness for departure? What if the engines were not turned on? All these 'what ifs' swirled in my mind. I had not intentionally set my timer to arrive back at a particular minute, yet my arrival was unconsciously timed to perfection because none of our crew were harmed.

The moment news of strange wave activity had reached the Captain just minutes before the actual surge of water, the motor was already engaged and the lines had been released of their tension. Somehow, we were prepared for something you cannot prepare for and I sat with that miracle for quite a while. I wondered if maybe I had been guided that day, if maybe there was a reason that four hours of shopping had finished at that precise moment. While I was moored in contemplation, unscathed, in our little pocket of Langkawi, word quickly spread that many people were not so lucky. The death toll was mounting. In fact, many people had rushed to the beach when the sea first sucked itself out and revealed the struggling fish as they flapped on the sand, stranded. Locals saw this free-for-all buffet as an easy opportunity to stock up on their diet staple. Sadly, many did not know this disappearance of water was a sign to run for the hills. Unfortunately, the situation was worsened because many Southeast Asians cannot swim, as swimming lessons for the young is not the cultural norm.

Within a day, an outpouring of grief eclipsed the world. While I experienced immense gratitude for the fact that the people I knew were all safe, it was mixed with confusion and a sense of guilt for surviving. Tragedy happens without reason or explanation, and I struggled to balance the joy of relief with the devastation that faced millions just beyond our waters.

Although nations around the world generously donated money and resources so quickly, recovery to the people on the ground was slow. Most news attention in Indonesia focused on the main city of Banda Aceh, where cameras could report, but fishing villages down the coast were being forgotten. Even two weeks after the initial shock, people were starving, just a few miles from the epicenter of all the chaos. Bridges were down, roads were out of action, and a lack of basic infrastructure meant that aid could not get through. The airport was damaged, and at the time, Sumatra was a twelve-mile restricted maritime zone, meaning boats needed government clearance to get in. Help could not just sail there and provide assistance.

Yet, filled with compassion, the local boating community became fired up to take action. Surrounded by experienced mariners, ideas started to surface and heads started to collaborate. Influential and resourceful people stepped forward. As the days passed, the beauty and buoyancy of possibilities unfurled. At first, I sat back as people who seemed more skilled and empowered rose up to be part of the solution. A group of doctors and nurses from Malaysia immediately volunteered to cross the sea and join the relief effort but had no transport. The possibility of sending a boat with supplies and medical technicians to those barely surviving started to form.

I was not medically trained and had no political influence. Yet, I was unable to sit with the anxiety that had infiltrated my core. The realization struck me, like a crashing wave, that I could allow my thoughts to tie themselves in knots and be swept away forever in a sea of "what ifs." At that moment, I was Ignited to take action. So, still full of insecurities, I offered my help, inspired to be a part of the beacon of hope. A band of misfits formed, propelled by the Captain of our yacht, the Global Sikhs of Malaysia, and the Dutch owner of a 150-foot wooden sailing vessel. It was an unexpected collaboration of a rainbow of cultures, bound together by a giving heart. We called ourselves *Waves of Mercy*. Our mission: achieve the impossible and get aid to those who were dying.

Soon after, a miracle showed her beautiful smile. We were granted permission by the Indonesian government to dock a vessel and disembark relief workers into Sumatra. Only two Malaysian charities were approved to enter Indonesia: *Waves of Mercy* and the Malay Red Cross™. It revealed to me the importance of connections, teamwork, and the ability to achieve goals despite almost insurmountable odds. If you get resourceful, a sea of red tape and an immense hurdle can be overcome.

Once I had raised my hand, I quickly found myself sorting the financial accounts, as I was happy working with numbers. Next, my provisioning experience came to use, and I took charge of sourcing and fulfilling requests for supplies. As the weeks passed, I woke up with a renewed spirit of purpose, bursting to embrace each day. I was lit up and keen to make a difference to people who had lost entire generations and every possession.

I recognized that though many events are beyond our control, we can always choose to be part of the solution. I loved how I upskilled and embraced new challenges. Suddenly, I was successfully convincing local businesses to donate their resources and co-ordinating cargo logistics on the vessels. I felt so empowered. My initial uncertainties were being washed away as I stepped into a new, more confident version of myself. Still, a small voice inside felt like my role was not enough because I was not on the ground in Indonesia, helping one-on-one, where there was almost unimaginable destruction. Those who went to Sumatra, the epicenter, were real heroes to me. One of them was my boyfriend, now husband, who witnessed death, loss, and the fragility of human life up close while recovering bodies of the deceased in Sumatra. I felt insignificant next to those who willingly exposed themselves to such trauma.

My heart ached as I heard details of individual stories, experiences that I could not fathom, that seemed to come out of a made-up horror film. There were accounts of people who had gripped poles with all their might as water filled the streets and neighborhoods. Others had to dodge floating debris that posed immense dangers. It was described to me how a 100-foot high wave had landed on a beach and reduced a once vibrant community of a thousand to merely a classroom size of survivors. The odd spoon strewn on the sand or water-drenched slipper lying in the puddles was the only evidence that a community ever existed. The enormity of the devastation of the earthquake and resulting tsunami that left millions homeless sat heavily in my heart.

Yet, there were also pockets of hope. Entire villages had survived because wise elders had known that when the sea is sucked away to a distant dot, it is the time to run like a cheetah and head for higher ground. This wisdom, carefully guarded and passed down, was able to save many lives.

Out of this tragic experience I saw compassion and cooperation. I witnessed an inspiring resilience and the un-*quash*-ability of the human spirit. In a time of darkness, I realized there is always hope, and it lifted my soul. I was warmed by the open hearts of the local people and the millions around the world who donated their time, money, and resources. I found a renewed sense of purpose and joy as I lost myself in the service of others. I reconnected with the resourcefulness and strength that lies within and how when you give out of love and kindness; it comes back to you tenfold.

It gave me incredible insight to what a life living with intention looks like and what it feels like to wake with enthusiasm to make a difference. Out of this hurt and suffering, I realized the value in generosity of spirit and making a direct positive impact in other people's lives. I was filled with excitement at being given a physical list of groceries of specific needs, not just what people think others *wanted*, but what people really *needed*. I loved sourcing and supplying these provisions, then loading them onto vessels. But the biggest blessing was hearing of the smiling faces as people received their requested food and supplies, nourishing their bodies and souls, and knowing that others cared. I loved this beauty of giving without expectation and sharing in a way that never needs to be repaid.

I appreciate that our unique skills and expertise are a vital patch in the quilt. I learned that whether on the field or supporting at home, a charity cannot run without the management, organization, and support of logistics. Becoming a slice of the solution unintentionally quelled the sandstorm of thoughts flying around in my mind. *What if the earthquake had happened the day before when we were on the beach enjoying Christmas day?* The tragedy could have been far worse. *What if we were stationed on a smaller, less sturdy vessel at a different dock?* There are so many "what ifs" in life that we can never ourselves answer, like *Why me?* or *Why not me?*

I am inspired by the quote from Nick Vujicic, the motivational speaker who was born without limbs. "You can't expect every day to make sense. Sometimes your days are just comical. Other days are tragic. But for better or worse, in sickness and in health, good or bad, it is just ridiculous that we are alive and breathing, isn't it? Life itself is a miracle." Focusing on the gift of being alive can be a great hug of comfort in times of darkness.

Trying to understand why an event has happened or unfolded in a certain way can lead us into a burrow of overwhelming anxieties and unanswerable questions. Life has its own agenda. I learned that we can breathe and step into the challenge that has presented itself, then remind ourselves that we are alive and have something to offer. I discovered giving to others can be a form of healing also.

I began to see that we do not have to work for a huge charitable organization to positively influence the world around us and find purpose. Instead, I drew more on the importance of *kindness*. Though money can make a big impact, our time, presence, and smile can often be the greatest gift of all. I discovered how when you raise others up, the joy that rebounds is simply immeasurable. Sprinkling our world with a little kindness can inspire others and we can all become part of an ocean of hope and create a positive, everlasting ripple effect.

IGNITE ACTION STEPS

- Take a moment to reflect on the difference you, and you alone can make in the world around you. What skills and experiences could you use to help others?
- What small act of kindness can you add to your day to make the world a better place? Bring a smile to every face your eyes rest upon today.
- Have you thought about donating money to a local or international charity? One I have taken much inspiration from is *Charity:Water©*, founded by Scott Harrison.
- Could you volunteer your time for a local or overseas event? Take a look at *Mercy Ships©*, a charity serving the world's poorest people.

Sarah Cross — New Zealand
Author, Mother, Coach
thestorytellingart.com
sarah@thestorytellingart.com
 Sarah Cross

Diana Lockett

"Surrender is not giving up on life, it is letting go of controlling the outcome of life."

LIFE THROUGH SURRENDERED PRESENCE

BY DIANA LOCKETT

My deepest longing is that you, the reader, will recognize that you can find your way back to surrendered presence, where you can trust and relax into life. Through this deepened relaxed state, you can welcome Grace in each moment and find joy, peace, and freedom in all the moments of your life.

The stillness of the air was met with my beating broken heart on that cold and blustery Friday morning. I arrived just in time to say goodbye, as my mom received her angel wings following a gentle, short journey of surrender to brain and lung cancer. For the six months prior, my family and I decided to support her palliative care at home and took "shifts," dropping into the role of her care provider. I bathed her, fed her, and shopped for her. I washed her hair and held her frail hand, worn from many years of her own unprocessed pain and betrayals. We sat and talked about life, often through tears of laughter and regret.

That season was a physically and emotionally demanding experience as I lived six hours away, had a young family, and worked. My life became very curated. Work for six days and care for my young family. Drive to my parents' home. Spend four to five days caring for my mom. Back in the car for the six-hour drive to my home. Catch up with my family and my work and, just as I felt alive again, I would be driving back to care for her. The journey to her home was often a fist-clenching drive through blustery winter storms trying to abort my mission. The trip home was equally treacherous, with my vision obstructed by my tears as I witnessed her losing her strength to live.

The night my mom exhaled her last, gentle breath, I felt both the relief that she no longer suffered and my own deep, painful grief. I had lost my Mommy. We would never get to play cards again or talk about life. I would never hear her say how proud she was of who I was becoming, or share in my pride over her grandchildren.

After her passing, I realized I was exhausted. I decided to take a trip with some friends to the kitesurfing capital of the world, Cabarete, Dominican Republic. If you have ever kite surfed, congratulations. I wish I could say "me too," but the truth is, I never made it off the beach. I tried. I tried with all my effort, strength, and determination. Each day I would go out there with a coach and survey the beach. I breathed gently as the sea rolled back and forth while the heat of the glistening sand baked my toes and the mighty wind mustered all its threatening force to create the ideal conditions for kitesurfing.

After a quick demonstration, I was given the privilege of holding the kite bar. I confidently began to pull on the bar, but every time the wind caught in the kite, it would pull me backward, forward, sideways, and to the ground. With each gust, I did what I always did in life. I grasped harder. I held tighter. I tried to control my fate by seizing the bar with clenched fists. The more I clutched with all my force, the more power I granted the wind to control my kite. What I learned about kitesurfing is that the harder you try, the more powerful the resistance becomes. How you choose to hold on or let go will create the ripe and perfect condition of being flipped in the air on a whimsical journey, or dragged across the water with a magnified force.

This defied my instincts. It was habitual for me to hold tight with all my might when something felt challenging. I had learned very early on that I could control life by working harder, faster, more than anyone else. Unfortunately, working harder and resisting the kite simply resulted in my being dragged, on my face, one hundred feet down the beach, with my coach racing behind me, trying to grab my feet to stop me. I giggle today at that vision.

After many tries, I remembered the teachings from my mother through her illness. *You cannot control life, and sometimes all you can do is let go of the reins and surrender to your destiny.* I softened the hold on my bar until I was barely holding on with four fingers. Soon, the kite began to dance in the wind in response to my tender grip. I took a big exhale and thanked my mother for that imprint. I never did get off the beach that week. Let's just say that my inner wisdom was certain that it would not end well. Yet, I never forgot the lesson of surrender and letting go from that kitesurfing experience.

Over the following many years, I would begin to catch myself returning to my habit of grasping life, longing to steer what was not mine to control. Each time I did, it would not end well. I would remind myself to consciously practice softening my fists, relaxing my shoulders, taking deep breaths, and trusting in the experience of life. I practiced letting go and remembering that the only thing that I could truly control in life were my responses.

Seven years after my mom's death, while in a circle retreat in Amsterdam, I was gifted with a fully surrendered experience that, today, remains one of the deepest impressions of my body, mind, and soul.

During the final day of the circle retreat, I came to realize I had played small throughout, watching others claim space for their deepest healing and needs. Since my mom's passing, life had imploded, and I had spent five years in a state of intense nervous system activation due to a bankruptcy and loss of my businesses, my home, my retirement funds and my friends. I was, once again, living in a state of fight/flight trying to control life. When I registered for the retreat, I knew that I needed to pause life and find my way back to myself.

Although I had many daily practices that allowed me to release a little steam each day and gave me just enough capacity to teach and serve, I was out of touch with what I needed to *thrive* in life. That unknowing followed me to the retreat. When the retreat began, I felt content being there, witnessing the courageous participants processing their desires and their pain simultaneously.

Each day, I stayed curious about what I might want to experience and express and had few answers. I wondered how others could be so clear and how I could be so bound in my doubt, fear, and ignorance of what I needed. Beyond the joy of watching others on their healing journey, the nourishing food, and the opportunity to rest without any responsibilities, I kept asking myself, "Why had I come here?" The answer was downloaded to me, gently and clearly on the last day, at the last hour.

I had seen others open up and share in the circle, reinterpreting the vulnerable pieces of their lives. As soon as the space opened up, I shot up my arm and jumped to my feet. I was ready. When asked what I yearned to enact, I expressed, "I want to experience a full surrender," followed by "and I know how it will look." The room laughed. I wanted to experience surrender on *my* terms and with my careful, comfortable, controlled plan. The facilitator asked me if I trusted him. "Of course," I humbly lied as I immediately regretted taking the space and time.

I was brought to the stage in the presence of an intimate group of forty people that I had come to know through a range of emotions including jealousy, admiration, judgment, and most of all, love. I didn't know what was expected of me as I was guided to a stool on the stage. I was invited to stand on that stool, and once standing, I surveyed the people below me, all of us silently curious. I could hear myself breathing. I felt shy, unsure, and immensely vulnerable at that moment. I drew my eyes to the ground realizing how high I was, standing at almost ten feet.

I was asked to select twelve men to stand in front of me. Men? I was afraid of men. Men had abused me, ridiculed me, betrayed me. How could I trust these men that I barely knew but somehow loved? I selected the men and they stood, forming two rows in front of me. They crisscrossed their arms, and a blanket and pillows were placed over their makeshift human scaffold. I was asked to turn so my back faced them. The song "Let Me Fall" by Josh Groban began to play. I instantly understood what was being asked of me. I was about to do a "trust fall" backward into the arms of these men. The ultimate act of surrender and letting go.

The music penetrated my ears, each verse louder and louder. My entire body began to tremble. My fists clenched. Tears streamed down my face onto the stool. I have no idea how long I stood in fear with the story in my mind that this was to be my inevitable and imminent death. My mind was telling me to run in full resistance, but my body knew this had to be. I had not only asked for full surrender; I had ached for it.

The facilitator stood in front of me, gently encouraging me as he held onto the stool. I inched my heels back until there were no steps left. The lyrics continued, "*let me fall, let me fly, there's a moment when fear and dreams must collide*" (Groban). Through my heavy sobs, I silently counted in my head, 1….2….3…Go.

I fell back and heard a curdling scream release from my body as I landed in the arms of the men, safely and quickly. "That was it?" I had created so much tension, fear, and a death sentence, and it was over. I began to laugh at myself and wondered about all the times in my life where my mind anxiously created frightful stories, or I had tried to control and curate life itself when it was not mine to manage. I thought we were done with the exercise, but my process continued.

The men gently lifted me overhead and softly walked me around the room while the song continued, *"And if I fall, there's no reason to miss this one chance, this perfect moment..."* I melted into their strong hold. I surrendered and trusted their powerful hearts as I sobbed, this time tears of joy. I was held in a way that I had never been held and I felt my nervous system, my body, and my heart fully release. After a while, they tenderly placed my feet on the ground while continuing to hold me. They formed a tight circle around me and lovingly guided me from one to another while every muscle in my body was fully relaxed; my soul fully nourished. I surrendered to them as I was soothingly passed around their circle. The last words that I heard from the song were, *"I will dance so freely, holding onto no one."*

Eventually, they helped me find my feet and we all found stillness. I gazed into each of their eyes; these men that I knew only a little about. One was a successful entrepreneur, one was a writer, one identified themself as a regretful rapist, and all were angels for me at that moment and in my life.

I looked around the room and saw that the other women were weeping. I knew I had embodied and experienced the surrendered presence that all these women were craving in their lives.

After the retreat, I returned home with a new perspective. I began to take more time and space for myself. I rested more. I danced more. I carved out time with my "sisters" and took the trips I had put off for ten years. I balanced my masculine practices of breathwork and yoga with daily feminine practices of surrendered and unstructured movement. I began to pay attention to the whispers of the Universe, inviting me to engage in life with open palms. I willingly experienced each moment as my GPS in my life. When my body required stillness, I stopped. When it needed movement, I moved. When I needed to breathe, cry, yell or love deeper, I followed those impulses and allowed myself to be penetrated by life. I dropped all care of what others think about me and started to live fully and authentically. I surrendered to life itself.

A few years later, my willingness to soften my fists and surrender to life was given the ultimate test as I navigated through a global pandemic, a painful end to my marriage and a cross-country move with my teenage son. I left a thirty-two-year career and said goodbye to my relationship, my home, and my large spiritual community. As I stepped into the abyss of this metamorphosis, every cell in my body was relaxed. I was in surrendered awareness and excitement about the wonder of life itself as I welcomed a new chapter in my life.

Today, I know with certainty that I am supported, that the Universe has my back, that I am always divinely guided. As I follow the breadcrumbs, I see how life has always happened for me, and, when I fully surrender to it, life truly happens through me.

Surrender is not actively giving up. Surrender is a full-body, tender experience that infiltrates our being when we let go of control. If control is the disease that was fed to us and resulted in tension, disappointment, armor, and defense, surrender is the wisdom medicine.

When we release control and surrender to the life that is waiting to reveal itself to us, we begin to awaken beyond our separate self and get a glimpse of the larger truth of who we are: expanded conscious beings. Instead of arguing with life, we get to create the inner art of presence and the ultimate freedom, rooted in love and trust.

The famous Sufi poet, Rumi, summarizes it this way:

"Be crumbled so wildflowers will come up where you are. You've been stony for too many years. Try something different. Surrender."

IGNITE ACTION STEPS

- Practice tracking your body. Take notice of where you are holding tension. Invite your breath to soften the parts of your body that are tight. Relax your hands, soften your jaw, and drop your shoulders while releasing any judgment that your current state is wrong. It is simply informing you that something is tense. Once you become skillful at tracking your body, notice how it feels when you let go of trying to control life.

- Release the *shoulds* that may have been imprinted in your life. Your life is unfolding perfectly. You are not stuck. You are simply holding on too tightly to something that may not be yours to hold. Be willing to see life as feedback, not failure. Take every experience as a gracious opportunity to learn a little more about yourself and how you relate to life.

- Where can you sense the wisdom of letting go of your thoughts, expectations, judgments, and fear? Meditation is a great practice to untangle from your thoughts. Find five minutes to sit in surrendered presence daily.

- Notice any obsessive worrying. Change your language of "worry" to "wonder."

- Become curious about your resistance to discomfort or pain. Feel the wisdom of being open to feeling all emotions and sensations.

- Surrender your story of not being enough and open to meeting your expanded, beautiful self that is lovingly rooted in the home of your heart. When you live from your heart, you become the joyful co-creator of your life.

- Listen to the gentle whispers that are always encouraging you to reach for freedom by trusting that life is happening for the evolution of your soul.

Diana Lockett — Canada
Transformational Communication Coach
dianalockett.com
🖪 *dm.lockett*
🅞 *dianalockettcoach*

"Understand your priorities, goals, what's important to YOU... and chase that!"

BALANCE IS NOT EQUAL

BY STEPH ELLIOTT

My desire is that you give yourself grace as you embark on your life's journey toward happiness, love, and purpose. Whether you're an entrepreneur, working for someone else, or a parent staying home raising children, I hope that my story helps you find clarity, acceptance, and BALANCE. Balance means everything is equal, and I want you to understand that it's okay to jump off the hamster wheel of what you've always done and chase your dreams.

"You need to find a work-life balance."

If I've heard these words once, I've heard them a thousand times. I've lost count of the number of times in my life my inner monologue screamed that I should do more for myself, with zero clarity on how or even why. When pressure comes in from every angle — get that money, care for those kids, fill your own cup — hearing "live your best life" is more infuriating than it is helpful.

I became a mom at eighteen, at a time I thought I knew everything: how to be an adult and how to make ends meet. Boy, was it eye-opening to find out I was pregnant at eighteen while already moved out of my parents' home. I learned what it was like to be in the real world, with car payments, rent payments, bills, groceries, diapers; all my money was spoken for before I had even received that week's paycheck.

Many people in my life at that time doubted my ability to be a successful mom and offer my child a wonderful life simply because of my young age. I took that as a challenge. The determination to prove them wrong was boiling inside my veins. When my beautiful baby girl, Makenzie, arrived, I immediately knew how transformational she would be in my life. That little 6 lb., 2 oz. bundle of pure bliss would inspire me to be the best version of me. Even if I didn't show up for myself, I surely would show up for her.

Showing up meant creating stability and developing a daily routine that ensured my daughter was taken care of and I was earning money to support her. Each day, my baby and I woke up and while she went to daycare, I went to my job. I was hired as a receptionist for a recreational vehicle dealership, and although I enjoyed the company and my co-workers, the paycheck was just getting us by. I wanted more for my little family and was the first to volunteer for any opportunity that presented itself to do more at work. Sometimes that meant overtime hours; sometimes it meant helping out in another role. I had a lot to learn in the work environment, but I was eager to do so, fueled by the challenge to show I was capable of being a worthy mother.

Quickly, I proved my work ethic and ability. A position opened for the role of finance manager, and it was offered to me. I was ecstatic! Now nineteen years old, my salary was higher than average for someone my age, with the opportunity for bonuses. I saw the light at the end of the tunnel and felt excitement rushing through my body, positive that this new opportunity would provide new adventures for my family to embark on. It was a thrilling anticipation of new memories that would be in the making.

Before I turned twenty, I purchased my first home and lived the life anyone my age would be proud of. And I did it on my own, with a baby. My sense of excitement didn't last long though, as I still felt like I was chasing a dream—a dream that was not yet clear in my mind. Without clarity on what I really wanted most, but the determination to keep doing what I had to, I kept living my best life. Each day was the same: wake up, drop Makenzie at daycare, go to work, pick her up from daycare, go home, eat dinner, have bath time, go to bed, then do it all over again.

I lived this vicious cycle, day in and day out, until a disastrous relationship and a betrayal with acts of incomprehensible proportions unfolded without my knowledge and caused me to move out of state. I packed whatever belongings fit in my small burgundy four-door car and left the rest behind. The beginning of a new life was ahead of us as we drove I-95 North out of Florida. It felt like a setback and came with numerous challenges, some of which were self-created and some of which were simply a part of this journey I call *LIFE*. I was scared—scared of not knowing where Makenzie and I would live or whether I would be able to find a well-paying job. Making enough money to support the two of us and fear of the unknown were always present in my mind. But what I did know is that I would not give up. Makenzie deserved a safe, consistent home, and a mom that could support her.

While I didn't necessarily always know what each day would bring, or how my life with my little girl would end up, the Universe certainly had plans for me. To my ultimate surprise, it blessed me with a second bundle of joy; this time a baby boy, Travis! I was now one mom with two babies under two. Wowzers! A new challenge. But just like before, I knew in my heart that even if I didn't show up for myself, I needed to show up each day for two beautiful humans that meant more to me than I could have ever imagined. So that's what I did.

I found a new job at a family-owned mortgage company. I felt that by working for a family-owned company, they would understand that as a single mom I would have things come up, sometimes planned, sometimes unplanned. And they certainly did. At that company, I learned about the mortgage industry, and it was rewarding seeing families become homeowners and feel the strength and sense of independence that it brings. But, I was still in that same cycle of chasing the dream that was unclear to me. The only difference was, I was doing this with two children instead of one.

Each day, we did the same thing. We woke up, the children went to daycare, I went to work, we went home, did our evening routine, went to bed and did it all over again the next day. Was there balance? Some may say yes since there was consistency. However, to me, it felt more like monotony than stability. I asked the Universe if this cycle of the same thing, day after day, would ever change; if I would find balance as a mom, individual, employee, friend, and daughter. *Would I find enough balance to be able to venture out and date?* That was always a scary thought. If I didn't have balance to be me and a mom, how in the world would I have balance to find love and add a loving father figure into the mix? As the months went by, my questions went unanswered.

Our daily routine got so honed, the kids and I had it down to the minute. I was seeing the same parents at daycare drop-off and pick-up and leaving no time to spare in arriving at work on time. I felt a lot of nothing to do the same thing day in and day out.

One evening that all changed. I found a babysitter and took the opportunity to go out with a friend. While my friend and I hopped from place to place in town and enjoyed the scenery, food, and beverages, the last establishment for the night was where I met someone. This man was a smidge younger than me, but I felt a connection. We exchanged phone numbers, and he called me the next morning. As we went on a few dates, the connection grew stronger. As time went on, I introduced him to my children. The four of us had a wonderful connection, and whenever we were together I did not want the day to end. Two adults and two children... could I have possibly found true, equal balance? I wondered until self-doubt blew in like the wind of an approaching storm. I thought to myself, and even said to my friend, "Who in the world would want to be with a woman with two young kids struggling to make ends meet?"

The Universe heard me and answered that question. The "who" was the man I met that night, Tyler—the man I call my husband today, fourteen years later. We figured out how to be a family of four and combine our lifestyles. In the midst of being comfortable with *our* balance, the Universe showed it had other plans for us. Soon came baby number three, a beautiful little girl, Sylvie! So much for that "equal balance" of two adults, two kids. Now we were outnumbered.

The best part was, this time was different. Instead of just me showing up each day for three little humans, I had Tyler showing up to divide up the responsibilities. But I was still looking for balance. I left the family-owned mortgage company and went to work for a corporate bank. I was still in the mortgage field but felt I had more of an opportunity to work my way up the ladder. I was doing more, making more, working longer, and still not finding the balance that I longed for.

Over the next few years, I started at the bottom and worked my way up. That meant working 40, 50, and even 60+ hours a week; taking calls any hour of the day or night and even on the weekends. I would see co-workers doing the same. We would stop at the coffee bar and chat for a few minutes while we waited for the caffeine to brew; it kept me going. As positions opened with the company, I applied and advanced my title and responsibilities one step at a time. I talked about work-life balance often, and I tried to establish it the best way I knew how. I made sure to log off work and run to one of the kid's school events or sports games, and when I got back home, I logged back into work to knock a few things off my to-do list, many times into the wee hours of the morning. This went on for years. While the cycle was still the same, I felt productive and successful. I thought that was winning.

Then I applied for the next position; one that required traveling. I was excited, my heart skipping as I thought about the change to my routine. The cycle would remain mostly the same, but this time I'd be adding to the cycle and seeing parts of the United States I had never seen before.

It seemed like a wonderful, much-needed change of pace after so many years of doing the same thing over and over. That was until a business trip arose that overlapped with my youngest daughter's birthday. I was anxious as I left for the airport that Monday morning, knowing her special day was later that week. Although we talked about it with her, that Mommy would be gone all week and this was part of my career, I felt terrible. After all I had done, for so long, to be a worthy mom, I felt like I was failing her this time. But it was part of the job, and I had no other choice.

The next few days went by quickly thanks to my busy schedule at the office, but the evenings in the hotel room felt like time was standing still. I was constantly having the inner thought in my mind questioning if I was being a good mom. I woke up sad, wanting to cry and stay in bed, but I fought through the emotional roller coaster the morning of my daughter's birthday. And because I was in a different time zone than my family, I needed to wait until the end of my workday before I could speak to her.

I felt like the end of my workday would never come. I must have looked at my watch every five minutes. I left the office that evening in a hurry to get back to my hotel so I could call home, but I wasn't fast enough. As I stopped to fill up the rental car with gas my cell phone rang. At home, they were getting ready to sing "Happy Birthday," blow out candles, eat cake and open presents — and there I was in a random town, standing under flickering fluorescent lights all alone. Instead of being at home celebrating with my family, I was on FaceTime™ singing *Happy Birthday* while pumping gas. How could this be winning when I was feeling so much loss and missing out on the most valuable thing that mattered to me; my family?

I chatted with the family for a few minutes, but of course, as any child would be, my daughter was more excited to dive into her new gifts than to talk to Mom. We hung up the call, and I cried. My heart ached with feelings of loneliness, and my mind was questioning my worth as a "good" mom.

Although I had attempted to mentally prepare myself for the day and pump myself up that all would be okay, it wasn't. I felt alone, isolated, and disconnected from my loved ones who were celebrating without me. While I thought I had found balance, here I was, yet again, lacking the feeling of things being equal. I felt like a terrible mom and a terrible wife. While I know my family missed me when I traveled for work, their daily routine stayed consistent without me.

When I arrived home that week, I apologized to them for missing such an important yearly event. They reassured me that it was okay. They knew and understood that their mom traveled to give them opportunities in life they wouldn't otherwise receive. That moment, feeling their support, was the first time I realized that *balance is not equal*.

Balance is an individual quest, meaning that what works for you does not always work for someone else. I had to let go of what I thought about balance and find what worked for my family. I had to stop comparing myself to others. I had to let go of what I saw in other wives and mothers and do what was best for us. I shifted my mindset and saw all of the beautiful experiences I was having with the family. I looked at all the things I was doing, the benefits I was creating, and saw that my time with them, big or small, was precious. Things didn't have to be a "certain" way. My husband was great at raising the kids, the kids felt cared for, and I didn't have to be there every minute for me to feel like I was worthy.

Over the years of long workdays and working on weekends, the kids never missed out on their events. Tyler and I always ensured the kids participated in sports. Makenzie cheered competitively, Travis played baseball, and Sylvie excelled in softball. Their cups were full. We went on family trips around their sporting events, visiting Disney World, taking a cruise, and seeing many beaches to create memories they still cherish today. Those times spent with them formed a connection that allowed them the comfort of knowing I was devoted to our family, no matter how much time was spent working either at home or on the road.

It is impossible to have a "50/50" balance with everything in your life; your career, being a parent, entrepreneurship, time with your partner, or anything else. While this next statement may just hit ya' where it hurts, it's the truth: stop looking for and chasing the equal balance. You will continue to be like a hamster running on a wheel. Equal balance doesn't exist.

What does exist, is YOUR definition of balance. Balance shows up in every-one's life and at different points in your life differently. For some, balance may look like a split of 80/20, 70/30, or 60/40... you get the gist. But if we are honest with ourselves, it's never 50/50. There are times, like me, you may miss a birthday or a special event. The scale will fluctuate, and that is okay. However you divide your time, do it with intention, talk to your family, let everyone say what works for them, *and* then find the winning combination that works for you.

Stop chasing equal balance, you will be on the hunt forever. You can find your own unique balance once you understand your priorities, goals, and what's important to YOU. Chase *that*! Believe in *that*! Once you find your true balance, let it empower you. You will start to see your productivity increase, goals reached, and you'll move closer to your dreams, as they become your reality. Balance doesn't have to be equal to be beautiful, it just has to be YOURS!

IGNITE ACTION STEPS

Set your schedule: Track for a week how you spend your time. If your time is spent doing things that don't align with your priorities and goals, re-evaluate how you're spending time going forward.

Set the expectation: Communication is key to success in ensuring our family and friends understand. Share with them your priorities and goals so it's clear that you're never ignoring them or avoiding them.

Set your stance: Always remember: "No" is a complete sentence. There is no interpretation. Everyone knows what "no" means. Some might not like what it means, but they understand it.

Set boundaries: Boundaries are important to set with others as it teaches people how to treat you. Setting boundaries with yourself is just as important. Boundaries will let you hold yourself accountable. What are those things in your life that are non-negotiables? For me, it's self-care. Establish what boundaries mean to you.

Steph Elliott — United States
Life Purpose Life Coach, Author,
Motivational Speaker, and Exceptional Mom
www.stephelliott.club
 @therealstephelliott
 @therealstephelliott

Dr. Jo Dee Baer

*"When you take care of YOU in your world first, the
world around you is EMPOWERED forever."*

FEEL YOUR REAL

BY DR. JO DEE BAER

The secret to wisdom is feeling "real" emotions in the present, but not being held captive to them. Instead, embrace them with gratitude. A life well-lived in the present with one hundred percent passion allows you to reach your fullest potential and experience your life in the winner's circle. May my story empower you to breathe joy into *your* life and truly feel the moments that take your breath away.

"Hey, Big Wheel Guys! Mom's got a snack!"

There I would stand, on the front porch, lemonade and cookies in hand, wrapped in the fragrance of my lush rose garden. I had everything I ever wanted: a husband, a growing career in the emerging field of alternative health and wellness, and the perfect suburban house on the cul-de-sac where my two young sons could ride their toy cars to their hearts' content. Life was both abundant and good.

Until it wasn't. Like a scene from a TV soap opera, I awakened one morning to a note on the kitchen table from my "Wasband" saying: "I'm not coming home." Nearly fainting, I slumped to my knees, gripped the table, and crumpled up the note. Somehow, I pulled up the fortitude within myself to shower, dress, make breakfast, and drop my sons off at school. Mustering all the strength left inside of me and faking the usual Mommy smile, I sent them off to school with the usual hug and salutation: "Make it a great day." All the while, my heart was racing, and my stomach felt like I'd swallowed a bowling ball. What was my next move for the three of us? Where do I begin to make our life great?

I was never one for stagnating or contemplating, so I did anything to create action and momentum. I THRUST myself into my elementary school sons' well-being by supporting their gift of competitive swimming. I coupled this with exponentially accelerating my health coaching career and submerging myself into the new calling of single sole-support parenthood. I was committed to raising my sons and giving them all they needed with just one parent.

Stepping into my forties, I had successfully launched my eldest son into a full-ride swimming scholarship at Georgia Tech in Atlanta. I was then at the precipice of triumphant single parenthood: one down and one to go! My focus was on achieving this SAME pinnacle and dream for my second son. His goal: The Sydney2000 Olympic Gamesome. After all the long and arduous hours, traveling the roads and airways of North America, grueling workouts, and years of focused effort, the coveted Olympic mark was not to become a reality for my youngest. He had achieved so much, but when he didn't make the team, all I could feel was the emptiness and devastation within him.

On the seemingly eternal drive back from Indianapolis to Atlanta, after he missed the mark, the air in the car was so thick you could cut it with a knife. Disappointment and then re-direction was the center of our conversation. What was next? He also had a full-ride scholarship awaiting him, so the answer was, "Let's pack up and leave for Knoxville tomorrow and the University of Tennessee!" Within forty-eight hours, he, too, was gone, and I returned home by myself.

"Hello? Is anybody home?" No one answered. It was only me. I could hear the reverberating walls resonating to my solo voice. I "excavated" from my son's bedroom numerous unidentifiable artifacts, which included a Burger King Whopper™ still in its container with a receipt dated six years prior, displaying his messiness, yet focus on his goal. I wandered up and down the hallways, now resembling the size of Buckingham Palace, and once filled with boyhood noise and laughter. What was "our home together" was now gone forever, and I thought: *What now?*

An unrecognizable ingredient in my DNA was my inability to sit still. I didn't feel the pain or grieve the abandonment. Rather than pause, breathe, and feel all those emotions — *feel the real* — and move into the next evolution of life, I THRUST myself again into another project. I dove into my own training, running seventy to eighty miles a week and competing in a marathon a month. With every pounding footstep, I RAN, but never took the time to ask myself, "From what?" Every step was just another step in staying busy and another step toward numbing my emotions. Once, the Mom who cooked mountains of pancakes in a single sitting, now, I didn't even turn on the stove until my sons came home for Thanksgiving. I was the queen of takeout from various neighborhood Cheers™ type restaurants. I'd sit at the bar, not to imbibe, but to engage with people.

Perpetuating a geographical run, I relocated from my home of twenty-two years in Atlanta, Georgia, to Miami, Florida. This empty-nester didn't listen to the emotions in her heart. All this over-exercising provided a wonderful experience in the outdoors, and the endorphin-induced high was amazing, except for one critical component of health. The arduous endeavor toxified my liver, exhausted my adrenals, and what ensued was more than an illness — it was a shattering wake-up call. For the first time ever, I was forced into a Life's Milkshake Moment™ of choosing different ingredients in my own life for ME. It was more than a tap on the shoulder; I was hit with a Mack Truck™.

While I was running in Miami, I went to a spa for my usual facial. During her customary examination of my skin through a magnifying light, the aesthetician shouted: "¡La masa en la piel es muy mal!" ("The mass on your skin is very bad!") Even with my limited Spanish, after hearing her passionately repeat that phrase for the tenth time, I knew that I would be in the dermatologist's office the next day. Prior to the biopsy, he almost assured me that "la masa" on my right cheek was malignant. The wait for the eternal biopsy report began, which was a different twist on endurance for me because we know how much I love patiently waiting!

How did I fill my schedule while waiting for my results? Of course, I plugged in *another* swim meet for my youngest son! With a two-inch squared patch on my face, I flew out to an NCAA™ qualifying swim meet at the University of North Carolina, where he was competing. I donned an orange-colored wig emblematic of the University of Tennessee, my youngest son's collegiate team colors. All the while, in my subconscious mind, I stared down the barrel of my dreaded diagnosis and feared my impending baldness while wearing my "fan" costume and cheering on the team.

After the meet, we attended a team banquet celebration. The exhilarating energy and testosterone of the team's accomplishments were a welcome diversion. As the parents and team were departing, I got a phone call from the doctor's office. "The spot on your face has metastasized into your lymph nodes, and it is probable you have only six months to live." I broke into tears and delivered the news to my son. His cavalier and endearing response to my cheek patch and anxiety was much-needed humor: "Mom, you'll still keep your own hair right? Because Tennessee orange is not your color," he joked, giving me a bear hug, and enveloping me in his full six foot seven stature.

Upon my return home to Florida, I attracted two holistic physicians that changed the trajectory of my life. Even as an alternative healer myself, I had gotten off focus with my own self-care. Oftentimes, the cobbler's children don't have their own shoes. This was certainly the case for me. Dr. Greg and his new associate, Dr. Mike, who was just beginning his practice, both encouraged me to "go deep" with acupuncture therapy and Chinese herbal medicine, as I'd taught so many of my own clients to do for decades. I chose to follow their advice and implemented an ancient traditional Chinese medicine topical remedy on my biopsy incision. When I told Dr. Mike that the other doctor gave me six months to live, his comedic reply was: "I am a competitive swimmer like your sons, and you're my first patient. I'm not going to let my record be zero and one."

I decided to reject traditional medical therapy but agreed to have the malignancy surgically removed. In the ten days before my imminent surgery, I continued to train and work out. During an interval session at the gym, while doing a vertical weight-assisted body pull, I felt a *POP*! There was an explosive thrust of force, radiating from my elbow, that expelled through my right cheek. It was volcanic. The silver-dollar sized, black, brown, and yellow mucosal mass on my cheek expelled outward, hitting the wall three feet in front of me. It was the unhealthy cells forcing themselves out of my body. I fell to my knees as my face throbbed. I sobbed, yet I knew I would live. At that moment, I chose not to believe the diagnosis: "You have six months to live." I chose life instead and drew the line in the sand for my own health and my life's destiny.

As Les Brown, the world renowned motivational speaker says, "Your diagnosis is not your prognosis." My life's trajectory took on this famous quote.

After surgical removal, and lengthy facial reconstructive surgery, I spent the next few months supporting my sons' collegiate swimming careers, and began my *comeback*; a *personal race,* the best journey of regeneration for me. I emphatically announced to my sons: "I'm going away." I embarked on a life-changing alternative healing, macrobiotic-vegetarian diet, and deep spiritual meditation at a remote retreat, over the next four months. I closed the world around me and took care of MY world first. I embraced only those who assisted my healing so my re-entrance to the world would be EMPOWERED. For the first time in my adult life, I could say that I could *feel the real.*

I turned off my "superhero" alter-ego Mom mode and turned my family nickname GO GO Jo-Jo upside down and around. I FELT my emotions: fear, abandonment, sorrow, resolution… and grief. I integrated the truth of those emotions on a cellular level and into the interspaces of my Being. I lived my "diagnosis is not your prognosis."

While on that spiritual retreat, I did nothing but focus, feel, and experience me: who I was, what I'd accomplished, but most importantly, how I could reclaim me. I delved into how I'd gotten to that point in my health in the first place. I asked the poignant questions that dove deep into the pain and loss of my marriage and intimacy with my "Wasband" over a decade, and experienced true grief. I felt the loss of my sons' daily presence, so I could rejoice in the accomplishment of their gifts and future goals. The practice of Qigong became an integral part of my revitalized life as I worked on all quadrants of me.

In my late twenties, I began my career as a certified health coach and holistic nutritionist, assisting people with their own health. Over the span of my practice, becoming a doctor myself, I helped others to lose over one million pounds of toxic fat. I assisted countless people to regain their health and achieve victories in an abundance of situations. I had to commit to my own personal transformation of the same epic proportions — to feel *the real* — to give the same care, self-love, inner peace, and vitality back to myself. Health isn't something you do, it's who you are.

That led me to believe in, to this day, taking care of you in your world first. You must listen to the warning signs of your body: the tap on the shoulder; the two-by-four that hits you before the collision from the Mack Truck. I needed to forgive myself for not practicing what I'd espoused, taught, and believed. I had to let myself off the hook. I wanted to feel the exhilaration and relief of experiencing "slow down to speed up." That brought forth my decision to live a life *ALL IN!* When my near Mack Truck experience finally pushed me to the brink, I chose to develop my own alternative protocols of yin and yang that have helped to Ignite massive lifestyle changes in millions of people. True transformation is an inside job. It started with me, and it has empowered thousands.

Prioritizing your health becomes a daily decision and once committed, you can heal yourself and rid your body of any unwanted toxins. Taking care of yourself means taking care of your health and your emotions. Health becomes **H.O.P.E. (H**ealing, **O**pportunity, **P**ositivity, **E**mpowerment) and who *you* choose to become along life's journey. I've had the honor of unearthing my clients' emotional pain that has often been left in the middle of junk food aisles at the grocery store; I have provided them a hunger to create their own foundational health of H.O.P.E. Many sweet milkshakes have now been expanded into something that transformed lives. I am devoted to my clients; nothing feels as good as a healthy body with energy, vitality, and longevity.

For four decades as an alternative healer, and for the twenty-two years since my *feel the real* moment, I've been consciously and competently practicing this mantra: "CONTROL your emotions and feelings. Feel them, feel the moment, but NEVER fall captive to them." Helen Keller said: "Emotions must be felt with the heart— But never be at the mercy of your emotions."

After decades of single living and moving nine times, I unpacked the boxes of a life with perfect focus. I created a bi-regional health-consultant company in Florida and Colorado. I settled into enjoying the sounds and surroundings of *me*. I split my time between a condominium in the Colorado mountains, and the beach in Florida. I made "health" my life and cherished my time alone, and transferred this joy to my clients.

I was a member of a popular dating site for so long that they offered me six months' free. Thousands of "to-go" boxes later, I released my longing for a relationship, and I wrote a simple relationship affirmation and placed it in my personal Book of Scriptures. It simply stated: "I will attract a man who keeps me excited past the appetizer; a man who knows what he wants and knows how to get it." Life came full circle while I was doing my life the right way, doing what I loved, and feeling the real me. While on my daily run on the beach, my now-husband Bob ran into me "full throttle" in the heat of July and the burning sand of the beach. In a premeditated maneuver, replete with his Department of Defense badge, he introduced himself and asked me out for a glass of wine. Let's just say, it was way more than an appetizer. Bob found me because I was *feeling the real*. After all that running — geographically, professionally, and personally — my soulmate was there all along; hiding in plain sight. He had been watching me on my beach runs, from afar, for weeks. He was my neighbor.

The wisdom that I've gleaned throughout this journey of multiple relationships, especially the relationship with myself is Life "lifes" on all of us. What we do at those times are found in my healthy teaching of the empowering P's:

Perseverance: Positive self-talk and saying this simple affirmation: "I WILL until." Spring and summer always follow fall and winter in life.

Patience: I WILL be okay. Be willing to slow down to speed up.

Passion: Feel your emotions without being emotional and live one hundred percent, all-out, all-in, no matter what.

Persistence: It beats resistance every time. You WILL WIN. The door to an abundant life is marked: P-U-S-H (persist until something happens)

Peace: Keep your mind focused and stayed on the eternal things from above. My life verse says: "All things work together for good, for those who are called according to His purpose." Romans 8:28

Power: What you're going through, you will get through. Visualize the other side and how you feel. Strengthen yourself to be the Band-Aid for someone else's pain.

Present: Art Rust Jr. said: "Yesterday is a canceled check. Tomorrow is just a promissory note. Today is a Present and is the only time we have, so spend it wisely. Give each day a chance to be your best, most adventurous, and joyful day.

All these P's were hiding in plain sight. And just like my soulmate, once I was finally still, they completely enveloped my life and liberated an unleashed joy I didn't realize I had been outrunning. We must grant ourselves the chance, the TIME, to experience each present moment because those minute-by-minute moments accumulate to become our lives. Listen for the whispers of your heart and wisdom. For in those whispers is life. Just give yourself daily permission to dive into the deep end. To *feel the real*. The water is just fine!

IGNITE ACTION STEPS

Feel your own world first. Schedule daily time to check your own "temperature" in all six areas of life: Spiritual; Physical; Mental; Emotional; Social; and Financial.

Spiritual: Mediation and prayer for the first ten to fifteen minutes of each day.

Physical: Doing a variety of physical fitness modalities; moderation is key.

Mental: Gratitude in real-time through a daily gratitude jar.

Emotional: Checking your energy and vibrancy connection by adding a scoop of wheatgrass in a glass of water.

Social: Expressing and accepting love. Hug someone and yourself on a regular basis.

Financial: Manifest your goals and dreams as reflected in your health/wealth accounts.

Dr. Jo Dee Baer — United States
Certified Health Coach, Holistic Nutritionist, PhD, Speaker, Author,
Philanthropist
www.healthcoachjodee.com
 jodee.nylander
@healthcoachjodee

Peter Giesin

"Don't be a lone warrior for a lifetime;
be a lone warrior when needed."

THE LONE WARRIOR

BY PETER GIESIN

Here's the thing, my friend: Every day... every moment... we're writing the story of our life. While we can't rewrite previous chapters, we *can* write the next one purposefully. And, perhaps more importantly, we can write the one we're creating right now. We can write more of what we've experienced that has made us proud of our story. We don't have to be stuck in our story; we can change the beliefs from the ones that didn't serve us, to the ones we love. That's what growth is all about; defining your story, your way.

Lying underneath the sheets, our hands are lightly clasped together; soft, tender music playing in the background. You can feel the energy still pulsing through the air. Our naked bodies, glistening with sweat, spent, yet every molecule radiating from the out-of-body connection that we just experienced. It is one of those magical moments that you only witness in the movies and then fantasize about for days afterward.

My wife whispers, "I love you," as she gently slides over and puts her head on my chest. After moments like this, we love to hold each other and simply talk... about our dreams, our passions. Like two giddy school children, we laugh and joke about who loves each other more. I tell my wife she is amazing.

In return, she loves to say, "If I am amazing, then you're amazing," and then we giggle and smile at each other.

In the aftermath of such a connection I know I should feel content, cared for, and satisfied, yet, something strange and eerily familiar takes over my mind and robs me of the moment. I can feel my energy shift from the blissful passion of two lovers cocooned in each other's aura to that of isolation. With a sinking feeling, I know what happens next will not be good. I start to brood. To pull away. The feelings of goodness become too much and our giggles stop as a more solemn look comes across my face. Still, in her blissful glow, my wife urges me to return to our playfulness. But I cannot stop the words from coming out any more than I can stop the tide from crashing on the ocean's shore.

"Don't make me smile," I say to my beautiful, loving wife; sucking the euphoria out of the room.

Like a black hole, any passion between us is immediately lost and severed. My wife stares into my eyes, at first with curiosity, and then heavy disappointment spreads across her face. She asks one simple question which haunts me to this day. "Why wouldn't you want to smile?"

My wife is absolutely right. *Why on earth would I not want to smile? What would cause a man who has everything to be so unhappy that he wouldn't want to smile?* I knew that if the relationship between my wife and I were to survive and be *Legendary in Love* as we proclaimed it on the day it started, then I needed to find the answer to this question, and pretty darn quick!

Taking several deep breaths, I snuggled up beside her, prepared to do whatever it took to claim my joy, find happiness, and be the self-assured man she truly deserves. As she responds to my cuddling, I profess in my heart that our sacred bond is worth fighting for. With a bit of trepidation, I shared, "I am sorry. I am a raving idiot. You make me smile every day. I know I stop myself from feeling everything, from being emotionally open to our connection… It's because I have never been taught how to process these feelings, and in fact, I have been taught to shield myself from them and bury them in a deep, dark pit within myself. I am ready to jump into that pit and face whatever stands in front of me. I am ready to LIVE my life with you… as a present, openly emotional, and authentic man!"

My wife cuddled me in return, but the moment between us was lost. I was certain I *wasn't* being the man I could be. Mainly because no one had sat me down and told me that I had stepped into my manhood, or taken me off into the wilderness to cast away my boyhood by skinning a wild beast with my own hands. I had passed a heap of potentially meaningful milestones so far in my life — graduations, awards, summer jobs — but nothing so far that left me with a glowing, definitive feeling of manliness. When it came to 'being a man,' the only feeling I could remember learning from my father was that men lived in emotional isolation and accepted loneliness.

I remember my father doing two things in his life: working in the barn or working in the fields. My father never played ball, took me to the park, or just read to me. The only quality time I spent with him was when we were out taking care of the livestock or chopping wood. Even during these times, I was left alone to do my tasks while he was off doing his. Two lone warriors in close proximity but with no connection.

Throughout my childhood, the belief that it was a man's sole responsibility to be the protector and provider and not let any emotions get in the way was firmly instilled in me. My job was to be the lone warrior that stood at the door waiting for danger. Just like real men are not supposed to cry, I saw that they weren't supposed to be emotionally attached either.

I have only one lonely memory of a time when my father set his manly responsibilities aside in an attempt to have a father-son moment. He and I drove into town to watch a movie, *Puff the Magic Dragon*, in the theater. I could feel the excitement in me grow and the love for my father as we walked into the lobby for the first time and then plopped into those big seats. With my father beside me, and a slight grin on his face, I beamed with anticipation and boyhood elation… It was magical. Until, halfway through the show, my father stood up and gruffly said we were leaving; that the movie was stupid and he had better things to be doing back at home. My heart dropped, and that black, lonely pit widened as I shoved my disappointment, my sadness, into it. Never again would I let myself experience such heightened emotions. At that moment, the old-school definition of masculinity, working hard, and sacrificing enjoyment, was firmly and forcefully ingrained into my entire being. I was simply *told* to be a man, and men don't show foolish, or disappointed emotions.

As I matured, I realized, Man is a social creature, and as warriors, we usually rely on a tribe or band of brothers to increase our chance of survival. However, a lone warrior chooses a different path; to lead his life on his own. This lone type of life was what I was shown, all I knew, and what I purposely chose to follow. Because of this solitariness, I had to develop different skill sets and coping mechanisms to (over)compensate for the loss of collective support. I learned to push everything, and everyone, away. Many people advocate this 'loner' way of living. I know this because I spent the majority of my professional career jumping across the world, being the expert who solved everyone else's problems. I was in one place one day and then gone the next; "wham-bam, thank you, ma'am." I believed getting things done "alone" was praised and got more respect. I didn't like asking for help, even when that was the better way to support others.

On the outside, it seemed cool to be out on the savanna by myself, a lone warrior, carrying the world on my shoulders yet looking as if I had no concerns at all. I felt that behind sharp and determined eyes, no one could see the pain I was enduring internally. I persevered and convinced myself that even in the face of endless expectations, a lone-warrior powers through life, no matter what!

If anyone were to ask me what it really feels like to be a lone warrior, I would tell them it is scary and even traumatic; believing that you face the world alone and have no one to turn to for support is gut-wrenching. Gabor Maté states that "Trauma is when we are going through something alone without the ability to share the inner experience with anyone." I have spent the majority of my life living by this solitary code. I knew no other and shared with no one. Unlike a true tribal warrior, I minimized as many relationships as possible. I thought I didn't need the bond of friends from high school, college, or places of employment. I was very strict about keeping my connections with other people at a transactional level and terminated them as soon as they were no longer needed.

As one would expect, this led to a very lonely life, even taking time away from my former wife and my young children. I would diligently spend days on the road traveling for work under the guise of providing for my family. I would bravely endure countless hours in hotel rooms and airplanes by myself, wearing each of them as a badge of honor. Yet inside my soul was crying for connection, wanting to see my children grow up, laugh with friends, socialize with my colleagues, and feel a deep, loving connection.

Then came a time, where the emptiness was too much, and I wanted to break from the shell I had put myself in. I began seeking others, a community, a tribe, a place to feel accepted. After six years of living divorced, unloved, and raising my kids alone, the Universe answered my prayers. I took a chance to explore and seek the connection of others. That was when a Moon Goddess heard my pleas and gifted my life with her most sacred muse to show me how important connection is to live a full and meaningful life. Yes, the incredibly patient woman, who I told not to make me smile, stepped joyfully into my life. In true Goddess fashion, she wanted me to experience the brotherhood of warriors, one that I took on pure faith and trust, testing my lone warrior resolve.

My new love and I took our entire family and traveled to Tallinn, Estonia, to attend a personal development conference. Unbeknownst to our friends at the gathering, we had plans to get married amongst them. Yes, I did say "our friends," but in all honesty, they were my beloved's friends. I had met them during the past year, but in lone warrior fashion, other than my Goddess, I had made no real friendships with any of them.

My wife-to-be's dream was to have a fairytale wedding, with a horse-and-carriage and hundreds of guests. And it was my desire to give her anything she wanted. This meant that we needed bridesmaids and groomsmen standing beside us at the wedding… five of each. For many men, this is an exciting day (and maybe a bit nerve-wracking) as they get to share this momentous occasion with their brothers; their closest friends. I had none of that, despite the friendly facade I had created.

Turning to my future bride, I asked her to pick five men she knew and thought would make good groomsmen. She rattled off a few names, some of whom I recognized and others I had not yet met. At this point, I was near panic. How was I, the lone warrior, going to ask these complete strangers to stand by my side on the most important day of my life? I kept thinking that if it were the other way around and some guy I hardly knew asked me to be part of his wedding, I would certainly say "No thank you" and pass. After a bit of time, with some insight and instincts, we settled on the list of five men we felt would be perfect for the occasion. I stalked off, willing yet skeptical, eager yet terrified inside. I wouldn't say yes to such a request; why would they? I didn't *really* know them. I hadn't made any effort to stay friends. My lone warrior wanted to get married by myself; who needs anyone beside me? I had to push through fears and conditioning. I had to summon every ounce of courage within me to step into what felt like the Colosseum, slay the Roman hordes, connect with each man and present them with the opportunity to be part of this joyous event. Much to my amazement, every single man said yes!

It was all settled. They would stand beside me during the ceremony, and it would be over, right? Wrong. I didn't know that these five guys had known each other for years. So, it was very much to my surprise when they informed me that they would be holding a bachelor party for me. I am not big on parties, especially drunken bashes, as they require way too much social interaction. But I couldn't say no to this new band of brothers. I was terrified and ready to run for the hills to be more comfortable alone. Expecting the worst, I begrudgingly showed up when and where they told me to. It was 11 AM, and I could only think about how *long* the day was going to be. I wanted nothing more than to slip away and hide from this lengthy interaction.

All of the guys were cheerful, friendly, and talkative as we passed along the ancient streets of the Old City Gates in Tallinn. We stopped in front of a small little shop with its doors swung wide open and an old forge with a huge fire raging inside. "We are here," they announced as they slapped me on the shoulder. At the door stood an elderly gentleman wearing a leather apron and holding a small hammer. He smiled and said, "You must be the groom. Congratulations!"

My five new friends and I spent the next two hours heating, pounding, reheating and pounding a large piece of traditional iron. During this time of forging the metal, we shared stories of past and future marriages, businesses, and adventures. This was something I had never, in my entire life, experienced before. These men, whom I had just met, were truly interested in me, my thoughts, ideas, and *feelings*. And they were authentic in who they were and how they felt as any man could be.

From all that pounding and sweating and forging, embraced by this new-found brotherhood, a horseshoe was created. In Estonian tradition, it represents a powerful symbol of protection, prosperity, and positivity.....all things I welcome in my life and my marriage. More importantly, in my life, that horseshoe has become a powerful reminder that I don't have to be alone, that I am welcomed and embraced by men who honor me. That I can step forward in my life... And that I don't have protection, prosperity, and positivity in my life simply because I am a man; I create it, foster it, and craft it in the things I do and the people I surround myself with. I also realized that I had forged a relationship with a goddess who loves me for my own heart. And that my feelings matter and are the true source to my happiness and joy in life.

The horseshoe now hangs in a prominent place in our bedroom, next to the same bed where I uttered that insane statement of don't make me smile, which in essence was don't make me feel or express my happiness. That horseshoe's raw, rugged, primitive texture is a reminder of the moment when five amazing men, in their raw, rugged caring, sat me down and told me that I was a man among them. It is a reminder of when I finally decided what it meant to be good at being a man! At last, I knew what it felt like to have a group of men who had my back, supported me, and wanted to see me happy. That gave me the courage to be happy and drop the lone warrior facade. I saw that if I set my armor aside, was present, and vulnerable, that magical things could happen. It enforced a new belief that I could live openly, express my full emotions, and be a great man.

The truth is that humans are a social species. We thrive when we are in a community. We excel when we feel like there are people who see us, believe in us, and have our backs. We prosper when we are supported and loved by others. Yes, everyone needs some alone time in their lives. There is nothing wrong with that. The problem arises when someone begins to identify as the lone warrior and slowly loses any sense of connectivity with others in their lives. I now see how it is so much more enjoyable to be connected with the many people who enter your life, and how that connection can lead to greatness in your life and theirs.

I want you to know that every thought, word, and action is the composition of your story. The decisions you make today are writing your story tomorrow. And, if you're wise... the character building, personal development, prayer time, skill acquirement, and moments filled will snuggles, giggles, kisses, hugs, 'I love you' and 'I'm so grateful you're in my life,' will all fall into the outline you're creating for your future story. You absolutely *can* create the story in front of you if you remain present and choose solidarity over singleness; intimacy over isolation. Yes, you can get by for a time, fighting and enduring as a lone warrior. But it is when you find a tribe and trust in them that you will finally truly thrive.

IGNITE ACTION STEPS

Here are three powerful ways that you can move toward thriving.

Create a Social Life. Allow yourself to cultivate a rich social life: go to events, join clubs and groups, invest in old hobbies that you love, and re-engage with old friends. Be kind to others. Share yourself vulnerably. This will likely require huge amounts of courage, effort, and time... and it will be worth it.

Offer Support to Others. Put in a genuine effort to continue to invest in those relationships. It's akin to watering a garden... put energy in and energy will come back to you. Reach out to your friends and offer them support. If you've done a good job at understanding them, and knowing their needs, wants, and goals, it should become easy to know or predict what they might need help with.

Ask for Support. We all need a little help from time to time. Allowing yourself to be seen, witnessed, and supported by your friends will strengthen the ties of your social connection Lean on your friends. Call them or meet up when you're having a challenging day. Report your mind to a close confidante when you notice your thoughts slipping back into a lone warrior-type state of operation.

Peter Giesin — United States/Canada
Author, Human Possibility Coach and CTO of Ignite Moments Media
peter@ignitemankind.com
 @pgiesin

Jenna Haji

"In fear, we fall. In love, we rise."

FALLING IN FEARLESS LOVE

BY JENNA HAJI

Life is full of sacred change: loss, transition, rebirth, and transformation. As you steer your ship through turbulent times, remember you are not alone. My wish for you is to bathe in your unconditional wholeness. Release the conditioning that stirs you to believe you are not enough. May you abandon fear and all its deception, and surrender to the joy that lies in possibility. May you kindle the courage to embrace your life from a place of radical love.

I was the textbook definition of a "perfect" child. Not in the boastful, bragging kind of way, but my childhood painted a very floral, rosy, vanilla-scented picture. I was born in the wee morning hours, one crisp Thanksgiving day, the first baby of a self-made car dealership executive and a young runaway bride who wore her heart on her sleeve. My birth certificate logs the details accurately, though, knowing what I do now, I'd contest the revision of one singular fact: I came alive at twenty-five. Not in the biological heart-beating, blood-coursing kind of way — I'd had a quarter of a century to perfect those basic functions. No, I was reborn the moment I witnessed death; devoid of power, barren of control, dissociated from my body, and in complete terror, as I watched the love of my life draw his last breath.

This was far from what I'd envisioned as the beautiful, romantic fairy-tale ending to my otherwise picture-perfect upbringing. It wasn't until my life fell to pieces that I naively remembered most cameras have an auto-focus setting that blurs out the details.

All my life, I'd been a rule follower and an overachiever, to say the least. I was the please-and-thank-you kind of girl who put others before herself; everyone's best friend, a straight-A student-athlete, and president of every club you could think of. The expectations were high, and I kept striving to surpass them. I was only as successful as I was busy; only as prosperous as I was productive.

I never asked for help. I had to uphold the perception that I had everything under control. Growing up, I was surrounded by models of self-determination, self-reliance, and selflessness, and they, too, seemed to have everything under control.

Prior to the loss of my partner, my grip on the future was so firm, it turned my knuckles white. More than food or water, I craved certainty and control. Planning was my superpower; multi-colored highlighters my weapons of choice. I spent countless hours and immense energy fervidly plotting out my life plan in order to create some semblance of safety and security, to convince myself that everything I did was helping me get to somewhere better. I thought I needed to do more, see more, learn more, and become more. There was always more to accomplish. It was never enough. *I* was never enough.

I got my first taste of true freedom when I went to university. I packed my bags full of clothes and books, keeping room in one for the guilt I would carry for moving so far away from home. And then, I did what I knew how to do best: everything all at once. I studied hard, played sports, ran for student government, and volunteered my time. I bobbed in and out of social scenes, being the best friend possible to whoever was next to me at any given moment.

I was losing myself in the hustle of life until finally, I met someone interested in who I actually was, rather than who I meticulously appeared to be; someone who focused on my needs while I so readily focused on everyone else's.

The next seven years were a blur. Somewhere along the way, I earned two degrees, got engaged, landed my first job in the field of speech-language pathology, moved into an apartment with my fiance in a new city, bought a house, and began packing up our life for the next chapter, while planning a wedding. I was doing it all; being the "boss lady" everyone expected me to become and a picture-perfect partner with a supportive man by my side.

What wasn't captured on film during those years were the layers of uncertainty that hovered beneath the facade of success. I had a desperate need to be validated by other people and affirmed by external achievements in order to overcome my internally perceived shortcomings. Anxiety, imposter syndrome, and low self-esteem percolated beneath the surface, emptying my emotional tank while fueling my belief that I had to keep achieving more.

I accomplished every goal I set my mind to, and I was swiftly ticking the boxes on my imaginary life master plan, but my heart still felt like it was missing something. Each night, I crawled into bed, and a sense of dread washed over me. I felt incomplete. I questioned every decision I made. I felt small in the vastness of possibility, like I would never measure up. I felt like I could still lose everything that mattered, that it could all fall away in an instant.

And then, it did.

My partner took his own life before my eyes, one sweltering, suffocating July afternoon. The details are tragic and gruesome and still make me queasy. Some days, I am still ripped against my will back to the sights and sounds and words leading up to the moment he died.

At the ripe age of twenty-five, as I watched one life end, I felt mine forcefully erupt. I was suddenly reborn. Disruptively awakened. What once was a pristine view from the peaks of mountains I'd climbed had become a landscape of darkness and hopelessness. I found myself immersed in emotions of an unparalleled range and intensity.

In losing my partner, I felt like I had lost everything, including my sense of self. My historical pattern of perfectionism and people-pleasing had led me to cling to my roles, duties, and accolades as the measure of my worth. I had come to believe that I only mattered if I mattered to someone else.

My loss thrust me into stillness. Time stood still, a frozen lake filled with lost moments trapped in ice. Every dream I held for my future became a memory, and every hope was laced with grief. Here, in the shattering of my past, present, and future, began the re-discovery of my unconditional wholeness.

I took nearly a year off from work. I moved back home with my parents. My sister and brother set up my childhood bedroom in anticipation of my return. My mom slept with me so the bed didn't feel empty. My dad played the soundtrack of *Hamilton* on repeat, so the silence didn't drown me. My aunt brought her famous dumpling soup. My best friends helped me pack up my apartment. People dropped by with flowers, bath bombs, books, slippers, and more flowers. I asked for help. I let people help me.

In the wake of the collapse, my body, mind, and spirit held an emergency meeting. The result of that collaboration was the following message: I simply could not do it all anymore. My capacity was tapped, and my nervous system was overwhelmed. The brisk pace at which I'd previously paraded through life was no longer possible. I had reached my human limit. Somewhere in the cascading revelations of my humanness, I realized one very important thing. Every single thing I had done until that point in my life was fueled by one force: fear.

The fear of getting hurt kept me from adventure. I steered clear of arguments and confrontation in fear of disrupting the peace. In fear of disappointing my parents, I over-studied to get good grades. I feared being ridiculed by societal beauty standards, so I over-exercised and micromanaged my diet. Fearing exclusion, I people pleased my way through friendships. I strove with every fiber of my soul to be the "perfect" partner, out of fear of being abandoned.

Fear was at the root of me constantly overextending myself. My choices were fed by the toxic norm to *do it all* and make this one life worth living. Now, in moments of clarity, I chuckle at the ridiculousness of having wanted to live a life that left me perpetually burnt out, feeling like I couldn't keep up, like I could never be enough.

Pre-awakening, life had been noisy inside my head because fear was the conductor, clashing the cymbals, alerting me to all the potential dangers that lay before me. After falling into the petrifying stillness following my partner's death, I landed in a state of existence that permitted me to *be* instead of *do*.

I felt liberated. I rallied to vote fear out of government and petitioned for love to reign. I wrote myself a manifesto, and it read:

I release my sense of control on the ever-evolving journey the Universe has in store for me, and welcome the unknown in all its beautiful uncertainty. I embrace the expression of my true spirit and release that which no longer aligns in harmony with my inner wisdom.

I taped those words to my foggy bathroom mirror, and then I set out to re-discover exactly what *did* align in harmony with my inner wisdom. If I wanted to start this new chapter of life differently, I was going to have to do the opposite of living in fear. I was going to have to commit to living life from a place of fearless love.

When I think of love, I imagine warmth, and that reminds me of the sun. That's where I began. I rose with the sun each morning. Even on the days when my vision blurred behind tears of sorrow, I opened the curtains and let the sunlight seep into my skin.

I read books about the isolation of grief. I found an incredible therapist. I watched old home videos and cried. I joined support groups. I bought some plants from a local garden center and watered them tenderly every day. I wrote letters in my journal, and I cried. I took photos of the fiery skies at sunset. I talked to the birds and dragonflies and asked them for signs from Spirit. I canceled my wedding venue and cried. I shopped for new furniture. I became a certified yoga instructor. I auditioned for a choir. I adopted a cat. And I cried.

Every time I felt myself grasping for an outcome, I took a deep breath, and I let go. I let every emotion pass through me as it needed to, at its own pace. The old me used to crave answers and predictability, and there I was, newly alive, radically choosing to surrender. As I fell away from control, I also fell away from fear. As I rose toward embracing love, I fell in love with my true self.

On this journey home to myself, I long to rediscover my sense of presence. In the wake of my grief, I yearn for peace more than ever. I ache to move through life mindfully and invest my energy wisely. With every breath, I cast anchors to keep my boat grounded as I navigate the often tempestuous waters of this awakening. The source of the wisdom I have cultivated is in the knowing that my healing journey is infinite in duration.

I now understand that the divinity that exists within me is constant, whole, and worthy of love. When I lose sight of that love and the fear sneaks back into focus, I remind myself to trust that what was meant for me will not miss me. I choose to believe that with every gold-filled crack in my essence, I am evolving.

If for a moment I slip into the depths of darkness, I do not run. I choose to be still and breathe, letting my shadows equip me with the courage to trust that the light will again return. Even in darkness, I bow inward to myself, knowing that everything I need is within me. I forgive myself with love and fearlessly set myself free.

You too, are free, with every breath, to awaken to your radiant light, your innate perfection, and your inner wisdom. As you face change, you are free to choose love and cast fear away. The lens of life's landscape is ever-changing — at times, you may lose control of the shutter, and the path ahead may appear blurred. Your power lies in letting love spark the flash and capture the moment in all its beautiful possibilities.

Ignite Action Steps

Remember You are Made of Light

As you become aware of your existence as the Universe embodied, you will begin to treat every moment of this life as precious and the waves of grief and worry will crest and fall more rhythmically. When life is overcast and hope is dim, look inward for light. The darkness and shadows will not dissolve, so look to them with gratitude, as they are the oil that burns your light brighter.

You can hold space for your light and your darkness at the exact same time.

Loosen Your Grip

Grant yourself permission to lose sight of the outcome of your every action and get lost in the process. The truth is that you cannot predict the future, everything is temporary, and nothing belongs to you. Don't let that scare you. From a place of surrender, you transform worry into wonder and move from a desperate place of uncertainty to a powerful place of possibility. Trust the timing of your life just like you trust the sun to rise each brand new day.

You must be willing to let die the carefully crafted plans and timelines so your true longings can be born.

Consider Your Energy as an Expense

Productivity does not define your worth. Schedule in time to rest. Slowing down may seem scary, but in doing so, you unlock your potential to connect to a bigger energy. See magic in the mundane, discover your inner power, and uncover your truth. Remember that every thought and action requires energy. Bypassing challenging emotions represses energy within your body and can result in irresponsible, unhealthy expressions of this energy. Treat your energy as currency and invest it wisely.

Abandon the urge to constantly do and embrace the beauty of being.

Swap Perfection for Peace

Have patience with yourself. Show up for yourself. Honor that some days will be good, and some will be good enough. In choosing to be human, your authenticity will allow others to live more freely. Any defeat to perfection you endure is a moment of awakening — of returning home to yourself.

Your pain is a portal to turn your purpose into peace.

Jenna Haji, H.BHSc., MHSc., S-LP(C), RYT- Canada
Speech-Language Pathologist, Yoga Teacher
Founder of Sunrise Studio Wellness
bit.ly/sunrisestudiowellness
🔲 Sunrise Studio Wellness
🔲 @sunrisestudiowellness

Rosemary French

"Live like a LION-ESS."

"LAY HEAVY, ROSEMARY."

BY ROSEMARY FRENCH

This is my journey of loss, healing, and self-discovery. My wish is that you find HOPE in my story, so you can look at the events in your life that brought you to your knees and see them for what they are: lessons, gifts, a journey back to your heart. When I thought I had lost everything... I found so much. The inside journey is hard but so worth it. It's there you will find life-changing Wisdom.

"We found a growth. It's cancer."

The hospital room went wavy as my breath caught in my chest. I couldn't tell whether I was holding my breath, or the breath just wasn't there. My chest was tight. All I could feel was FEAR. My husband, Peter, had just gone in for routine tests when we got the terrible news. He had cancer. Cancer had been all around me: my parents, his father, and now my beloved Peter. To think of losing my husband was inconceivable. I loved this man from the moment I saw him in high school. I married him and raised two beautiful boys, Michael and Daniel.

They removed his growth and because they found it early, no further treatment was required. After one year, Peter went for a full round of tests and his doctor gave us the all-clear. We finally exhaled and celebrated by taking a wonderful vacation to the beaches of Mexico. We were so happy knowing he would be alright. We were playful, laughing, holding hands as we walked the beach, enjoying every meal and every moment together. We felt so lucky, thinking everything was going to be okay.

After returning from our trip, Peter started feeling unwell. At first, he seemed flu-ish, stuck in bed with a fever, and we were sure he had just picked something up in Mexico. But after two weeks, he still wasn't getting better. One day, unexpectedly, he said with worry, "Rose, I can't *see*." Tight-chested again, I rushed him to the hospital.

Shockingly, a new type of cancer was diagnosed, and they told us that they wanted to start treatment immediately. That was on a Wednesday. On Friday, in the middle of the night, the hospital called and asked us to come immediately. I knew it was bad. Why else would they call at 3 AM? "It's going to be bad," I kept repeating as friends drove Michael, Daniel, and me to the hospital. As we walked down the hall toward my husband's room, the nurse said, "I'm sorry, Peter died during the night." I instantly buckled, tears streaming. As we walked to his bedside, my sons and I wept in complete shock as we held Peter's hand and said goodbye to my husband and their father. He was fifty-two years old.

WHAT JUST HAPPENED? HE WAS FINE. I was in SHOCK. I was numb. It felt like I was having an out-of-body experience. I could not understand what was happening. People talked to me, asked me questions… my brain was not working. I could not make the smallest decision. I felt cloudy and fuzzy and lost. It was then that FEAR overtook me.

We held his funeral, a funeral mostly organized by my friends because I couldn't cope. Surrounded by people, I still felt so alone. I was lost, unable to make the smallest decisions or make the smallest movement forward. After the funeral, I sat alone in my living room, staring at Peter's chair, at a standstill while everyone else seemed to be moving. I didn't know what to do. But I knew ONE thing: I didn't want to feel my pain. The hurt was so big, so deep, and so dark that I felt it would swallow me up, and I wouldn't find my way out. So, I did everything I could to run from it.

I went back to work within two weeks because I needed to escape. I was an associate vice president for a large financial services company. I poured everything I had into my work because it was the only thing that felt safe and constant. For brief moments, focusing on work allowed me to forget the pain inside and that my life at home had just blown up and was unrecognizable to me. I continued to avoid my heavy sorrow, and I paid a heavy price.

The reality was, I couldn't hide from it no matter how much I wanted to. Each day, as soon as I left work, the same feelings of fear and panic overwhelmed me like a dark cloud. Because I knew I would be alone in the home that used to be *ours*. I would grab a bottle of wine on the way back, ready to open it the moment I walked in the door. Anything, just to calm my nerves and numb the agony I felt inside.

I didn't know that grief feels like fear. It does. I didn't understand what was happening to me. I tried to hide my feelings and did everything I could to show the rest of the world that I was okay. I was not okay. I replayed a toxic, negative mantra: *I can't do this, I'm scared, I'm alone*, repeatedly in my head. The only way I could find at the time to quiet the sound was excessive cigarettes and alcohol.

As this continued, my closest friends and family were getting worried. My son said, "Mom, stop drinking and smoking. I just lost Dad to cancer — I can't lose you." I was scaring him. I was scaring myself. I just couldn't stop because that meant that I had to face my grief and my pain. It meant that I had to carve out a new life, and I didn't want to. I didn't know *how* to. This pattern of denial and neglect went on for several years.

Finally, at my friends' insistence, I went to see my doctor, took depression medication, and went to therapy. I began a very slow road to healing. It was a roller coaster of sadness, desperation, and fear, followed by moments of normalcy that lasted minutes and then days, only to fall into hopelessness and desperation again.

During this tumultuous time, I met a wonderful man, Tom. His love, kindness, and patience gave me hope. I began to think, *I'm going to be okay.* I had something to look forward to, a light in my very darkest days.

Looking back, I could not have predicted just how important forming a relationship with Tom would become. One day, Tom mentioned he had felt a lump in my breast. As soon as he mentioned it, that old familiar fear rushed back, taking my breath away and paralyzing me. My thoughts swirled, *This can't be happening to me. I just met him. I'm just starting to feel okay.*

Instead of facing it, I did what I always do… I avoided it for months. New words were on repeat in my head: *No, it can't be. It's not going to happen to me.* But the thought of the lump kept haunting me, so I got it checked. A few weeks later, Tom and I heard the doctor say, "Rosemary, you have breast cancer." As the words came out of the doctor's mouth, I FROZE. All I could say was "no." I started to heave big tears, and I continued to cry: tears for me, tears for the loss of my husband, tears for the loss of my parents, tears for my children, tears for my past, and tears for my very uncertain future.

A million fears raced through my brain.

I cried out to God: "I've lost my father, husband, and mother to cancer in the last five years. I don't want to die! How can I tell my children? They've lost so much. Who will take care of them? I am an only child; who will take care of me? I don't want chemo. Why me? Please, God, not my hair! What about work? AND what about Tom? He lost his wife to breast cancer. He didn't sign up for this."

I was terrified. I needed to run somewhere, but knew I couldn't run to drinking this time. I googled "cancer support," and thank God, I ran to something positive: Wellspring Niagara™, a local cancer support center. Very quickly, I was wrapped in warmth and support from people who had walked this path before me. That evening, I was invited to attend a breast cancer group. There, surrounded by people going through cancer themselves, I began to talk about my feelings and fears, and it felt good. I needed to be with people like me, and once I was, I could process the inside journey I had to take.

At the beginning of my cancer journey, I received a card from my girlfriend that said, "I didn't know what BRAVE was until I saw it in my friend." Every time I read her card, it makes me weep, though it took me a long time to figure out why. It's because I DIDN'T feel brave. NOT one bit. I was terrified and overwhelmed and could not stop crying. I didn't want cancer. I didn't want the treatments and quite frankly, I wanted to run away. I hated that everyone's life kept going, but mine felt as if it had stopped. I did not feel brave. I felt overwhelming fear.

"Lay heavy, Rosemary," my radiation technicians would say to me. I had to lay on the radiation table as two technicians would push and pull me on the sheet below: centimeters one way, then centimeters another way to get me positioned within millimeters of the radiation light source. I would get impatient and always reposition my body and move myself to make it go faster. They would always smile and say, "Lay heavy Rosemary. We'll do all the work." Each time I moved my own body, I made it worse and we had to start again. This happened every day for thirty days.

Eventually, I learned to surrender and let them do their job. I thought about all the things I've worried about and tried to control in my life for fear of having them go wrong. Work, kids, finances, relationships, cancer. I finally realized that I had no control over any of those things. Lying there on the radiation table, I had to accept that I could not do the technicians' job. And at last, I had the thought that set me free. "I'm tired of doing God's job. I don't want it." I surrendered to Him and the Universe and realized that He doesn't make mistakes. I might not like it, I might not understand it, but once I accepted it, I was able to say, "Okay," and begin moving forward.

By stepping forward, I started to look at my life's events differently. Cancer showed me the power of LOVE. When I got cancer, I was terrified and worried about who would take care of me. I strongly believe that I am standing here today because Tom and a beautiful tribe of women friends showed me love and compassion that I have never experienced before. One by one, they came around me, encircling me with their support and kindness, their encouragement and time. They lovingly came without me asking and were the family that I needed.

Tom came to every single doctor's appointment and every chemo treatment. He held my hand for hours during treatments and tried to make me laugh so I could forget, for a few moments, how scared I was feeling. He watched me lose my strength and my hair. He brought me to his home and took care of me after my surgery. I kept thinking, "He did not sign up for this," but he never seemed to mind.

My girlfriends organized themselves like a S.W.A.T. team and started a meal drop plan. They came running when I called them weeping. They told me, "You've got this, Rosemary," when I didn't want to have another treatment. They never asked, "What can I do?" They just came. They told me I was beautiful when I lost my hair. They kept talking about all the trips we were going to take so I could see, feel, and touch my future. I saw God in each one of them.

Cancer taught me to take care of myself with a vengeance. I have spent most of my life pleasing other people. I was a "good Italian girl." I was taught that taking care of others, pleasing them so they were happy, and protecting their feelings was my job.

I spent the first half of my life making my outside look good. I wanted the second part of my life to be different. I needed to heal my inside because I hurt, but I didn't know how.

I started talking to God, asking him for what I needed. Sometimes I asked in quiet prayer, sometimes I wrote it, often I begged and cried alone in my bed at night. I asked, "I want this pain inside to stop, but I don't know how," "I want to live," "I want my body to heal and be strong," "I want to feel joy," "I want to feel Love so big it swells my heart." "And God, when my hair grows back, I want hair like a LION-ESS!"

Through cancer, I began to focus on ME as I learned about different ways to heal. I tried everything. It became my mission — my job was to heal ME. I learned about and immersed myself in Reiki, energy healing, hypnotherapy, healing circles, meditation, tapping, positive affirmations, writing therapy and yoga. I decided to write my personal story, knowing it would help me and someone else heal. I learned that each technique healed me in different ways and at different levels. My teachers became my guides and an integral part of my journey back to health. I discovered that this is the way of the energy world. It's how God works.

I began to uncover and peel back all the layers of pain, guilt, and lies that I picked up along the way about myself. As I explored my deep feelings, pain, and grief, I cried a million tears. I would go to the graves of my parents and my husband. Alone, I wept. At first in anger that they left me, then in gratitude for the wonderful years we had together and the beautiful children that I get to see grow. I let my tears come and flow down my cheeks, tears from heaven. I started to question everything about myself, my beliefs, what's right for me and what's wrong. I began to question what beliefs were mine and which beliefs were imposed by my parents and other people. I learned to say "no" to things that weren't right for me. I asked my inner guide for answers. I learned to trust my instincts and recognized that it was not my job to please others.

As I started to heal, my desire for those unhealthy things that I used to cloud my mind and numb my pain lost their power. Cancer forced me to STOP. STOP… to grieve, evaluate my life, change the destructive behaviors, and ask myself who I am and who I want to be.

In some crazy way, cancer saved me and changed me for the better. I spend more time with my children. I do things that make me happy. I speak my truth. I cry when the tears come. I rest when my body is tired. I sit in quiet to meditate. I focus on positive thoughts. I am so grateful for everything. I talk to God. I've learned to love and be loved. To take care of myself. I've learned that I am strong and I am BRAVE. And once I let go of the fear that lay heavy on my heart, I could finally live the abundant life that had blossomed all around me.

There is the belief that cancer is lonely, but not because you are alone and not surrounded by people, but because you are forced to go inside, and you are the only one who can do that. If you embrace that journey and be brave enough to discover your freedom, you'll learn the truth and beauty in you. After you have cancer, you have a new appreciation for life and the courage to "Live."

Live life with clarity and conviction. Live life with gratitude and gratefulness. You will find strength and know your power, beauty, and magnificent worth.

IGNITE ACTION STEPS

- As soon as you can, TALK about what's going on. Keeping your story and your pain inside is toxic. It's important to get your feelings and tears out. Don't be embarrassed about your emotions; they are real and part of who you are. They need to be expressed and get out of your body. Find a friend, search out a support group, or connect with family. Do not be alone. You have to share your feelings. Talking about it helps.

- Find your TRIBE. Create a group of people around you. Ask people for help; they want to be there. Friends, family, support groups, neighbors, coworkers are all invested in your well-being. Ask people to come to visit you if you need the company. Ask someone to drive you to treatment. You don't have to be alone. There are cancer support centers and resources in your local hospital. Make a list of all the people you know will be in your corner if you ever need them. You'll be surprised to find how many people will be there if you ask.

- Accept the TRUTH about what you can control and what you can't. Use meditation to be quiet and still. Let this practice bring you closer to your center, inside your body, connected to your breath and inner strength. Breathwork teaches you to use the power of Life Energy and will help you stay calm, grounded, and healthy.

Rosemary French — Canada
Lover of life, Entrepreneur, and Inspirational Coach.
rosemary_french@icloud.com

Victoria Rader

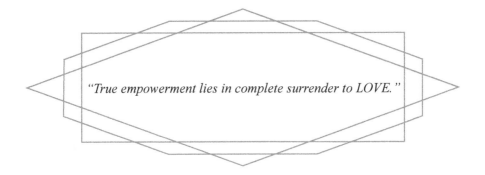

"True empowerment lies in complete surrender to LOVE."

LIFE AT THE TIP OF A HAIRPIN

BY VICTORIA RADER

I am opening my heart widely and vulnerably to take you on my journey of life, death, and true empowerment. You will find me feeling powerless through resistance, just as we all do when we feel life happens *to* us. You will find me feeling power-hungry through resilience, just as we all do when we claim that life happens *for* us. Finally, you will find me feeling empowered through surrender, for we gain empowerment when we experience life as the energy of love happening *through* us. I invite you to live the power of the statement *I am mE!* Where mE is who you are as mortal Eternal, matter Energy, material Essential, manifesting Expansive, bright light of creation in your physical form.

The second I opened the door to my house, a heavy feeling immediately swelled deep within my heart. I knew. I had known for a while. I had been trying to resist it. For the first time since we adopted and brought him home over eight years ago, my English foxhound Amos was not greeting me. I could feel his lingering presence in the air as I called his name and ran upstairs. I found him lying on the floor in my husband Randy's man-cave. "It's okay, Amos, now that you cannot come and meet me, it is my turn to come to you. Can you hang on till Dad comes home tomorrow so he can say goodbye to you?" Tears were running down my cheeks as I was hoping Randy would make it home from Japan in time. I knew it was time — not only time to say goodbye but my time to choose complete surrender. Life had been building me up toward this moment of surrender for decades.

Thirty years earlier.

I am five. Mama and Papa are both at work, and my grandpa Volodya, my "Dedushka," is babysitting me for the day. I know better than to upset Dedushka, so I try to be quieter than quiet, playing house in the bedroom. I sort through my toy items, looking for something tiny enough to hang a doll's dress on. A metal hairpin is the perfect size. As I look for a place to put it, I discover the thin holes of a nearby electric socket are the ideal place to wedge this new miniature hanger.

Electric shock!

The static in the air vibrates thick with Dedushka's fear. He stands at the door, seeing that I am alive, yet paralyzed with silence — the loudest kind of silence, deafening, with fear beyond any words. Fuses blew, and so did my grandpa right after the original deadly silence. "Are you insane? You could have died! Never do this again!" I do not hear his words. I am absorbing his fear of death and his anguish over the possibility of losing me. Within seconds, my childlike passion for life is shifted to living in fear of death. It is shifted to survival.

A few short months later, I felt the similar static of anguish in the air once again. Loud shouting and screaming of one name, Valera, overtook the otherwise completely quiet, isolated beach on the Black Sea. We had hiked with my parents and found this absolutely secluded private spot, tucked away behind the rocky shoreline. We learned that this name we were hearing, Valera, belonged to a master swimmer. He was so confident in his swimming skills that he swam past the fishing nets, then became entangled. Powerless to break the hold, he drowned and was brought back to the shore by the waves. His friends were trying to revive him, shouting, "Valera, Valera... please!" Then came the defeated, suffocating silence of complete realization they had lost their friend. The anguish caused by death. Absorbing the events in front of me, I was unaware and unable to receive the comfort coming from my mom and dad. I formed two devastating patterns: fear of death and fear of water. *To stay alive, I must resist water. Resistance is the way to survive.*

Powerlessness caused by this internal fear of water kept me captive through most of my school years. I avoided any activity that involved any possibility of swimming. Often, this powerless feeling left me completely isolated. One year I went to the athletic camp, where we lived in tents and cooked over the fire, taking baths at the nearby lake. Between training, all of my friends would go swimming, while I sheepishly stayed back.

No more, I won't let this fear keep me afraid. With my mind all made up, and with zero swimming skills, I jumped in the deep water off the pier on a dare from my friends. Both paralyzed by fear and with a complete lack of muscle memory, I froze and started to drown. I don't remember anything beyond the jump. Clearly, I was pulled out and saved. But now the fear was validated and settled even deeper. In this moment of power-hunger, of desire to reclaim my power back, I had failed and withdrew back to being powerless.

Due to my fear, once I had my two kids, I made sure they took swimming classes and were excellent swimmers. While I was empowering them by equipping them with the necessary skills, I continued feeling pretty powerless when it came to water. The feeling culminated when we were on one of the excursions off Santorini in Greece. The boat brought us to some healing hot clay pools formed within the old volcano. All we had to do was to jump into the water and swim fifty yards to the pools. Not only did I not jump in, but I also prevented both of my kids from doing so. I was terrified that, despite them being good swimmers, if they struggled in the water, I wouldn't have been able to help. My fear was not only suffocating me, but it was disempowering my kids. I was resisting life to keep them in survival mode, thus preventing the joy of life from happening through them. There had to be a better way.

I was hungry to reclaim my power back, and knew that I needed to have practical skills backing my burning desire. I took basic swimming classes, then went even further. I got certified in Emotional Freedom Techniques and Theta Healing, while learning to release my deeply embodied fear. Step-by-step, and year after year, shifting from resistance to resilience, I became more and more whole, more comfortable with the water. I learned to truly enjoy the freedom you feel when trusting your body weight to the support of the water, loving the water, and letting go of fear. I finally felt empowered in the water.

My shift from powerless resistance to power-hungry resilience was to be tested. My fear of swimming was just a cover for a much deeper fear of losing a loved one to death. A frequent visitor throughout my life, death really came knocking on my door in 2013. I lost eleven people that were dear to me throughout the year. The first call of the year came with news about my aunt Luyda, who died unexpectedly from a heart attack in Moldova. Mom and I, still in complete shock from the sudden loss, flew over from the United States to say our final goodbyes.

In March, as we barely returned back to the US, I heard someone come to my house. I smiled as I saw my dad. Dad was not smiling. "You need to sit down… Grandma just called… Alex died". Alex was my cousin, with whom I grew up as a child; both of us lived at my grandma's house for a while. Panic enveloped my body; the familiar thick static of anguish in the air. I felt completely numb and frozen once again. Alex *drowned*. We do not know the circumstances of his death, other than he was alone and heavily intoxicated.

My grief engulfed me. I did not resist it. I trusted it to show me the way to healing. I leaned into my grief. While mourning Alex, during one of my morning meditations, I was taken to a vision of a pure stream of water. I palpably felt myself floating through it, feeling the freshness and the coolness around me, seeing the river rocks on the bottom of the stream. All of a sudden, I had a feeling of being lifted up from the water and carried up into the open sky. I could feel the breeze. I felt weightless, light, filled with immense hope and radiant joy. A quiet knowing that Alex was at peace filled every fiber of my being. I knew that what I experienced was the sacred transition of his spirit, his eternal energy, and essence, out of his mortal body and into the light and love of our Creator. I was comforted and uplifted. I felt the healing power of love beyond my ability to deny it. I knew not only through my faith, but also through my very experience that death did not interrupt life. It simply framed it to teach us how to appreciate our every moment. Death invites us to surrender to LOVE, or as I identify **LOVE**: Life-Originating Vibrant **E**-motion (Energy-in-motion).

Death after death, I was learning to surrender deeper and deeper to LOVE. Each upcoming month throughout 2013 brought a new transition of a family member or a friend as I was further letting go of resistance to pain and developing resilience through surrendering to LOVE. And then a call came from Anya.

Anya was my best friend from college. She was there when I met my husband in Ukraine at the Mohila Academy. She was there when I was expanding my intuitive abilities reading coffee cups and cards every Saturday for a group of friends in my apartment in Kyiv. She was there when I fearfully shut all of those abilities down when I foresaw the death of a friend's father — not knowing how to voice it or whether I was to prevent it — then witnessed him die within days of my intuitive feeling. Anya was there when I turned to God for guidance about my gifts and when I turned over and surrendered my fears to Divine Power and dedicated my life to be a vessel of God's light.

I was reading a book when the call came in, "Hi, Vica, it has been a while…

They just diagnosed me with stage four advanced throat cancer. Can you heal me?" The peace and the knowing came immediately. I lovingly connected to Anya's energy and asked to witness a healing. She was instantly enveloped by the most brilliant light. I saw angels descend and surround her. I saw her spirit ready to walk through the iridescent light door. The healing she was being granted was not for her physical body, but for her immortal soul. I no longer had to hide my light in fear of death. I was able to convey to her with great love that she would soon find relief from the pain and suffering; that soon she would find healing peace. That was the last time I talked to her. She died a few days later, welcomed by the same angels that I witnessed in her healing.

I felt deep grief and even deeper peace. I was expanding my ability to accept death as a sorrowful yet beautiful part of life, so that I could live fully and invite and guide others to do the same. That year of death brought the birth of my company: named YU2SHINE™ as an invitation to allow for the light within to be shining brightly without fearful resistance.

We resist life because we fear pain, and because we fear death as the ultimate version of pain. Resisting pain leads to suffering. Accepting pain resiliently leads to deep joy. By welcoming, understanding, listening to, and thanking our pain, we can then fully accept healing. We can accept love. We can accept life. Pain creates an opening within our heart that the light of LOVE fills. We become empowered as we resiliently surrender our resistance to the flow of Divine Power. *True empowerment lies in complete surrender to LOVE.*

Surrender was a big, BIG trigger word for me. For my Ukrainian/Russian genetics and history of wars, surrender as a concept was simply unacceptable. Surrender meant captivity. It meant both the loss of freedom and the loss of dignity. *You fight, or you die.*

Yet surrender is not weakness. Surrender is giving up your force to gain Divine Power. If you sit on a bench and lift your feet, you give your weight to that bench and let it support you. Surrender is a powerful choice you make, and it can strengthen you as it unburdens you.

Even as I am writing this chapter, Russian troops have invaded my homeland, my beautiful and free Ukraine. Ukraine is resiliently resisting the darkness, while fully surrendering to LOVE, as prayers and healings of light are sent to create a hope of peace from all around the world. I know the light will prevail. I surrender to LOVE.

My final moment of surrender to LOVE came in 2014, when I had to say my final goodbye to Amos. He was my canine soulmate. He responded to my every thought and reacted to my every feeling. The bond between us was felt by all. As I walked through the door of my home, I knew it was his time to be set free through death, and my time to be set free through life, trusting LOVE to carry us both.

After burying him as a family in our backyard, I laid on the couch, staring into the ceiling. I was allowing for grief and allowing for healing. Praying, asking, and inviting LOVE. "Please, please, I surrender my grief. Show me how to live even more fully, with deeper joy and deeper awareness." And every day since then, the great Creator of All that Is has been showing me, guiding me, on how to continue to surrender to LOVE and live fully — one day, one person, one act at a time.

All those years ago, I was spared from a 230-volt current because of the resistance in the fuses. Resistance saved my life. Think of it, the same amount of power is offered to all of the outlets in your house. It is the resistance within each appliance that allows for the amount of power through. Hence, some bulbs shine at forty watts and some at one hundred! Like electric devices, we all have equal power of light and LOVE offered to us through our Creator. It is our resistance to the flow of that power that dims us. It is our surrender to that power that shines through us brightly. And connecting to that power does not require something massive; it only takes the tip of a hairpin.

IGNITE ACTION STEP

I invite you to surrender your resistance to LOVE. Right now, I invite you to choose true empowerment through this **Re-plugging Empower-mE Visualization.** Record this on your phone in your own voice, and use it to shift out of feeling powerless to truly empowered.

Take a deep breath in, counting to six – 1, 2, 3, 4, 5, 6; and out – 1, 2, 3, 4, 5, 6. And again. In for six counts… Out for six counts… And one more time. In for six… Out for six... Closing your eyes, imagine that there is a beautiful, brilliant spark of light deep within your heart's center. Imagine connecting to that bright light and going deeper and deeper into it, being pulled and welcomed by the light. The deeper you go, the more welcome, the more at home you feel. Home, deep within this warm light that is the very Source of all love. Imagine how this love enfolds you, allowing you to relax fully. Feel your shoulders, neck, and whole body relaxing into this loving light.

Now feel this love expand down to your solar plexus, your light center, connecting yet to a brighter light. Imagine the energy between your heart center and your light center travel back and forth, creating a beautiful number eight pattern, the pattern of infinite flow of love and light. Gently flowing up and down and expanding through your whole body.

Now to your LEFT, imagine a still image of a situation that is disempowering in your life. Notice how there are currently power cords leading from your light center and to the image.

Now imagine to your RIGHT, a bright endless source of light. Quickly and effortlessly unplug the cords from the disempowering black and white still image on the LEFT and re-plug them to the empowering bright source of all light on the RIGHT.

Repeat: *It is done. It is done. It is done. I surrender to LOVE. I am empowered.*

See and feel how the energy of light is being poured through you, creating a new image that is coming to life on your RIGHT with vibrant details of the outcome you desire. Feel the way you wish you were feeling: free, empowered, fulfilled, and happy. See the picture brighten up as you imagine all the good feelings you are feeling in that image.

Continue in the joyful space of empowered creation… then, take a deep breath in, and out. Now open your eyes.

Victoria Rader — United States / Ukraine
Possibility Coach ™, Founder of YU2SHINE™, Best-selling Author, Speaker
Empower mE ™ TV Show Host
www.yu2shine.com
 yu2shine
 vica_rader

Melanie Summers

*"Do not let lies from your past
become the truth of your now."*

UNMASKING TRAGEDY: MY JOURNEY TO TRUTH

BY MELANIE SUMMERS

Memories are sometimes sad and sometimes joyful; at times peaceful, or occasionally traumatic. Our personality is reflected by flashes of memories and emotions we felt at the time they were made and echoed through feelings of either misery or contentment in our current life. It is my hope to prove that untruths and tragedies of yesteryear don't have to define *you* now.

There I was, slouched over my desk, chin in hand, pondering my life. I often sat like that, squeezed into overly tight clothes, which accentuated my tummy rolls, a frown pasted on my lips. This version of me would look at others and ask herself, "Why is that person so angry? Why is that person so heavy? Why is that person so stubborn?" as well as many other "Whys." However, I should have directed those questions at myself. Subconsciously, I saw imperfections in others that were really reflections of me. How did I go from angry, overweight, and stubborn to being strong, well-rounded, and a healthy human being? Let me share.

I guess I should take you back to my formative years, sometime in the mid-1950s. I was the third child of four children living on a farm overlooking the Ohio River Valley, in West Virginia. I never appreciated how stunningly beautiful my home was because of all the hard work it entailed. From early spring into late fall, we worked in the hayfield, mucked out barns, cultivated the huge garden, and did chores around the yard. We traded food with my uncle, who owned a dairy farm: his spring peas for our green beans; Dad's beef for his milk, cream, and eggs. Astonishingly, it was years before I learned that milk, eggs, and vegetables could be bought in a grocery store!

We woke up before the sun, in time to catch the bus for school. When we got home in the late afternoon, we changed clothes then did evening chores. After the dishes were washed, dried, and put back in the cupboard, we completed our homework around the kitchen table, took a bath, and went to bed. Life was very structured and repetitive; however, I often felt alone and unloved and turned to food for solace. That was partly because solace wasn't going to come from my dad.

Dad was a WWII veteran, who we now know suffered from PTSD. We learned early to stay out of his way when he was "in a mood." Some of the lessons I learned were probably not what he intended. For instance, one time, my chores were completed early, so I went to the neighbor's to play. Since we were gleefully whooping and hollering in their apple orchard, I didn't hear Dad call me to dinner. Finally realizing he was shouting for me, I abruptly stopped and scampered home. He was waiting at our property line, belt in hand, fuming.

He demanded, "Why didn't you come when I called you?"

Fearfully, I said, "I didn't hear you."

He whipped me, shouting, "You're lying! You were ignoring me, weren't you?"

To stop him, I screamed, "Yes! I didn't want to stop playing!"

That is the day I learned to lie. It's also the day I began to hate my father.

Another time, an older cousin molested me sexually. Knowing I was afraid of Dad, he threatened to say it was my idea to "play doctor," and I believed him. Therefore, I held it inside and hid anytime dear ole "Cuz" was around. My imagination triggered nightmares over these situations, eliciting terror — terror that caught my breath and squeezed my insides so *hard* I couldn't breathe. Alas, the deceit did get uncovered, and there is no other way to describe Dad's anger than the military term "DEFCON 1." Needless to say, my punishment was grim.

I hated life on the farm, but I had one spot of heaven I adored — I owned an Appaloosa horse. I claimed her the day she was born and named her Polly. In my spare time, I'd go to the pasture and whistle, and wherever she was, Polly came galloping! I'd just grab a handful of mane and jump on her back, tearing off on an adventure, no bridle, no saddle. We were one with the sun. On those days, we'd wander wherever our path chose to go. Sometimes, I'd sit on my favorite spot overlooking the river and dream of what I wanted to do and where I wanted to go while Polly cropped grass and occasionally blew in my hair.

Years later, when I was in college, Mom told me Dad had sold Polly. I saw red! How could he just *SELL* the *one* thing that meant more than the world to me? I harbored lifelong resentment toward him until a random phone call from my younger sister revealed what really happened. Polly was mortally injured during a thunderstorm, and Dad had to put her down. Rather than allow me to picture her in the throes of death, Dad concocted the story of her sale. Epiphany! It must have been tough on Dad to shoot my baby, then resolve to keep that terrible scene from my memories! Maybe he'd learned, too, that sometimes it's safer to lie.

When I was miserable, to make myself feel better, I ate. A LOT. By the time I was in fifth grade, I wasn't quite five feet tall but weighed 150 pounds. Trust me when I say that kids can be cruel. "Bully" is just a word until it is put into action! I lost a good bit of weight during junior high. Frankly, I finally wanted to fit in. Sadly, the boy I liked had no interest and said horrible things to me, so I drowned my sorrow in food and gained back all the weight I'd lost.

I lost weight again during my senior year of high school; I wanted a date for the prom! I did well until I went to college with my boyfriend, but he broke up with me when he found another girl. Again, I overindulged in food, and again, I wound up dieting. When I caught my first husband in a compromising position, I don't have to tell you what I did. This happened over and over throughout my life.

On October 9, 2017, it happened one final time at the age of sixty-two. It was the first time food was not the solution. Let me explain.

I was a forty-two-year veteran schoolteacher from three different states, working at a charter school, and at the top of my game! During fall break, I received a phone call from a nearby school district asking me to interview for their math and science administrator. I said no, because I didn't have an Arizona teaching license *or* a master's degree in mathematics, which is the law for public schools in Arizona. The principal insisted, "I'm *positive* the district will work with you! Your resume is impeccable!"

He described the perks that came with the job: my current salary would double; a possible $5,000 bonus at the end of the year; I'd share an office and a secretary with the language arts administrator. SWEET! So, I agreed to an interview. Three days later, the principal called and offered me the job, so I scheduled an appointment to break my good news to my current principal.

There is an old saying "Don't count your chickens before they hatch." Minutes before my appointment, my phone rang. It was the principal from the other school. He began, "I'm afraid I have some bad news," and my stomach flip-flopped. Contrary to his initial claims, I couldn't be hired unless I obtained my master's degree in math from an Arizona accredited college. I *knew* it had been too good to be true! When we disconnected, my first thought was, "Wow! It's a good thing I haven't officially resigned from THIS job!"

Well, there is another old saying — something about "waiting for the next shoe to drop." There is a letter that one school sends another to verify your work history. The owner of my current school got *that* letter *that same morning,* which angered her. She *supposedly* called my principal and said, "She obviously doesn't want to work at *my* school; fire her!" Despite the impeccable resume I boasted, I was told to gather my things and leave. I was dumbfounded. How could they fire me?

The following morning, a former coworker called me. Proverbs 16:18 comes to mind: "Pride goes before destruction, and a haughty spirit before a fall." She revealed my ex-principal had lied. She did *not* have to fire me; she was given a CHOICE. Her boyfriend needed a job, and the best way to get him hired was to create a vacancy. My co-worker clarified, "The District actually left the decision to her because they knew you two were friends." I immediately called the District, who confirmed what my coworker said.

Cue the anger! Cue the tears! And cue the binge eating!

About six months after *the incident*, my new husband said something about a picture of me on Facebook™. I remember I was fixing dinner when curiosity made me stop and take a quick peek. There I stood, my 200-pound body resembling the Stay Puft Marshmallow Man! I was mortified! Gasping for air, I broke out sobbing, my tears sizzling as they dropped into the frying pan. I felt I had been pulled into a colorless, motionless vacuum, as the truth I'd been hiding from smacked me in the chest: "Melanie, you are committing suicide by food." I knew with absolute clarity, if I didn't get a handle on me, myself, and I — *I was going to die.* I knew I *had* to make some personal changes, or my future would involve doctors, hospitals, and taking handfuls of prescription medications every day. Was that the vision of my future I had all those years ago daydreaming with Polly?

With this awakening, I took deliberate steps into the first day of the rest of my life.

I realized this repetitive cycle occurred every time something traumatic happened; I gained a lot of weight and then lost it. THIS time, instead of trying yet another fad diet, I took a long look at myself in the mirror. What did I want to do with the rest of my life besides eat and pretend all was well with the world? I read an article that led me to realize the only way to stop this cycle of self-abuse — and that's what it was — I HAD TO STEP OUT OF THE "CIRCLE." I had to find out the real reasons I always resorted to this unhealthy pattern every time something tragic transpired.

My truth? My issues stemmed from all the trauma and drama from childhood. Unconsciously, I felt anger and shame for so many things that had never been resolved. I kept those issues bottled up inside, allowing them to fester whenever I felt unworthy. I didn't realize I was a very angry person, and angry people can be ugly inside. I combated nasty comments directed at me from childhood with uglier comments in response. Things said to me didn't feel good, but a plateful of brownies tasted good. I soothed myself with milkshakes when I felt sad and unloved. I protected myself, first with dishonesty, then with comfort food.

Eventually, I came to terms with several different issues I had been carrying around with me like an overstuffed suitcase. First, Dad acted the way he did every time he was angry because of the culture of post-WWII. Men had to show strength, never show weakness, and lie to themselves and their loved ones just to get by. Also, he didn't really know he was angry.

Shortly before he died, Dad told me his harrowing story. He was left for dead, lying unconscious in a pool of his own blood with German bullets lodged in his liver. Decades later, he died of cirrhosis among other terminal diseases, stating, "That German finally got me." Knowing his story, I finally forgave him, but just as importantly, I forgave *myself,* too, for hating him.

The cousin who molested me died years ago. Because I couldn't change anything or confront him, I let it go. I have no feelings of guilt now and can say out loud, "I was molested," and not feel ashamed, dirty, or unworthy of love. Nor do I have to use food to hide behind.

Next, looking back at the principal who fired me, I realize she did me a huge favor! If not for her, I probably would still be seeing my life as a half-empty glass, eating my way to an early grave, instead of where I am on my life journey today. Just look at me now, writing about my wisdom in this book!

Finally, I had to confront the woman in the mirror and the food in her fridge. After the humbling, crumbling moment of staring at that social media picture, I was determined to resculpt myself. While watching my daughter compete in bikini bodybuilding competitions, I noticed there were several categories for women over fifty, which got me to think, *I can do this, too!* I began by joining a gym, training like crazy, and learning all the keys to nutritious eating. On my sixty-fifth birthday, I did sixty-five military-style push-ups as the folks at the gym counted them off out loud! I recently turned sixty-seven years old, am eighty pounds lighter, and *so* much stronger, both mentally and physically, than I was in 2017.

Letting go of all the hurt from years gone by and forgiving others and myself was very cathartic. For the first time in my life, I felt at peace, and all was right with my world. I could redefine who I was and where I wanted to go. I *can* become more.

The old me died on October 9, 2017, but I was born again a new person six months later, freeing myself from all the emotional issues that stemmed from the lies of days gone by. I am only four and a half years old, looking at life through a child's eyes, but with the wisdom of experience. I want to be remembered as a kind person who loves to give, has a smile for everyone, and doesn't just hear others but *listens* to them. I want to be remembered as someone who is willing to help people, even if they don't ask or are ashamed to ask.

This is what I want because it is the truth of who I am.

I am grateful for the big things in life and the very small things, too. I am not in competition with anyone, not even myself. I am the one who is driving my life, and I put my past in the rearview mirror. I can only live in the now, so I sit in the driver's seat and steer my life with purpose today, looking forward beyond the windshield to the future.

Snap your fingers… that action is already in the past and cannot be undone. But, you *can* create the life you choose to live and be happy. Like me, let go of negative energy, set high goals, and dream big! Give yourself grace; be grateful for every moment in life. Associate with people who support and care about your successes! You are smart, strong, and a marvelous human, so let today be the first day of the rest of *your* life. Seize the day — seize your NOW!

Ignite Action Steps

- Make a list and write down the things you remember that are negative memories. Be a devil's advocate. Examine these memories from the other point of view. Admit to yourself the mistakes you made, and then forgive yourself. Forgive others who may have been involved. Then burn the list.

- Establish a morning routine that is meaningful to you. Write down five things you are grateful for. Put them beside your bed and read them every day before you get up. Add to the list.

- Visualize the goals and dreams you think about. Think "I *will* go to ____; I *will* have ____," not: "I *wish* I could" or "I *hope* I can."

- Make a vision board. Find pictures of places you want to go to and things you want to buy if money was not an issue. Glue them on poster board. Hang it up somewhere where you will see it every day. Include those things you think about from above.

- Meditate. YouTube™ has lots of videos on meditation. Choose one that speaks to your soul. I meditate with healing, soothing music.

- Practice in a mirror saying out loud: "I am strong. I am smart. I am a marvelous human." (Add any other positive descriptions of you.) Look yourself in the eyes when you practice. You are the first one you need to convince.

Melanie Summers, M.A. Ed, C & I — United States
Educator, Certified Health & Fitness Coach, ASFA
A Mellie Moment, owner
www.amelliemoment.com
amelliemoment@gmail.com
 Melanie Summers
 mellie_moments
 @Melanie81345198

Jane Kilpatrick

*"Surrender to the wisdom of your higher self.
It is where all truth resides."*

YOU ARE WISER THAN YOU KNOW

BY JANE KILPATRICK

I am consumed with compassion for you as a fellow traveler on this journey called life. It is my deepest desire that my story and the lessons learned within it will support and guide you to live a healthy and fulfilled life. Listen to your higher self, intuition, or gut; it will always lead you in the right direction. Once your higher self reveals your path, hold firm, and walk it with confidence.

Little did I know that the vision I had when I was nine years old would become the story of my life.

It was the most radiant, sunny, cloudless day. The afternoon sun scorched the sidewalk as I walked downtown, without a care in the world, swinging my briefcase in rhythm with my steps. I was wearing a pale pink suit with a white blouse, striding effortlessly and confidently along in white patent stilettos, firm in my purpose. I was elated and happy, knowing that I was walking my life path.

Abruptly, as quickly as the vision appeared, the vision ended; there was no more road ahead. To this day, sixty years later, it is as clear as it was back then, but it wasn't until much later in my life that I realized its purpose and understood why the road had ended.

In 2014, I awoke one morning and, to my surprise, saw a pimple at the corner of my left nostril. I smiled, saying, "Sixty ain't so bad; look, I still get acne!" However, I heard an insistent, small voice inside, which I will call my higher self, whispering that I was dealing with more than acne. Over the next three weeks, the pimple would almost clear up, only to reappear and start bleeding again. I went for a biopsy.

After waiting ten tense days, my dermatologist confirmed that the pimple was basal cell carcinoma, a form of skin cancer caused by the sun. Heart pounding, I asked him what my options were. He replied that I would *not* like the scar that surgery would leave. Instead, since we detected it early, he recommended a less invasive, monthly treatment called photodynamic therapy (PDT). I was not comforted by his recommendation, and I told two friends that I was terrified at the thought of losing my nose. Both were quick to respond that I was behaving like a "paranoid idiot."

As so often happens to those of us who are medically illiterate, I chose to defer to my doctor's expertise and accept the alternate treatment, his recommendation playing straight into the hands of my vanity. My gut, which was like neon lights of red, green, blue, and yellow flashing across my brain, was saying, "Get the surgery now! Get the surgery now; early detection is the key." Did I listen to my higher self? NOPE. Not listening to myself ultimately led me down a path to much more than just a scar.

Nearly two critical years had passed without making any headway to kill the skin cancer. My gut had been screaming the whole time, but it wasn't until I had a botched and terrifying round of PDT, which sparked an infection, that I finally chose to listen. I demanded surgery, and in May 2016, I went under the knife to remove the basal cell carcinoma.

With my dear friend, Maureen, by my side, I sat terrified and fidgeting, waiting to be called into surgery. The surgeon performed a MOHS surgery, which is a precise surgical technique used specifically to treat skin cancer. During MOHS surgery, thin layers of cancer-containing tissue are removed and examined until only cancer-free tissue remains. After three hours of procedures, I returned home with a massive, unsightly bandage covering my nose. My surgeon told me he had obtained clean margins, but my higher self was not buying it. I asked whether or not the basal cell could return, and he explained that only 2% of the population had a recurrence. My heart sank, and while I frantically prayed I was wrong, I felt a dense blanket of fog closing in on me, knowing *it* would be back.

About twenty-four months later, I heard the insistent voice again, alerting me that the cancer was back. There were no visible lumps or bumps, but this time my higher self and I agreed there was no time to waste, and I scheduled an appointment to have it re-examined.

Despite my knowing, my inner critic was yammering at me, wondering if I was losing my mind. A war raged inside me. I asked my surgeon to perform another biopsy, which he did, and sure enough, the cancer had returned. This time, the skin cancer had traveled from the original site on my left nostril up to the corner of my left eye. I learned that I had a rare and aggressive basal cell that had tentacles enabling it to spread. During the second surgery, I pleaded with the doctor to expand the margins because my gut was shrieking at me that he would not get it all. But did I hold firm to my instincts? NOPE.

In 2018, within an eight-week period, I was dealing with unexpected levels of heartache and disbelief as my life spun out of control. I faced a recurrence of skin cancer, lost my job of fifteen years, and lost over six figures from my financial investments because I trusted my financial advisor. Everything that mattered was gone. It ripped my heart out as I asked myself, "What else could go wrong?" I was lost and feeling hopeless. Buried in total darkness, I clung to the glimmer of lights in my life, my amazing son, my twin brother, my sister, and my closest friends.

Like clockwork, two years later, in June 2020, I lay in bed accepting that it was my third surgery. The sun streamed through my curtains as I faced my reality. It was 7 AM when I arrived at the hospital. I detached and watched myself step off the fifth-floor elevator. Stunned at my levity and calmness, there was a lift in my step and a smile in my heart. "What was I thinking?" I asked myself, knowing I *should* be scared as images from my first surgery inundated my mind. But I knew the drill. I knew to walk along the hall from reception, turn left, turn right, and right again. I took the only seat available, right up front and faced the waiting room full of blank-faced skin cancer patients already donned in their drab blue hospital gowns. I could feel all eyes on me, looking at my attire, a black leather jacket, white shirt, black jeans, and over-the-knee black leather boots. I was ready for anything and felt confident.

By that time, the cancer had spread its tendrils into my sinus cavity. Again, my surgeon performed a MOHS surgery. I went in and out of the surgery room five times. Each time that I returned to the patient room, waiting for the biopsy results, I noticed more patients had been discharged, and I wished I was one of those lucky ones. I waited, wondering how many more biopsies lay ahead.

By 2 PM, I was alone in the dreary, colorless room shaking and petrified, as tears rolled down my cheeks. Finally, my surgeon advised that he had obtained clean margins. Because I elected a certain type of skin graft, my surgeon turned me over to his colleague, a different surgeon, to close the wound. To my dismay, that surgeon assigned me to his intern, who he would supervise. I was shocked. This was my face, my personal identity, and an intern was about to put it back together. Surely this could not be happening. I wanted the best and most experienced surgeon to repair the wound with as minimal scarring as possible. I trusted my original doctor and followed his referral despite my trepidation.

When the surgery was finished, the intern proudly handed me a mirror and said, "I want you to look at yourself and see the work that has been done before you go home." I got a sense he wanted me to see the results when I was not alone. I resisted and then reluctantly took the small hand-held mirror and held it up to my face. I gasped, stunned at the horror of my disfigurement. I burst into tears and spiraled into utter numbness.

It was about six months later when I noticed the inside of my left nostril was not healing properly. I panicked, and my gut urged me to act. I went to see my surgeon, yet he refused my request for another biopsy. Rather than pressing the point with him, I accepted his opinion, went home, and kept putting Vaseline™ on the area, massaging it daily.

Despite the exceptionally accurate wisdom my higher self had developed from my past, did I hold firm on that knowingness and insist on another biopsy? NOPE.

But I was granted a moment of undeniable truth. Before seeing my surgeon, I sat quietly in the waiting room where two ladies were talking. One was explaining that she had many recurring basal cell carcinomas over her body, but never in the same spot. She was a patient of an advanced cancer center, where she had undergone multiple PDT treatments and explained that they were painful, yet successful. She then commented about the laser center I attended for several of my PDT treatments, saying that they had a much lower efficacy rate than the one she attended. My head spun because I realized where I had been going for treatment had a much lower success rate. I felt the air sucked out of the room as I grappled with the truth I had always known, the truth I was facing for ignoring my higher self in 2014 and not asking for surgery right upfront. I finally had outer confirmation of my inner beliefs, and I marveled at the mysterious ways that life will present us with the truth. I knew it deep inside, but hearing it from her was the kick in the butt I needed. I leaped into action, sprinting down the hall to find my original doctor, requesting that I be his patient again, to which he agreed.

It was time to deal with my six-year quest to fix the disfiguration of my nose. I was referred to one of the best surgeons in North America. He advised that the only permanent way to restore my nose was to have a forehead flap nasal reconstruction surgery. I had been resistant because the nose is a major focal point of our face, and this surgery is considered the most complex of facial reconstructions.

The procedure involves cutting a strip of tissue from my forehead, starting at my hairline to the corner of my left eyebrow, rolling it into the shape of a straw and pulling it down over the corner of my left eye. This structure is extended and connected to the new left nostril, which is formed by taking cartilage and tissue from my ear and forehead. The structure also provides the blood flow to the new nostril.

I told the new surgeon that given my history with the basal cell returning every two years, I wanted to be certain that cancer would not return before undergoing any invasive reconstructive surgery. He agreed. I listened to my higher self and felt relieved.

Sure enough, my premonition came true again. While away from home on a weekend in September, something shifted in my nose. Again, there was no obvious change in its appearance, but my gut said, "Oh oh, I'm in trouble." I could not eat or sleep. I immediately scheduled an appointment and asked for another biopsy.

I visited the surgeon who had recommended the forehead flap nasal reconstruction because I had gained a significant level of trust with him. I showed him that when I opened my mouth my lower lip slid to the right… a worrisome new occurrence. Over the six years, I had asked multiple doctors for an MRI but had been refused. Yet when I showed my surgeon the issue he said, "You are going for an MRI now." That procedure was completed on November 11, Remembrance Day, 2021. *A most fitting day to end the war on cancer,* I thought. This must be a good sign.

The war wasn't over, though. My biopsy results indicated that the skin cancer had returned for the fourth time. The thought paralyzed me that my life had become "death by a thousand cuts." This was not the kind of notoriety I wanted. This time I was advised that radical steps were required. Within weeks my left nostril was removed, and just one week later, I underwent the invasive forehead flap nasal reconstruction surgery that I was so frightened of.

As I was moved onto the operating table, my surgeon told me that something had shown up on the MRI regarding my lower lip, but no one knew what it was. He assured me that he would investigate thoroughly and do whatever was required to get a diagnosis once the operation was over. After a successful forehead flap surgery and another reconstructive surgery, it was time to get a diagnosis of my lower lip.

I have recently learned that not only am I in the rare 2% of the population with recurrent basal cell carcinoma, but I am now in the 1% of the population where cancer has spread to the submandibular salivary gland and has infiltrated the surrounding soft tissue.

Skin cancer presented me with an opportunity to delve deeper into, and give more thought to, the truth, the wisdom of my higher self, and imperfections in my life. I now choose to take the lessons I have learned and let them guide me to live a much different kind of life, still full of meaning. If it weren't for this experience, I would have never authored this story, which I trust will facilitate me to continue speaking publicly and helping others.

Here's a great irony. I have always been concerned about my appearance and did what I could to be the best possible version of myself. Like the woman I saw in my vision when I was a nine-year-old, I never left home without my stilettos, as I carried myself through a brilliant career in human resources, helping individuals and organizations reach their potential and exceed what was previously thought to be unattainable. Skin cancer has forced me to reframe what the best version of myself is now. It has also revealed the beauty of the life I currently have. Jordan, my son, has been with me every step of my journey with cancer. As I reflect upon his consistent, calming support, my heart is bursting with love and gratitude for all that he is. And I am reminded by my incredible friends and family that my true beauty has always stemmed from the inside out, part of which is my cheerful outlook, courage, and strength to face reality and, in this case, to face the challenge of skin cancer and its ugly consequences.

There is so much beauty to experience and appreciate in many areas of life, from nature, art, science, and simple everyday human interactions. Nothing will prevent me from trying to make the world a better place for everyone I encounter on my life's path. I strive to be an example of someone who has learned to deal with a serious life challenge through seeking and finding grace in others while helping to improve the health of our planet.

Among the most beautiful things in my life, is the truth that I have confidently rediscovered my higher self by finally listening to my inner voice. It is that small, loving voice that was always there, helping me deal with the unknown and guiding me on a path to follow. So, is this where our truths and wisdom reside? I think so.

The gift of wisdom was within the vision that my higher self showed me when I was still a young child. It is astounding to reflect upon how that image became the roadmap of my life. I now know why the road ended; the life I knew had to end for a new chapter to begin. I've come to realize that my future is filled with many unknowns and yet also many unforeseen possibilities. Instead of letting fear and disappointment deter me, I choose to pay close attention to my higher self, and follow its guidance while developing the courage and curiosity to see what magical things might be in store for me.

To all of you who have suffered from human life events, please find the will to rebuild and live the life you have been given. Seek your truth and listen to the wisdom of your higher self, for it will lead you in the right direction. Life sends us countless invitations to listen to our deepest intuition. You have the answers deep within you. What is your higher self telling you? Listen to it. Pay attention and respect what it wants you to know. Trust it. Nurture it, and follow it as it will lead you to your truth. Then never look back!

You have all the wisdom you need. See yourself for the beauty that you are. When you embrace your higher self, a new confident you will emerge.

IGNITE ACTION STEPS

- Love yourself and your uniqueness. No one knows your body as you do. Listen to it and pay attention to the messages from your higher self.
- Accept your reality. Act now because wasted time can cause irreparable damage.
- Tell your truth with compassion, even when you do not know the solutions. Find your voice and be your own advocate.
- Frequently, a decision isn't required in the moment, and the sense of urgency we feel is a limitation that we've placed upon ourselves. Know that it is okay to step away and breathe.

Dedication: To Mom and Dad, who gave me life. To Jordan, who made my life perfect.

Acknowledgment: I want to celebrate and thank the people who stood beside me because it is your wisdom, unconditional love, and support that made this possible: Dr. Cassia Braulio, Dr. Nowell Solish, Jordan, Susan, Ted, Arlene, Beth, Bre, Cassie, Cristina, Dorothy, Gillian, Haak, Lauren, Mau, Nancy, Pat, Paul, Rob, Frank and Hallie, Mike and Jayne, Ron and Joyce, and my Ignite family.

Jane Kilpatrick — Canada
President of Touchpoint HR, Human Resources Consultant, Coach, Speaker
https://touchpointhr.ca/

Marla Ford Ballard

"Go as guided. Just jump."

WHAT VOICE?

BY MARLA FORD BALLARD

Nothing I tell you is the truth. All I can give you is my current perspective on my current experience, my version of the truth as I know it. It's up to you to decide what's true for you. Trust the still small voice within. Trust when everything in you feels like yes. And trust when you feel yourself holding back or hesitating. Don't try to talk yourself into this person, this situation, this opportunity when it feels like it's anything less than perfect for you. Go as you're guided because everything you've ever been through matters, and you have the wisdom of it within.

At twenty-five, I was in a pickle. I had married the wrong person. Certainly, I'm not the first person to do that, and I'm sure I won't be the last. But I had really gone against all guidance. Everything in me knew I shouldn't have done it, but I was young, and I didn't know how to get out of it. I had married a controlling, physically abusive person with a serious drinking problem. And after four years, I realized that if I stayed, only one of us would be walking away. Getting pregnant or having children was out of the question. I couldn't bring a child into that. I had to go. It had taken a while, too long, to take ownership and responsibility, but the voice inside me was clear. *Leave. Leave as soon as you can and make yourself safe.* And it was getting louder after every drunken bout. It was starting to scream at me, *Leave! Leave, or you will die here!*

Four years into a bad marriage, I finally took the guidance. I waited until he left town, and as soon as he was too far away to come back and catch me, I was gone. I was scared, and I wanted to hesitate. But the voice insisted *You know. It's time. Now jump.*

I was so relieved it was almost a feeling of elation. I was terrified about having left; I could only let go and trust my intuition and instincts — only me and my inner guidance. Only the voice. *Go here. Stay here. Now leave. Quickly. Trust this person, but definitely don't trust that one.* It took a long time, and a lot of mistakes before I could feel safe. I still didn't trust ME, but the voice was all I had during most of that time.

I would love to tell you that was when I became wise. But that's not really true either. You see, "wise" would have been not to marry him when everything in me said not to. But I didn't take that guidance. I was too unsure of myself, and I simply lacked the strength and the courage to trust it and say no to him. I talked myself out of believing I was right. And what a price I paid for that.

I remember when I could trust the voice I heard inside me when I was brave. I was little, maybe four or five. It was a cool, early evening in spring. My mom, aunt, and uncle were sitting on the porch steps talking. It had been warm and sunny all day, and the sun was starting to slip back towards the earth. There was a heavy, sweet smell of the big pink lilies on both sides of the sidewalk in front of our house where I was playing. I leaned in to smell the lilies, brushing against them, and nine bumblebees landed on me. The voice whispered, *Just relax, and standstill. They don't want to hurt you.* I knew that if I stayed calm, it would be fine. I froze and quietly called out to the nearby adults. My aunt came over first, saw the bees, and completely freaked out. The voice said, *Stay still, don't move, don't panic.* When my mom saw the bees, she immediately started waving her arms and shouting for my father, soon joined by my aunt and uncle. Maybe I should panic and shout too? But I trusted myself. *Stay still. The adults are going crazy, but you and the bees are fine.* The voice wasn't reckless. It was brave. So, I was brave also.

My father walked up slowly and calmly from across the yard. "Well, what do we have here?" he asked, stepping away from me, breaking a thin branch from the maple tree nearby; its woody scent combined with the sweet, heavy perfume of the lilies. He gently began to scrape the bees from my arms back onto the flowers. "They are just sleepy," he said, "They got cold, and you were nice and warm." I took his hand. To this day, I love bees. We garden together. It's peaceful, and we have no desire to hurt each other.

When I was little, I could clearly hear the brave voice. But over time, there were so many other voices. Voices of fear and panic, chaos, frustration, old wounds, all shouting, *Better watch out!* I started to hear them more than I could hear myself.

I remember victimhood and betrayal, feeling targeted by those around me. Girls in high school goaded me into saying something bad about another girl, then used it against me. Employers made promises but provided less money, less vacations, and less promotions. People said they'd keep my confidence and then used it to embarrass me. The man I married when I was young promised to cherish me and then repeatedly hurt me. I realized at some point that for all those betrayals, the first act of betrayal was always against me. At times when I felt sketchy, I heard that little voice inside saying something wasn't quite right, but I didn't listen. Or, at times when I knew one thing would make me really happy, I chose another thing because I was afraid to be honest with myself.

When I stopped betraying myself, no one else could be in a position to betray me. I simply didn't allow for it. I decided that in spite of my hardships and difficulties, I would be happy. Once I was choosing what felt right for me and what made me the happiest, I could no longer be a victim of anyone or anything. In leaving that behind, the strength and courage I lacked before developed in spades... even if it was intitally difficult.

I started to be honest with myself, which made me more honest with others about what I needed and wanted.

Of course, I wasn't very good at first. Not because the voice was flawed, but because I had broken trust with myself. It took a lot of time in the dark and the quiet to really hear what felt right and trust it. After about five years of hearing the inner guidance, sometimes trusting it (or sometimes wishing I had), I came to know what that voice was. I could hear it. I could hear ME. *Yes, do this, no, don't do that. Aw, seriously? See, I told you. You should've listened.* I felt into it more, becoming more still and tuned in. *What do I really want? What is right for me? What is the experience I'm having, and what experience would I prefer?* For years, I practiced listening. I'd make a choice about a person, place, timing, or opportunity, and I'd check-in and wait for the voice to respond.

Then one day, it happened. The voice got SO loud, and it told me to *just jump.* This time I didn't argue. I didn't hesitate. I just leaned in. I didn't know it, but I had met the love of my life several years earlier. We even went on a date. No doubt I liked him, but my life was still in total chaos from the divorce, and I knew I hadn't figured myself out yet. I wanted to be with him, but the voice said, *This isn't the time. Not yet.* I let it go. He was my best friend's brother and a really good guy… a GREAT guy. Instead, I chose my best friend over needing a new relationship. *Not yet*, the voice assured me.

Three years later, her father died... I knew how important her dad was to her. The voice said *You have to go and be there for her. You have to go — just jump in the car.* Even after a long week at work, I listened and made the four-hour drive to her family home. I didn't make it in time for the funeral, but I did go to their house to pay my respects and to take a Dr. Seuss™ book to my friend's baby girl. It was late in the day and late in the year. The fields were cut and brown, and the low sun still burned brightly above the horizon. When I parked the car, the air was crisp and smelled like earth and hay, casseroles, and funeral flowers.

I went inside. Of course, I knew he'd be there. It'd be interesting to see what kind of wife he had and whether he was on .5 or 1.5 kids with her. But never mind that, I was here for my friend. Like the aftermath of any funeral gathering, the family was tired but peaceful. I, too, was tired from the drive. My friend, despite her grief, greeted me and quietly escorted me to the buffet line to get an iced tea.

And there he was standing among the casseroles... And there I was. He looked good. And no wife and no .5 kid.

He thought I seemed familiar but couldn't place me, so he asked me my name. Not what I expected at all, given we'd been on a few dates three years ago before I got scared and stopped returning his calls. The inner voice laughed at the blow to my ego, but I relaxed. Good. Maybe I was incognito. My voice said *That's wishful thinking*. I cringed when recognition hit, and he knew exactly who I was.

I took my tea and sat down in a chair with my friend's baby girl. He brought a plate of food and sat next to me. Baby girl and I opened the book, and I read it to her, snuggled in the chair until she fell asleep. Since I was pinned to the chair, he and I made conversation while she slept. The voice said *This is an interesting development.* The five faces of his adult siblings would randomly peek in from around the door of the adjoining great room with mischievous grins. *Oh, boy, what is happening?* Then one of the adult in-laws appeared wearing a barely contained coy smile and carrying another sleeping child. He stated. "She wants her uncle," and deposited this child in my future love's lap. We were in it now. Willingly trapped under sleeping children, we just talked. It was easy, even though it should've been weird as hell, especially given we were at his father's funeral gathering. I don't remember a single thing we discussed, but I do remember the voice saying, *This is nice. We like him.* Once the kids were awake, and I had paid my respects to the family, their faces brimming with bright-eyed curiosity, I left. Only, my best friend didn't walk me out. Her brother did. All the way to the car. *Hmm,* said the voice, *there is going to be some family ribbing in his future.*

Don't let the moment pass. Do it, do it now. I offered my number. He said, "No, this time, you call me." Crappola. He did remember. More laughter from the voice.

I knew I had met, or re-met, someone important. I was completely rattled. How could I call him? What would it mean if I did? What would it mean if I didn't? Of course, I didn't trust myself, look at what a mess I'd made the other times. But I checked in and the voice said, *Do it.* I was dialing, itchy and sweaty and filled with doubt. But the voice was brave. I tried arguing. But by now I had learned that talking myself out of things when the voice said otherwise only led to self-betrayal and regret. Besides, I had to know how the story turned out.

We went to lunch the next day. And I got excited again. Then I became afraid; proof that sometimes the body can't tell the difference between fear and excitement. I got still, I checked in and the voice said, *This feels right, see how it goes.* I didn't really perceive that I was happy yet other than for a few bright shining moments a day, but I knew I could be; I wanted to be, and I had made it my intention to be. I was no longer a victim now. I was being brave.

By now, I had begun to trust myself just enough that I had actually started to like myself again, and I knew I could be happy within myself. I trusted that if it didn't work out, I would be okay. At lunch, I put all my cards on the table. We both did. I trusted the guidance, and I opened up to trusting someone else. I heard the voice, and I listened. And everything it said was, *Yes.* Then it urged me to, *Pay attention, take a pause, and see how you feel.* I realized what I was ready for and what I was not. I let him fly back across the country. And when he called me from the airport as soon as he landed, I knew. The voice knew. This wasn't just a "temporary weird weekend making an odd decision at a funeral" type of thing. It was real for us both.

Things happened quickly. We saw each other again just a few weeks later. He flew back across the country, and we met up out of town. I only told two friends about it. I knew there would be judgment and criticism, but the voice knew. I knew. I had to be with this man. I knew what I needed to do, and I knew I could be happy. If it didn't work, I could always go back to where I was. *But what if it did work?* the voice kept saying. *It will, and it feels right.*

People around me had their caution, reservations, and hesitations. When I told people at work that I was engaged and leaving my job, the questions flew. Co-workers asked me repeatedly if I knew what I was doing, while some flat out told me I didn't. My family asked, "Are you sure you can marry an army guy? He's going to have so many demands and be so militant." They reminded me I was untidy and questioned whether I could be regimented. "How will you live together? You will drive him crazy, and he will be too controlling." And, of course, they echoed my old fears, "Are you sure this isn't a worse mistake than before?" They wanted me to be safe. But what's safe in this world really? I had certainly learned the dangers of refusing to listen to myself, that other people's opinions that opposed my voice were not safe.

I went against the guidance again. But this time, I went against everyone else's voice — and I trusted mine. I had some very long conversations with that voice. I would say, *I'm taking a leap of faith here and trusting you. Don't let me down, and promise you'll catch me if I fall.*

I asked my new beloved many of the questions that everyone was asking and then listened for any red flags from my voice just to make sure. Every phone call was a new adventure, as I asked whether he bounced a quarter off his bed after it was made, where he put his dirty clothes, and whether his canned goods were lined up in perfect rows; questions that were met with his deep, dulcet warm laughter. I asked where we might live, whether I would have to be the rock in the relationship, and whether he loved dogs. With each answer, my voice became more sure. I became more sure.

My voice said, *Just jump!* And I listened. I JUMPED. We'd only spent eleven days physically together since the funeral before I moved across the country and married him. We've been together 19 years and counting.

By trusting my voice, I married not only the love of my life but a man who already had the deep wisdom to trust his own voice. Unlike me, he could listen to his internal guidance often without question or hesitation. I had found a partner who helped me deepen my ability to hear and trust my voice. Whether something lit me up and excited me or someone caused me to pause and question, he would encourage me to listen. "Your instincts are good," he would say. "They're spot-on. Trust them." So I did. Not always, not perfectly, but intentionally, and increasingly often.

In doing so, I became wiser, and helped others tune in to their voice so they themselves could be wise. Sometimes I was floored by how willing people were to trust me and my guidance, as I was still learning to trust myself. But he said, "Of course. People trust you because you're trustworthy." That became a short-term mantra. *I trust myself, and people trust me because I'm trustworthy.* Going as guided got me through many more difficult times and many more successes, bringing me opportunities that have created incredible love, joy, prosperity, and happiness. So when my clients ask me, "What do I do?" I say, "Let's check-in."

When something feels perfect... like the earth is singing and the stars are fully aligned... like it's so right... a full yes... trust yourself and jump. When you feel that something's not right... that it shouldn't happen... that it's not a full yes (which means it's a no)... trust yourself and don't jump. When you just aren't sure yet... trust you are allowed to take time to think it through. Ask yourself what you want, what works and what doesn't, and what will make you happiest. Know you are powerful enough to find it; all the love, validation, and wisdom you need is within you. As you tune into that inner connection, you strengthen your connection with others. As you hear your voice, others will hear and trust it, too. Your voice is wise, and the more you hear and take guidance from it, the wiser you become.

Everything you've been through, every experience you've had, all of your learning, training, unique gifts, talents, and experiences — all of who you are — is important. It matters. It matters... because it's you. Trust the still small voice within you. It's wisdom. It's wisdom... because it's you.

IGNITE ACTION STEPS

- Consider what you intend to feel and experience in your life, not just now but five or even twenty-five years from now. Do you want to feel happy, healthy, and have love in your life? Or do you want to hang on to resentment and regret, recreating them? You choose because once you are conscious of your intention, your mind and voice will support creating it.
- Once you've set your intention, take a deep breath, close your eyes, and look within to connect to your heart. Ask yourself, "What does my heart want most right now?"
- Each day, each week, as new opportunities and options present themselves, examine and trust what your voice is saying. Is this a full yes? Recognize that anything that is not a full yes; is a no. If you are at no, let it go. Be honest with yourself about that and ask, "What would I like to experience instead; what IS a full yes for me?

Marla Ford Ballard — United States
CEO of Jump Off Point International, Professional Enlightenment Trainer,
Speaker, Author, Certificate of Science in ThetaHealing®,
Free-Me™ EFT Instructor
www.jumpoffpoint.net
 @jumpoffpointconsulting | @ @marla.ballard

Cindy Tank-Murphy

"Through immense tragedy comes great clarity."

Little Voice on the Prairie

by Cindy Tank-Murphy

My story is one of love, loss, redemption, and gratitude. Love that never ends, even through tragic loss. Redemption by way of finding a lost voice, and gratitude for the gifts of wisdom that emerged along the way. My wish for you is to recognize that in the most tragic moments of your life, you can emerge with clarity and be inspired to transform yourself. By tapping into your innate power, wisdom, and strength, you can become the next best version you desire.

As a little girl, I watched episodes of *Little House on the Prairie*® and thought how amazing it would be to have Pa Ingalls as my father. With his soft, kind expressions and warm, generous heart, Michael Landon perfectly portrayed the wholesome, loving, problem-solving father on the television show. So well, in fact, that my innocent eight-year-old mind thought the character, Charles Ingalls, and actor, Michael Landon, were one and the same. As I'd watch the drama play out in Walnut Grove, I'd envision myself as Laura Ingalls, the fiesty, courageous, outspoken daughter. The Ingalls' life seemed easy, carefree, and while there was always some sort of mishap taking place on the prairie, everything turned out fine by the end of the show. If there was a fight, the combatants would make up. No matter how dreadful or hurtful the situation was, there was always consolation at the end. Why couldn't it be that carefree in my home on the prairie? I wanted so desperately to be seen by my father, the way Laura was validated by her Pa.

My father loved me tremendously, but it was a confusing, complex love. There was a certain amount of dysfunction that muddled my little-girl mind, like a hopscotch pattern changing position in mid-jump. How could this hero I called Daddy, who would take me on adventures and play imaginary games with me, also be cruel, abusive, and vicious at times? We would be giggling under the bed covers one evening, and by the next, he'd be angry, wielding the threat of using a belt to scold me. Amongst laughter and good times, there was something awful lurking in our home.

I was confused when he would act erratically. I'd stay up late at night with my mom waiting for him to come home, believing he was just working late. I'd struggle to keep my little blonde head from hitting the pillow, sure that I had to keep my hazel eyes open long enough to see him walk through the door. I didn't realize until my teenage years that my dad dealt with mental illness his entire adult life. Dad would have bouts of depression which would last months, followed by jubilant upswings, providing a false sense of hope. It was like living with two Dads: loving Dad and resentful Dad.

It became a routine occurrence for Dad to come home late and smell of alcohol. An argument would ensue with Mom, who, distraught and furious, believed he was out carousing. I vividly recall him being drunk, hostile, and violently aggressive toward my mother after one of his bingeing excursions. I wanted so badly to take control of the situation and end the drama like my alter-ego Laura Ingalls would. I knew what Pa Ingalls would do when confronted by his daughter. He'd immediately realize his mistake. He'd embrace her, holding her close to his heart, caressing her hair, tears rolling down his cheeks as he'd sorrowfully apologize to her.

I mustered up my Laura Ingalls strength, swung open my bedroom door, and marched down the hallway of our ranch-style home straight toward the kitchen. While my father held my mother by the top of her head, pulling her hair and shouting down her throat, I entered the room, and in my best Ingalls voice, I firmly demanded, "Please stop fighting, and leave Mom alone!" He looked at me, and while I don't recall what he said or did at that moment, my demand wasn't met with the same contemplation and apologetic response I'd envisioned from Pa. My words had not cut through. I ran back to my room, slammed the door, and hid in the dark until the shouting stopped.

At that moment, I lost my voice.

That night, I realized my world wasn't always going to play out the way I wanted it to, no matter what I said or did. It began my silenced years. Years of finding it hard to be right, questioning myself, and seeking validation from someone else.

I grew to be a substitute caretaker of our household. Someone my younger siblings could count on when things were rough. As I grew older and moved out of the house, I helped them get jobs, bought some of their college essentials, and took them into my home so they could get a good start on their careers. By the time I had children of my own, in my thirties, I felt like I had already raised one family.

While everyone leaned on me, there was one person I let close enough to be *my* shoulder. Sweethearts since high school, my husband and I built a beautiful life together. It was what some would deem a successful life. We both had good paying corporate jobs; two courteous, smart, and athletic young daughters; a beautiful home in the suburbs; and a neighborhood filled with friendship. We were best friends and teammates in raising our children; the couple who hosted neighborhood parties, went on exciting vacations, had few financial concerns, and a rock-solid marriage. We felt lucky to be at this pinnacle in our lives, and excited to be moving into a new home in a well-to-do neighborhood where our girls would be able to attend some of the best schools in the state. We had arrived, or so we thought. We had obtained a certain lifestyle that required us to continue to work the jobs that had gotten us to that point (whether we liked them or not). Nonetheless, we were about to move, and there was excitement about the next chapter.

Two weeks before the closing date on our new home, I received a call that would change my life forever.

The call came on a Tuesday evening in late July. I didn't notice Mom had phoned around dinner time, so I knew nothing until my aunt left a strangely ominous voicemail. "Cindy, you need to call your mother right away," was all that she said. As I dialed Mom's number, I felt a sick, nauseous sensation in the pit of my stomach.

Mom answered the phone, "Cindy, he's gone." It was all she could say. I didn't need to know more. I knew exactly what that meant. I was terrified by the news. I stepped outside to let out an excruciatingly pained wail. My neighbor heard me from across our backyards and came running to console me. As she embraced me, I fought to get air to my lungs; to slow my breathing enough to be able to speak. Once somewhat composed, I went back inside, and being the oldest of four, I dutifully made the calls to my siblings to relay the news. My father had lost his battle with the demons. He was gone, and he had chosen his exit door.

Losing a parent for any reason is difficult, but when the death is a suicide, there is an added element of ugliness. Shame, guilt, disbelief, anger, and questions of how this could happen add layers upon layers on top of the devastation. It takes a great deal of strength to continue forward after losing a loved one to suicide. It was a strength I still was developing.

For the next several months, I went into reaction mode. There were decisions about our childhood home, what to do with Dad's antiques, and how we would care for Mom. I disengaged from friends, pushed away my husband's affection, lost touch with my career goals, and couldn't connect with my daughters as well as I had before.

Everything I had accomplished before his death was now a farce, a sham. None of it mattered. I started to see the world around me differently, and I realized how sheltered and ego-centric my life had been. I started to question everything. I began to ask myself, "What is my true purpose in life?" I certainly knew it was no longer climbing the corporate ladder, having a bigger home, driving nicer cars, or losing ten pounds so I'd look better in a bikini. I had been in total denial, asleep for several years, thinking this was the best life had to offer. Those things seemed worthless to me now. I needed to redefine the word "purpose" entirely.

Life was too short to continue living small, insignificant, and voiceless. My perspective of who I was was forever tainted. I went from feeling successful in my career, marriage, and parental responsibilities, to feeling unimportant and lacking any real substance in most areas of my life. There had to be more to give and more to gain.

Prior to losing Dad, my siblings and I had been discussing a business idea. The dream of starting a venture provided a healing space for us to come together and a way to honor our father, an entrepreneur himself. What we started was something special. It gave us great joy and purpose again. A year and a half into the project, I made the decision to quit my corporate job and pursue the business full-time as well as begin a journey of healing. I named this phase of my healing process my "Leap of Faith," because it started with making a conscious decision to listen to my intuition and allow it to guide me. Thus began a transformation that would lead to personal growth far greater than I'd ever experienced.

Less than a month after ending my corporate job, I received an email about a female leadership event in San Diego that coming summer. The experience would be recorded for a web series as a combination between self-discovery, humanitarianism, and adventure all wrapped up into one trip. My intuition told me I needed to go, even though my mind was saying, *Are you crazy? A reality show? Pushing your limits and public speaking? No Way!* This wasn't something I'd ever done before, but I was willing to put myself out there in hopes of connecting with other influential businesswomen. I finally decided to let go and say "yes," figuring I had nothing to lose.

I was mistaken. I had a lot to lose. I needed to shed my comfort, personal space, and inhibition. I had to become vulnerable in order to gain something much greater and more powerful. I learned some of my most valuable life lessons over the course of eight days with thirty strangers. I conquered my fear of heights in literally one day. In twelve hours, I led a team of five women on a scavenger hunt around San Diego as we fundraised over $10,000 for a local children's foster care organization. I proved my physical and emotional strength to a somewhat skeptical Guinness World Record holder. He's the oldest person to have reached the peak of the highest mountain on each of the seven continents, including Mount Everest. I felt instant validation as I lifted him on my shoulders to "safety" across our fictitious electric fence during a team builder. As he climbed from my shoulders, he professed, "I just fell in love with you," and I freely accepted, finally recognizing myself as someone worthy of being loved. Up until that point, I believed love was conditional. He broke through an impenetrable shield of self-protection with those simple words.

I was right about living too small for too long. I was ready to continue to step into my purpose and regain the voice I'd silenced years ago. Coming home from that experience in San Diego, I knew I was onto something greater than anything I had ever achieved in the corporate world. I was transforming myself into a better, upgraded version of me. When the next opportunity presented itself, how could I say no? I knew I needed to continue to discover more about who I was becoming and what this transformational journey had in store. Off I went, halfway across the world, to speak on an international stage. The trip scared me a great deal, but nothing feels too massive to achieve when you've awoken from your slumber and are Ignited.

I knew I needed to use my newfound voice to tell my story — the story of losing my father to suicide — to another country that was dealing with a suicide epidemic. I boarded a plane from Chicago to fly twenty-three hours (with two layovers) to New Zealand. There, I was amongst some amazing life coaches from around the world, many of whom were well-versed and comfortable speaking on stage with years of experience in metaphysics. Several were not only teachers and life coaches, but also gifted empaths and psychic mediums. Some of the speakers had studied under the likes of Tony Robbins and Don Miguel Ruiz, legendary giants of public speaking and self-improvement whose books I had only read. I felt like a minnow in a sea of worldly traveled and gifted whales. What value could I offer these brilliant, conscious leaders?

Little Cindy would not have asked such a question. As a child, I'd allowed even the simplest things to feel magical. I'd spend hours playing outside in a ditch full of rainwater, or sit and watch tadpoles swim around in a small pond until it was dark outside.

What happened in between that innocence of my childhood and my awakening was no surprise. I was chasing material dreams. I lost my belief in knowing I was right. I began to question myself and allowed other people to misguide me or, worse, speak on my behalf. In giving control to other people's voices, I had allowed myself to be silenced. My inner Laura Ingalls had been stripped of her bold courage, and my egoic mind was spewing lies pretending to be useful. I gave the microphone back to my intuition, knowing my present self would always guide me to what was right.

A sense of peace and calmness came over me as the plane landed in Queenstown. I decided all I needed to do was show up, be my authentic self in every situation, and speak my truth. Even though I didn't have the same credentials as most of my travel companions, I knew I had something to share, or I wouldn't have grabbed hold of this opportunity.

On the day of my speaking debut, I felt fear and excitement coursing through my body. Our bus arrived at Forsyth Barr Stadium in Dunedin, and the reality sunk in that this was it. Just shy of three years after losing my father, I was about to step on an international stage and share the story which had brought me halfway around the world. I learned I'd be the first guest to speak; that it was *my story* that would kick off our team of conscious leaders. My message would set the tone for the entire event. It was up to me to provide the feeling and flow for my esteemed colleagues to confidently share each of their messages that would follow.

I stepped on stage, a maple tree waiting for my tap to flow my sweet syrup, took hold of the microphone, and owned my story. With an empowered voice, I shared what I had been holding back for so long. I had not only found my voice, but I had also been profoundly heard.

The Persian poet, Rumi, beautifully said, "You have to keep breaking your heart until it opens." I would add that one single tragic act can crack your heart open in a millisecond. I didn't know how to stand in my power until my life was unraveled by heartbreak. It forced me to make a choice. I could allow shame, guilt, and sorrow to swallow me whole, or I could seek to find a new version of myself through vulnerable self-discovery.

I'm grateful I chose the latter; to have experienced the enormous lessons which brought me to where I am today. My reinvention began the moment I tragically lost my father, jolting me to the greatest clarity. I accept that life had to sucker punch me to get me to this place. I had to go to the deepest and most vulnerable parts of me in order to rise. I unlocked my hidden wisdom to live a fuller, more authentic life. I'm no longer afraid of being vulnerable. It's now one of my greatest strengths. I love this new Version 2.0 Cindy, but I am still a work in progress. The difference is I'm now writing the script of the house on the prairie I want to envision, and it feels perfectly right.

Your voice matters. If you've ever felt it's been silenced or quieted, due to an emotional trauma or crisis, now is the time to step into your power and reclaim your voice. When you speak, what you know is your truth; you open yourself up to new possibilities. You find unconditional self-love and true, inner acceptance. Know that what you have inside is all that you will ever need. From that knowingness, your deepest wisdom will unfold.

Ignite Action Steps

- Listen to the nudges. Intuition is golden.
- Just say yes! Especially when it scares you.
- Let down your guard and allow yourself to be vulnerable.
- Own your story and share it freely.

Cindy Tank-Murphy — United States
Sales & Marketing Professional, QPR Certified & Mental Health First Aider,
Adventurer, Speaker, Entrepreneur
www.thestrengthtolive.com
cindy.tankmurphy
@cindytankmurphy, @thestrengthtolive

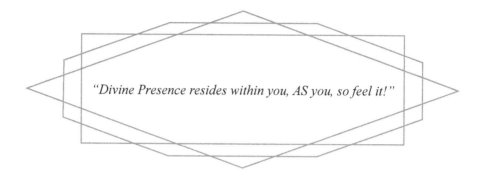

"Divine Presence resides within you, AS you, so feel it!"

Your Presence is Requested

by MaryAnn Swan

My wish is that you don't have to wait for the challenging times to wake up to the truth of you. Start to dance now with the Divine Presence already and always within you. Look back on the events of your life and see those places where you were given nudges, or in some cases, a cosmic kick in the pants. Awaken to the visceral knowing that Divine Presence is expressing into this earth plane as you. With an awareness of this, you can shift your reality at any moment, find love and compassion for all of your journey, and engage with others from the unconditionally loving Presence that you are.

"Look at her. She has the perfect life."

There was a time when anyone who knew me would have spoken those words. I was living the dream in an idyllic, suburban, cookie-cutter neighborhood. I had a secure job as a classroom teacher; a contented, loving marriage; was raising beautiful, thriving twin boys; and surrounded by a fulfilling and fun social circle. Everywhere were reminders of my many blessings. Until it began to unravel.

I was in a period of questioning if regular classroom education was really for me anymore after twenty-five years of teaching kindergarten to grade eleven. My relationship with the students uplifted me, but the workload overwhelmed me. I was suffering from depression and burnout and was on a leave from work in the spring of my fiftieth year. Since I was not working full-time, my husband and I were having financial struggles. We were in the process of selling our house; using the profits to clear a long-standing debt and reset our finances.

One mild and sunny Friday morning in April, my husband of twenty-one years — my friend, my partner, the salt of the earth, and the one who I thought always had my back — announced that once the house was sold, he was leaving our marriage for a woman twenty-five years younger than us (we were both fifty, and our twin boys were seventeen).

In that moment, my world fell apart. Time stood still. I was immediately aware of my heart pounding as nausea and light-headedness set in. The shockwave overtook me. How could this be happening? Our eyes locked in a deafening, frozen silence. I blurted out, "Who are you?!" He continued to stare back at me, and for the first time in two decades, I did not recognize the person in front of me. "Who does this? What about our family? What about our wedding vows?"

I could not wrap my head around this new reality. I knew our relationship was under stress and figured I had loads of time to set things right. But the fact that he had already taken up with another left me with no recourse to save us. It was over. He was leaving. This stunning, tragic news arrived seemingly out of the blue, given who I thought my husband was and who I thought we were together.

Over the next few weeks, I hurled ugly tirades at him and experienced paralyzing moments of terror, panic, anxiety, and despair. To cope, I isolated myself from family and well-meaning friends, numbing my shame and guilt with too many bottles of wine and getting lost in other people's dramas by binge-watching useless television.

Of course, this was not my first experience with loss or tragedy. Even before the demise of my twenty-one-year marriage, I had experienced the death of a sibling as a child. In the years that followed, I lived through the loss of home and work, my amazing, now grown children no longer "needing" me, and the death of a parent. Each of these intense losses and setbacks were followed by long periods of depression, anxiety, self-doubt, isolation, hiding, and just surviving rather than thriving.

Even in the years before my marriage ended, I was on a personal development and spiritual journey. I'd amassed many resources: healing practices and energy work, yoga, dance, and various types of meditation. I was able to get off prescription medications for depression and anxiety, embracing more natural remedies and holistic dietary solutions that supported my physical, mental, and spiritual health.

The most impactful and accelerated times of my healing came to me from working in experiential group settings, retreats, and workshops focused on being in the truth of the moment. They allowed me to be anchored in my body, own who I really am, notice and share what's moving in the moment, express my desires and longings, and be heard, felt, and met in my expressions.

The first time I felt myself as Divine loving energy was five years after my divorce. I was four days into a seven-day "accelerated awakening" retreat in the Netherlands and feeling deeply connected to the group. Our energies had synched up, and the amplified energy field was rich. Although, a part of me was aware of a growing frustration, because we were so far into the healing process, and still, there were people who weren't willing to dive in and surrender to their transformation. They didn't see how amazing they were. Several were mired in their collapses, and I was in my own judgment about them not "getting it." The circle was getting energetically tense, and a derailment of the group's cohesion was brewing.

As my frustration built, all of a sudden, I felt an energy take over me, and I exploded from my seat without signaling that I wanted to share or getting the group's agreement. I started ranting from the center of the circle about how they were missing the point of the gathering; they weren't seeing all the juicy, golden nuggets that could relieve their suffering and help them heal from their woundedness and conditioning.

"Why are you still not feeling safe? Do you think anyone here means you harm or doesn't hold you in high regard, love, and acceptance?" I called out.

The leader didn't stop me as I started to zero in on individuals, emphatically sharing and raving about how amazing and precious they were. I wanted them to see the beauty I saw within them. I don't even recall what I said, but I couldn't stop the wave of passion and love pouring through me.

Eventually, I ran out of steam and softened, and the group energy felt instantly lighter. That episode was dubbed "The Love Bomb," and I was known as "The Oracle" (like the character in *The Matrix*) for the rest of the event. I had never expressed my love in that way before to a group of strangers, and it showed me that I was honoring my emotions and speaking what needed to be said.

A year later, in another circle-based, multi-day retreat, I was challenged to awaken a foreign emotional range for me around sensuality. I was in a paired exercise where we were to move with our partner in a "queenly" or "kingly" way, and we were to encourage each other to do more, or less, of what we were witnessing in each other. When the instructor told us to dance seductively for the other, I had no idea what he meant. This was a range of sensuality that I found awkward to express with anyone, let alone with the numerous other people in the room.

In the years after my divorce, I had not made any effort to attract a special someone into my life. I didn't consider myself sexy or desirable because I still held a lot of guilt and shame from believing the end of my marriage was my fault. This exercise was not enjoyable for me, and I was confused by what being a queen would look like. As we rejoined the circle to debrief the exercise, I asked what it would look like to "be a queen," knowing the risk of being singled out for asking. I had witnessed others, upon expressing a curiosity or confusion, become the focus of the next activity.

As I suspected, I was invited to come to the center of the circle and take my turn to do a solo exercise. A piece of music was selected. My instructions were not to *perform* but rather to feel into my body and slowly move with the music. No dancing, just letting the music move me.

I closed my eyes and felt the impulse to move my body, absorbing the lyrics and the beat. As I began to sway, my breath quickened. I felt intensely charged pulses, a buzz; a tingling began to arise within my body. I moved faster and faster, the energy building and radiating throughout me. The music reached a crescendo, and suddenly I felt a cascade of electricity shoot through me, a *whoosh* of tingly energy surged from my head to my feet, and my heart was blown open in euphoria. I was in bliss.

All at once, I was spinning in the center of the circle, my arms wide. The instructor encouraged me to open my eyes, take in the people surrounding me, and just allow my sound to come freely. I surrendered. I cried out, emitting moans of ecstasy and laughter, and I felt tears of joy running down my face. As I looked into the eyes of those in the circle witnessing me, I could see *their* joy and hear their laughter cheering me on.

That's when I knew what it meant to truly love myself and to fully, viscerally feel within my body the divine LOVE that I am.

For the remaining days of the event, I was on a high. I returned home a changed woman. The worries I carried before had dropped away, and I was able to stay present each time my mind attempted to bring my concerns back. I was able to tap into the LOVE that I had experienced; the LOVE I realized was ME, the LOVE I now call Divine Presence.

My journey since has been about being in my body as much as possible to stay connected to how I am responding to the present moment. I often ask myself, "How am I feeling right now?" and "What's really happening here?" I experience this level of moment-to-moment Presence in many parts of my day. It keeps me in the reality of what's going on and calms me when I get agitated, stuck in pondering past events, or fretting about the future. Being present helps me navigate my egoic thinking or relational challenges as I drop into the moment and attune to the other, listening carefully and truly BEing with them.

Expressing myself in that circle is what I consider a turning point for me. It allowed me to reflect on other times in my life when I also "knew" and was present to the Love that I am; that deeper knowing of my connection to others and a collective consciousness. Since then, I have been present to more moments of greater awareness. In the first few months of the pandemic, when we had stay-at-home orders, I took an online silent meditation retreat. In one session, while in a space of expanded awareness and stillness, I perceived myself in a void. Suspended in the stillness, I heard the sweetest voice say, "I like being you; I love feeling life through you." It was so comforting to hear those words, proof I was connecting to the Divine.

Recently, I moved out of the city, and while organizing my books, I came across old course notes and journals. As I flipped through them, deciding what to keep or toss, my eye settled on one of my reflections from a meditation course I took several years ago. In that program, I'd spent two years zeroing in on the guiding voice that has been with me my whole life. The one-lined entry jumped off the page at me: "I love being you." I had totally forgotten this. In finding that journal, I realized Divine Presence had always been there and was showing me that I was forever precious, valued, and loved.

Over the years, small and big cosmic kicks in the pants have awakened me to the truth that I'm much more than this "bag of bones and dirty water," as one of my teachers used to say. As I look back, I can see the breadcrumbs leading me to the realization that I am a divine spark of the essence of the Universe, and when I drop into this knowing — when I'm present and in my body, I can see the beauty in everything and everyone, and I can choose what thoughts to focus on and manifest in my 3D reality.

This is the same power that flows through you. You are always Divine Presence, and it's easy to embrace this when you open your heart and feel the sensations of your aliveness running through your body. Perhaps you sense a warmth radiating, fluttering in your heart area, jitteriness in your belly, or a buzzy tingling. When these are alive within you, YOU are present and a gift to those who receive your attention from this awareness. Being in Presence with someone is the attentive consideration you give when you spend time to experience them and really take them in. You're able to see them with fresh eyes, looking past any perceived flaws, wounds, or less than healthy behaviors. They become innocent, and it becomes easy to love them unconditionally, just like Divine Presence does.

My wish for you is that you find ways to bring yourself into present moment awareness and the truth of your NOW. There is much peace in the present moment, attuning to how your body feels, your emotions, judgments, needs, and what's going on around you. YOU are not your thoughts, your body, your past, or your wounding. You are all of that and more. Even better, if you're with others, attuned and in the moment, that present interaction allows for clearer, more authentic communication. As you see and feel yourself in their presence, you will receive the gifts of their attention.

You are a queen or king, just like me. We've been through a lot, and we are still, at our core, queens and kings, the physical embodiment of Divine Presence and Love. Trust that knowing this brings true acceptance of all your earthly parts, transmuting behaviors and energies that once limited your experience of yourself as the Light, into radiant, powerful expressions of the Divine Presence that YOU are.

Ignite Action Steps

Tune In to Connect - As you go through your day, take time to tune into what is true in the moment as often as you can. Stop where you are, take a slow deep breath, and exhale even longer. Notice the sensations running through your body; areas of tension, ease, thoughts, emotions; and any triggers and judgments that are running. Notice the physical space around you. What do you see, hear, and sense? Continue to breathe and allow your breath to calm you. While in the presence of others, notice how you are feeling in your body. Does their conversation trigger you? Are there contractions in your body or is it easy and joyful to BE with their energy?

Move Your Body - We know the health benefits of regular exercise and movement for keeping a healthy body. Also, seek out opportunities for slow mindful movements that allow you to tune into your inner sensations and energies. It's a way for your body to communicate with you. Tensions need your loving care; expansion and ease is your natural state.

Communicate Clearly - Have a dialogue practice where you keep your responses related to your experiences. Use "I" statements and speak from what it means for you in the present. When you talk about yourself say this: "A part of me feels… " or "I notice a part of me… " This will help you not to identify with any one aspect of yourself and keeps you in an observer role, rather than enmeshed in your drama. It then becomes easier to love and accept all parts of yourself without making any part of you wrong.

Create Community - Find your tribe; the groups and mentors that you can feel safe with, who offer opportunities to explore your relational communications. It took others to create your conditioning and wounding, so it makes sense that unwinding that and feeling whole would be most effective in the presence of others, in a safe, nurturing environment where you can be seen, heard, felt, and met. And while this can certainly occur in the presence of a loving and supportive one-on-one coach or therapist, there's nothing like the impact of an amplified energy field in a group situation for accelerating your growth and healing.

MaryAnn Swan — Canada
B.Sc., B.Ed., Relationship Coach, Group Workshop Facilitator, Author
www.maryannswan.com
 maryann.swan
 agatheringofhearts.toronto
 agatheringofhearts

Loree J. Kim, PhD, Esq.

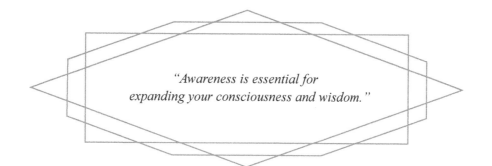

"Awareness is essential for expanding your consciousness and wisdom."

THE KEYS TO RE-INVENTION AND LIBERATION

BY LOREE J. KIM, PHD, ESQ.

If you want to recreate "your life" but are experiencing a lot of resistance, know that your social conditioning is probably the root cause. It's possible to transcend your limiting self-identity and create a new life by transforming your self-concept and realizing your true essence. Your unconscious attachment to a manufactured identity may be delaying your beautiful transformation. My hope is for you to see that increasing your self-awareness can help you soar toward realizing your unlimited identity.

"Extraordinary" is how I would describe my forty-fifth year, for what unfolded as a painful "tragedy" eventually transmuted into "enlightenment" a decade later. That year, checking into the Emergency Room on three occasions left me feeling like I was living in the Twilight Zone — experiencing someone else's life. On the first ER visit, my debilitating pain was diagnosed as "a rib fracture;" on the second visit, flu-like symptoms were labeled as "a bad summer cold." On the last ER trip, my feverish weight loss was diagnosed as a "thyroid infection." My weight dropped from 105 pounds to 92 pounds in a single month, and I feared my body was dematerializing into bones. Without certainty that my thyroid would reset to normal levels, I wondered, *Is this how I'm going to feel when I'm seventy-five?* For decades, I had enjoyed near-perfect health, not needing any medical care - no pills, no surgery, and no doctors. *Why is this happening to me NOW?*

Over many decades, I trained my body to tolerate high stress and pain (physically grueling workouts and high professional performance). My passionate career as a corporate intellectual property attorney had consumed nearly all of my attention and energy, fading any sense of a work-life balance. Even outside the office, my mind was always on work — the next steps, the next plan, the next strategy, the next skill, and the next ACHIEVEMENT. For decades, my mind was conditioned for overworking, as were my adrenals.

Immobilized and depleted by a hyperactive thyroid, I felt like an energy vampire had latched onto me, slowly draining away my life force. Instructed to allow four months for healing and hormone rebalancing, I felt helpless and internally restless. With low-energy reserves, low-grade mental activities such as speaking were exhausting. Walking to the restroom required forty-five minutes of prior visualization to muster enough energy. Shampooing my hair felt like an Olympic feat since I could barely raise my arms.

Bedridden and bewildered, I thought: *HOW and WHY did I become so compulsive?* Over decades, I had programmed myself to strive for the abstract standard of perfection. I didn't need external motivation to achieve hard goals; I programmed myself to be intrinsically motivated. To get through challenging tasks, I repeated the mantra, "no pain, no gain." This "tough" mentality became part of my self-created identity. The truth is, I pushed my brain and body for nearly thirty-five years prior, trying to become "self-actualized" in the spirit of Maslow's Hierarchy of Human Needs. I was conditioned by Western education to believe the highest peak of personal achievement was to "reach" self-actualization. I hadn't consciously investigated whether this self-absorbed, career-obsessed lifestyle was the best strategy for true satisfaction.

Deeper self-reflection revealed this compulsive habit of "striving." It started in childhood with maintaining a spotless bedroom and closet. My next goal was a perfect attendance record in school. The next goal; becoming the president of my elementary school. By campaigning diligently, I won the election, even though I was an immigrant who spoke imperfect English! My father thought I should learn to take risks, even if I might lose; this proved a valuable lesson at an early age. My peers' affectionate labels, "the bookworm" or "the brain," shaped how I perceived myself. The positive reinforcements from teachers fueled this compulsion to keep adding more achievements to the fire. My over-glorification of work and endlessly striving for self-improvement started early. This was the easiest identity to adopt for a very shy, quiet-speaking intellectual girl.

But *WHY* did I become so compulsive? Intense introspection revealed my compulsion was caused by my painful, traumatic childhood, the truths my peers and teachers didn't know. At about eight years old, I noticed the bruises on my mother, HER arms, HER legs, HER back, and HER shoulders. Asking how she got them, I was confused to learn Father did it. Around nine, the number of fights escalated and the conflicts became louder. My sisters and I heard the fights through the walls; fights that led to the painful and haunting sound of HER cries. We hid — too scared to stop him while fearing for our mother's life. Under the covers, I wanted to shout, "STOP HURTING HER!!!" But I didn't because I was terrified. His violent outrages always resulted in shattered furniture, dishes, and glass scattered everywhere — like a demolition site in the wake of a raging tornado. After the mayhem, while cleaning up his mess, I often burst into tears because the senselessness of it made me deeply sad. I inherently knew his behavior was NOT normal and continually worried for my mother's survival. After learning in Bible class that we could ask God for help, I started praying for mother's relief - compulsively praying for HER safety after I woke up, during school, on the bus, before starting homework, and before going to bed. All I wanted was to save her.

Nevertheless, the physical and psychological abuse continued, though less frequently. Still, we didn't know when Father would explode again. None of us relaxed when he was home. He was like a human machine, working six or seven days a week, fourteen to fifteen-hour days, running their business, threatened by the possibility of economic failure like most immigrants. Once over dinner, Father said he wanted sons and was *disappointed* with daughters. I wasn't sure whether he said this to insult my mother or hurt us, but regardless, it was obvious that he didn't have any filter. His words stung. I watched my sisters' reactions. Their faces said the same - *some thoughts you keep to yourself.* Didn't he realize his words and actions could scar us?

For the most part, Father raged on our mother mainly, except on a few occasions. Once, he was irritated hearing that my mother couldn't sleep due to our playing loudly. She'd mentioned it casually, not as a complaint, but Father's face turned bright red. Standing closest to him, I was an easy target. Without notice, he kicked my legs so violently that I instantly buckled to my knees before slamming my face hard on the carpeted floor. As a former captain in the Korean Army, trained in boxing and advanced martial arts, this was no ordinary kick. I was stunned by the burning pain below my waist as tears welled up instantly. I thought, *Get up and go to your room.* I wasn't sure if he would kick me again, so I knew I had to get out of his reach. Petrified, I couldn't stand up. I dragged my limp legs, pulling myself forward with my arms across the carpeted floor to my room.

That slow and strenuous crawl, was witnessed by my parents and sisters. I felt utterly humiliated. Sitting on the floor, I wept silently in the darkness, paralyzed with excruciating pain. Fearing I might not walk again, I thought, *Did he break my legs?* Other than my mother checking on me, I don't remember much, except thinking, *I will NEVER let anyone hurt me like that again.* Intuitively, I understood how much pain my mother endured during the first decade of her arranged marriage. That single blow was all I needed to get a bitter taste. At nine, that marked the bleakest moment.

Reflecting the next morning, I felt scared, trapped, and desperate. I decided not to rely on God or anyone to rescue us. Like a prisoner in a camp, I felt an uncontrollable urge to "do something" instead of waiting for Father to change. I begged my mother to run away with us. "We can't," she said, explaining the harsh economic realities of being a new immigrant in the United States. Although she had attended the best university in Korea in her youth, she knew it would be nearly impossible to find a professional job to support three girls despite her education. Fearing Father would find us, I got the impression she never seriously entertained the thought of escaping. Sometime thereafter, I stopped praying and going to church, dismissing them as a waste of time. I wanted more immediate relief to reduce my misery.

It was no surprise that unwarranted violence against my mother, our pets, and myself (and siblings) compounded my fear and re-emerged as nightmares from childhood that continued into adulthood until about the age of thirty-two. A recurrent nightmare was Father killing my entire family in one of the homes we lived in, leaving a bloody trail through the house as I walked from room-to-room fearing the worst. I woke up streaming tears and screaming.

When suicidal thoughts emerged at fourteen, I deliberately "threw" myself into all-consuming studies to avoid feelings of pain and hopelessness. I noticed when I kept my mind busy with reading and studying; I felt less pain. Since I loved stretching my intellect, academics were my favorite "path of least resistance." The positive feedback from teachers helped to reinforce these habits. By activating my imagination, books were portals to pretending that I didn't have any problems. I felt empowered by learning to focus my attention and energy towards realizing any desired outcome. Even as a child, I was mysteriously guided by an innate source of wisdom. I also read tons of self-help psychology books to "undo" Father's damage. I absorbed the knowledge that we can consciously choose to focus on the "good" or the "bad" on a moment-to-moment basis. Better choices get us closer to what we want. Any behavior can be deeply rooted by clarifying our intentions.

As I deepened my maturity and continued self-reflecting, I finally understood how it was possible for me to have accomplished so much despite the uncontrollable chaos and despair at home. I had witnessed my mother miraculously and consistently "collecting" herself after Father "kicked" her down (literally and figuratively). HER spiritual resilience was HER invisible armor. My mother survived those challenging years by aligning with the higher virtues of truth, love, and beauty shaped by Christian beliefs.

I don't recall her staying in bed or indulging in self-pity even through illnesses. By witnessing how she dealt with her suffering and challenges, I learned a significant lesson that shaped who I became. By holding onto her dignity and composure through her darkest moments, she inspired something deep inside that made me realize I could do the same: *Keep trying no matter how tough it gets. If she can do it, so can I!* This is how I got through the darkness, and how I picked myself up off the floor anytime my spirit became deflated by adverse circumstances.

Knowing my mother was denied a career, I felt a deep desire to succeed for *both* of us, so actualizing my potential meant actualizing HER potential. By aligning with this clear intention, I graduated as a top-tier performer from elementary school through high school. I could *produce* straight As and so much more! I repeated the habits of self-discipline (ability to control my thoughts and emotions through self-awareness) whenever I needed to perform my best, which required silencing destructive self-talk, harnessing laser focus, and strategically planning the next steps. Discovering this innate ability for focusing energy didn't feel "exceptional," but learning how to access this innate ability anytime felt gloriously empowering.

I became fascinated with uncovering other dormant abilities in myself. Since I breathed learning, I excelled in university studies. By listening to my professors' recommendations, I applied to quality graduate schools and earned my Ph.D. in Biochemistry. I learned more powerful analytical skills as a biomedical scientist, publishing my research in peer-reviewed journals. Feeling self-confident, I was ready to try something entirely different by pursuing a career as an intellectual property lawyer.

Learning to think like a lawyer changed my self-concept in more expansive ways. I realized I could accomplish anything by INVESTING my attention and energy. I shifted my practice focus from representing Fortune 500 and 100 corporations as a patent lawyer in large law firms to advising innovative startups and soul-aligned entrepreneurs as an intuitive branding strategist and trademark lawyer.

Recently, I felt called to serve soul-aligned business owners as a transformational coach by leading with my intellect and heart. This process of re-inventing myself, over and over, has been a natural way of being and has fueled my expectations for myself. We feel our best when we allow ourselves to grow unconditionally. I've learned to deeply trust my intuition to guide my life and professional choices.

That meant when my health crisis showed up unexpectedly in my forties, I sensed a deeper meaning behind the "existential knocks" that were impossible to ignore. The debilitating pain was a divine message guiding me to evolve spiritually. The forced "stillness" of being bedridden invited higher self-awareness directed at understanding how my self-created identity formed over decades. The extreme challenges caused by Father forced my consciousness to expand. Although I grieved losing my "innocence," these early challenges *accelerated* my growth. Through the lens of spiritual maturity, I appreciated that "my" personal and professional accomplishments were NOT created by "myself" as the ego consciousness tries to tell it, but by Grace, involving divine support in countless ways. This decade-long process of heightened self-awareness, leading through a spiritual awakening, further evolved my being. I profoundly altered my perspectives on the meaning of life itself. I learned to trust the existence of a Universal Consciousness (*i.e.,* God/Source) for everything I need. This transformation was enabled by absorbing spiritual teachings, watching thousands of hours of training videos, and faithfully meditating to transform from the inside out. It felt like I was literally "re-organizing" my perceptual and belief systems.

Prior to my physical collapse in 2011, I was experiencing life through the lens of an ego-identity, which was filled with anxieties and an endless list of "future" projects to further build a socially conditioned "identity." I neglected the existence of an inner source of boundless joy, love, and peace — the realization of TRUE WEALTH. For nearly five decades, my *false* self-concept was limited to a physical body and a psychological self: all my beliefs, knowledge, experiences, and opinions.

Understanding that we are spiritual beings, in essence, was a life-transforming revelation. I'm beyond grateful for receiving the divine "knocks" that cracked my ignorance. As an awakening being, I appreciate the wholeness of my being without needing to add more to "my life" to feel meaningful. I don't have a life; I AM life!

By intentionally practicing self-awareness, I received countless perceptual and energetic shifts that contributed to my unshakable sense of physical and mental well-being. I released any desire to change anything from my past because the adversities were necessary to allow the emergence of a wiser consciousness.

People lacking spiritual maturity try unsuccessfully to avoid and resist pain instead of evolving through it. Our perceptual abilities for pain (and activated self-awareness) are necessary for survival and for expanding human consciousness. Without this understanding, unawakened humans choose either to medicate their pain away by addictive substances or avoid feeling them by distractions and escapisms. Yet pain is a powerful catalyst for opening possibilities by expanding our consciousness. Consciously creating one's life by making conscious choices through "soul-alignment," can be a powerful and authentic lever when cultivated with increasing self-awareness and heightened intuition.

In the awakened state, my soul feels aligned with the Universe, appreciating the countless ways that our collective well-being is supported. I AM the light, love, and peace of the Universe. So are you! God-consciousness is available to all humans by tapping into our soul-inspired activities. This is the "miracle" that most are seeking without knowing! *There is nothing more significant than you realizing your truest essence. This empowers and enlightens all of us.*

IGNITE ACTION STEPS

IGNITE Your Witnessing Powers: Protect your quiet time and quiet space by removing all distractions. When you meditate, the intention is to "empty" your mind. Let go of your concerns and completely relax. Start by sitting comfortably so you can be *more aware of the changes in your fields of attention and energy.* Note sensations in your body. Allow the revelations to emerge by directing your attention to them as they arise.

IGNITE Your Presence: Pretend you are a child exploring your environment for the first time. Stay intensely curious while exploring with your senses. Notice things e.g., birds singing outside your window, squirrels dancing on your fence, or a fallen leaf on your deck. You can awaken your senses by re-conditioning your whole being to notice many "aspects" of people and things ignored or overlooked for decades since childhood.

Loree J. Kim, Ph.D., Esq. — United States
Trademark Lawyer, Branding Strategist, Intellectual Property Consultant and Trainer, Transformational Empowerment Coach, Business Advisor/ Coach, Manifestation Coach
www.flexipcounsel.com | www.innovetta.com
❚ *@flexipcounsel, @innovetta*

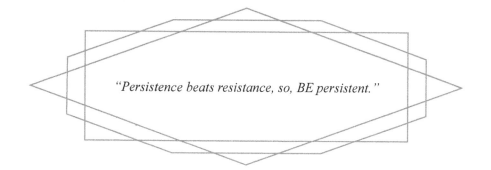

"Persistence beats resistance, so, BE persistent."

DECISION POINT

BY DAVID "DJ JUSTICE" SMALL

There's always a second chance and an opportunity to rebuild yourself. Be accountable for your life, and believe that you can make it, no matter what is going on. When you persist, you prevent doubt and fear from the opportunity to take root, and you can be the champion of your life. Loving yourself, forgiving yourself, and having the tenacity to move forward will be the determining factors in your life. Your next move *is* your best move. Your next decision *can* be your best decision.

Not many people can say they were born on their twenty-second birthday, but I can. I experienced rebirth on that day; the day I was released from prison. I emerged as a different person. After four long years, I was finally able to breathe unjailed air. Freedom. Opportunity. I was stronger physically and mentally, but I was scared of the unknown; the obstacles before me that I could not have seen coming. I had no idea the battles were just getting started, and I was late.

I have always had examples to follow. As the youngest of four children, I was blessed to see the experiences of my siblings. My two older brothers were my protectors and providers. I loved them dearly, even if they were sometimes difficult to live with. My father — the quiet, gentle giant whose presence stood like a mountain in the room — was someone that knew everything and, at the same time, questioned every decision. My mother's passion, drive, and sense of compassion was unmatched by his. My family was loving and supportive, but I still couldn't resist the temptation to mess up my life in multiple ways, all at the same time.

As a child growing up in North Carolina, I was exposed to so many things; many possibilities and many positive outcomes. Throughout my life, I was always a risk-taker and a motivator. As the youngest child, I was able to gain a broader perspective of some of the great things to do and some of the not-so-great things to do.

As a kid, I was outgoing. I had an entrepreneurial spirit that was ingrained in me from my earliest days. With admiration, I credit my beginnings in business to my mother. I watched her work, manage a household, and still build her own business. She was never afraid of opportunity and even inspired me to start my own business. I watched her work as an Avon™ lady, and I carried many Avon boxes as we set up and did vending shows all over the Southeast, selling Tupperware™, artifacts, history materials, T-Shirts, and books — we sold everything.

I began my first business at the age of seven: a jewelry company. By the age of twelve, I was featured in a national publication as a young entrepreneur, an "inspiration." In my teenage years, my love of music sprang forth like a rocket. As a young man, I remember an experience hearing the great Les Brown speak about being a DJ. I absorbed his story of taking chances in life to put himself in the right position at the right time. I learned from his story of working at a radio station and having to be ready; how he took his shot and made his break in that time of readiness.

After hearing Les's story, I knew I wanted to be a DJ, and I had an ever-present role model. My family was very large, with a multitude of relatives that were adopted into our clan through my parents' work in the community, their activism, and their position as field leaders in the NAACP™ (National Association for the Advancement of Colored People). I had a lot of aunties and uncles that weren't necessarily blood-related. One of those uncles is the incomparable DJ, P.G. Smooth, a.k.a. Pat.

To understand a little bit more of my story, you have to understand Uncle Pat: he was *smooth*. As a child, I remember when he would come to the house in his "T-top" sports car, he always had on a suit, gold watch, and money in his pocket. His sense of discipline he earned as a United States marine, but his style — that was all P.G.

I was determined to be a DJ like Pat because DJs were cool. At about the age of thirteen, I started navigating and exploring the possibilities of being a DJ on my own. Being an entrepreneurial young man, I was always down to make some money and didn't mind putting in the hard work. I've carried crates of records and very heavy wooden speakers — the old JBLs™ because they were the best. I remember saving up some money from doing odd jobs and going to my mother with a catalog from a pro sound company in California (at the time, California was a very far away place). I showed her a set of Gemini™ turntables that I HAD to have and some Gemini speakers. I worked very hard and saved up what money I could, and my mother, believing in me, advanced me with what I needed to get the equipment of my dreams. That was when DJ Blue Star was born. It would take many years of hard work studying the craft, going from fifty-dollar backyard birthday parties to, over twenty years later, being on international stages. In the entertainment industry, I have truly almost seen it all.

As a teenager, I did many events and festivals, growing in my art. But at the same time, being that ambitious entrepreneur and a hard-headed teenager, I was called and pulled in so many different directions. I didn't even know who I was or who I had become.

As a handsome, charismatic young man, I began to explore more than I could understand. I had a larger-than-life persona at times, captivating rooms with conversation, and I believed I was truly grown. By the time seventeen came around, I was ready for my freedom, or so I thought. I had engaged in a relationship with an older woman and was soon expecting to be a father. Throughout my life, I made many decisions, sometimes choosing the wrong paths, but leaving home at seventeen years old was the worst mistake of them all. I thought I was smarter than the average bear and began to do what I felt I had to do to survive, if only it was day to day. I began to challenge everything I knew to be right. I saw a path to easy money, or so I thought, and began to commit robbery. My series of bad decisions caught up with me. Five days before my eighteenth birthday, and four days before my oldest son was born, I found myself sitting in the county jail with no one to turn to.

It is often said that teachers' kids, preachers' kids, policemen's kids, and politicians' kids are a very *special* group of individuals. I can truly attest to that since my mother was a teacher, civil servant, and former police officer, and my father's career was in law enforcement and public safety. I knew better, but there I was, the result of several bad decisions, facing time that I could not imagine. Think of sitting in a jail cell doing long division with no paper when you hear your potential sentence in months versus years. I stood in many courtrooms alone because I knew I should never have been in that situation.

Once incarcerated, I had a lot of time to think and a lot of time to look in the steel plate mounted to the wall they called a mirror. When that door closes, and you know full well you cannot get out, the gravity of your decisions takes hold in your mind. There's a very small feeling that envelopes your entire body when you know your life's on the line. It caused me to study, not just myself, but the ideas behind the consequences I faced. I researched everything I could about justice: what it means, who deserves it, and how it can be achieved. The idea took hold, and I became a person who quested for justice, eventually claiming it as my name.

When I was released from prison on my twenty-second birthday, I was a new person. I had decided to turn my life around. I needed a plan, and I needed to move quickly. Having no real idea of what to expect, I searched for a job, thinking I had "paid my debt to society." I was wrong. Interview after interview, I struggled for over three years trying to find work, doing all types of odd jobs just to get by. I even got up the nerve to run for political office in an attempt to be a voice for the voiceless. Unsuccessful, but still impactful, I came in third in a primary for North Carolina's House of Representatives. I reminded myself to not let my current situation determine my final destination. I had to develop a winning attitude and go all out for my dreams.

About a year after my rebirth, I was sitting on a park bench with two dollars in my pocket, at one of the lowest points in my life. I was looking for hope, and a way to move forward to what I knew in my heart was my destiny. I was exploring Les Brown's recordings and heard him talking about possibility. He said, "Life has no limitations except the ones you make for yourself." At that moment, I knew I, and I alone had to have the self-determination to decide my path. I listened further to the great Les Brown say, "It's possible… but you have to be HUNGRY." That was truly a turning point, a moment that changed my life and redirected me to push harder than I've ever been pushed before. In that moment, I knew I had to be the driving force for my own transformation.

I started to apply what Les said, as I realized sometimes when no one will hire you, you just have to become your own boss. I returned to my true self, falling back in love with music, and began to DJ small parties and events. But this time *DJ Blue Star* had grown up, and *DJ Justice* was born. And this DJ took his skills further, working even harder, and proved how HUNGRY he was. Mastering my skills in media production has been one of the most gratifying accomplishments in my life.

As the years went by quickly, my life changed again as I became a father to two more sons. I really had to step it up, not for me but for my family. But even trying to be the best man I could be, I was met with all kinds of resistance. There were obstacles. My oldest two boys' mom, being many years older than myself, wanted to stay in my life; however, that wasn't an option. Navigating the legal system to be in their lives has been a difficult path, to say the least. But fighting to be the best father and a positive example for them while still feeling "not enough" was a challenge that I was determined to take on. I had to be persistent.

As my journey continued, I was blessed to be able to travel as much as I could and eventually made my way to New York City. As a DJ, I negotiated my way to provide music for a conference in Brooklyn, New York, that truly changed my life. There, I saw the meaning of a relentless pursuit of excellence. Rubbing shoulders with successful business owners really gave me hope and inspiration. I continued to master my craft and myself and take my shot. I was, and still am, a serious student of success.

At that event, I met another man who would be a mentor to me and believe in me, a stranger, like no one in his shoes should have. He gave me an opportunity to shine and showcase my DJ skills on the last day of the conference. As I sat in the back of the room, cold and tired from the drive from North Carolina, I felt a tap on my shoulder. At the time, I was not really interested in hearing from another network marketing company. But this tap came from one of the presenters who had been very passionate and inspiring that weekend. I mentioned to him that I was a DJ and had my equipment with me. He replied, "Show me." Thankfully, I had loaded a hotel luggage cart that morning with all my gear and parked it at the end of the hall outside the conference center. After he saw all I had stacked on this cart, he turned and said to me, "Okay. You got your shot tomorrow morning." Pure shock, but I was going to make it happen!

Early the next morning, on the last day of the conference, I came to the hotel conference center. I set up in the back corner with one turntable, a mixer, and one speaker. As the doors opened and people came in to take their seats, I began to play some smooth hip-hop remixed in jazz. As the day continued, I kept the crowd engaged, clapping and moving in their seats. When the presenter started speaking, I heard, "It's going down y'all" as he introduced a new product, and all I heard in my head was Flo Rida's song, "It's Going Down for Real." With that thought in my mind, I pulled the song up on my laptop and cued the hook of the song up in my headphones. The decision point was here, that moment of self-determination Les Brown talked about. When the speaker said it the third time, "It's going down, y'all," I held my breath, turned up my speaker, and scratched the record for just a second before letting the song fly. "It's going down for real!" The words blasted through my speaker, and the room's energy changed. A spark was lit by my decision, and this was going to be really great or really bad. Either way, I was committed. He looked at me from the stage, and the crowd began to move. The room erupted in energy. It was magic… magic I had created. We kept that energy for the rest of the conference. After the event, he pulled me to the side and asked me how I knew to play that song. I replied, "I heard you."

He told me, "You've earned your shot."

That man who tapped me on my shoulder and gave me my shot to DJ was the renowned entrepreneur and coach Jay Noland. I was beyond excited for whatever was to come next with him. The following stages of my life found me performing my talents around the country as the personal DJ for one of the most successful entrepreneurs in the world. He is a great man and mentor who taught me much about business and health, which are some of his life's work. I went from being flat broke to doing what I love in Los Angeles, Las Vegas, Orlando, Nashville, and so many other places. Experiencing that electric energy transfer was mind-blowing, and I knew without a shadow of a doubt that I would dedicate my life to being an example of what is possible. If you decide to go all in on yourself and all out for your dreams, you can achieve the unimaginable.

Stepping into my thirties, I was faced with a discussion of what to do next in my life. After years and years of trials and triumphs, a longing for more weighed heavy on my spirit. I was truly at a crossroads. In a stroke of pure genius and blessing, I decided to try my hand at a new and emerging industry. Drones. I bought my first drone and began teaching myself to fly. Knowing the elements of film and music production, I believed I could bring a new perspective through the air. And I did.

Utilizing my hustle and relationship-building skills, I approached a real estate developer and convinced him that he needed social media and drone videos for his business. He agreed, and with that first contract, I was in business. Skyline Video Pros™ was born. After a few months (and several crashes), I had got the hang of being a drone photographer. Over the next few months, the grind and workload were hard and fun. I traveled to many places and captured an aerial perspective of lands I had never known existed.

Building a business is never easy. There are many things to account for and decisions to make. But I wouldn't change it for anything. As I have continued to master my skills, I have now traveled around the country several times doing large motivational events, and filming documentaries and commercials. I've been blessed to have some great mentors whom I listened to and who gave me opportunities that really set a foundation for my path.

The persistence you decide to show in the face of resistance will be your path to your greatest dreams. Similar to what Robert Frost says in my mother's favorite poem:

Two roads diverged in a wood, and I—
I took the one less traveled by,
And that has made all the difference.

Never be afraid to take your shot and live your dreams to the fullest.

IGNITE ACTION STEPS

Accountability: Being real with myself about the decisions I had made that landed me in prison was a major step to where I am today. Be accountable to yourself, forgive and learn from your mistakes. You will find peace and hope in all that you do!

Be teachable and coachable: Be hungry for greatness and persistent toward success. As the great American football coach, Vince Lombardi, once said, "You must be relentless in the pursuit of your personal perfection, knowing full well you are not perfect, but in the pursuit of perfection, you will attain excellence." Write down your goals and go after them with your whole heart and mind.

BELIEVE! Believe in your dreams, your goals, your faith, yourself. Believe that the greatest version of you is yet to come. Believe that whatever you seek most typically gets found. Seek Greatness, Seek Hope, Seek Joy, and Seek Love. For the greatest of these is love. Love yourself and know that what you believe in, you can achieve.

David "DJ Justice" Small — United States
Son, Father, Husband, CEO of Cathedral Enterprises Inc. & COO of Skyline Video Pros
www.MyJourneyToGreat.com
www.SkylineVideoPros.com
www.SkylineSolarPros.com
🄵 *iAmDjJustice*
🄾 *DavidSmallCEO*

Malissia Woodall

"God doesn't get it wrong."

COMING THROUGH THE FOG

BY MALISSIA WOODALL

Your gifts are important; God has a purpose for your struggle. Let Go and Let God; the wisdom of God is inside of you. Your magic IS the miracle of God. Your story is your ministry. How it all unfolds is the divine discovery of who you are and what you have to give to the world!

I couldn't quite get out of the front door. Try as I might, resistance had set in, and I could find everything to do but get on the road. I had decided this three-week break in my work schedule was the perfect opportunity for God and I to have some alone time. The original *21 Spanish Missions* along Highway 101 down the California coast, the El Camino Real, was to be my road to clarity on why I felt stuck and out of place, not knowing what to do next.

I was in a fantastic job that I enjoyed for the people and travel, but it did not Ignite my passion. Taking this road trip to Los Angeles to change my destiny was the answer. A good friend, who lived in a spacious apartment in LA, was going abroad to Tuscany, Italy, and offered me her place to stay for a week. I was ready for change — to figure out a new career and life path. I was looking for answers in other people, external approval, and validation of my dreams. Anything to feel better, because although I had money in the bank and a dream career, I was unsatisfied and becoming depressed.

Another friend just happened to be reading about the original 21 Missions when I mentioned my need for a little getaway with God. She gave me the map and told me I should visit the mission in LA for inspiration. I had never heard of it but needed some guidance, and her suggestion planted the seed of an idea in me. Next thing I knew, I was planning a road trip for three weeks down Highway 101 to see not one but ALL of the 21 Missions. Apparently, people do this as a pilgrimage over a lifetime, but as an overachiever, seeing all *21* in three weeks seemed aligned with my nature.

Yet, there I stood, bags mostly packed, coming up with excuses like, *what books should I bring?* Once I realized I was allowing this silly necessity to delay my departure (by now a whole day), I decided to grab the biggest worn-out duffel I had and throw in every book I could possibly be inspired to read — easily fifty books — and get on the road.

The car was packed; a library nestled in my trunk, plenty of spiritual music and audiobooks at the ready, and fasting snacks in my vanity cooler riding shotgun. I was ready to set off on my road trip with God.

It was already dusk on that fine February evening in 2012, and God and I were officially "Holy rolling." I didn't make it far before I stopped at a roadside motel to get some sleep, my reward for at least having gotten out the door. I'd get an early start the next morning.

At sunrise, I got on the road to get through Oregon and into California to make up the lost time I had squandered faffing at home. I had driven into California by evening, and the sunset was immaculate. Being on the road for a full day was sublime. I already felt more free and whimsical, having said yes to that adventure.

As I was driving, I began talking with God, as I so often do, and asking: "What is mine to do; my purpose?" I couldn't see my life path clearly, and I was praying for guidance to clarify my next steps. Asking and talking turned into praying and seeking as I began to feel discouraged and frustrated, not at all enjoying myself as I drove past sunset and into the dark, barely able to make out the scenery.

As I was passing the Big Lagoon and praying to God for clarity, a thick fog suddenly set in like I had entered a cavern. I went from being unable to see my life path, to being unable to see *anything*. My car was in a tunnel of fog so thick and dark. All I knew was that there was a truck somewhere ahead of me and a car somewhere behind me as I navigated this winding, unfamiliar road on the edge of a cliff.

I went into an immediate panic! *Should I stop?* I couldn't see where I was! *Would the car behind me see me in time or hit me? If I keep driving, will I hit the truck up ahead of me? Had they stopped because of the fog? Or worse, would I drive off the side of the cliff?* All of this went through my head in seconds as I frantically tried to decide what to do.

I was suddenly back in 1983. I was eight years old, running through my favorite aunt's house. It was a gorgeous summer day, sun dappling through the cherry blossom leaves, as I threw myself down on her red velvet bedspread, listening to the dozen wind chimes she had hanging along the gutter at the back of the house. It was a perfect day. I had just been playing outside in the sprinkler and now was ready for my mid-afternoon nap with God. I loved to talk with God, my "invisible best friend."

Born into a faithful family of Southern Baptists and registered Native Americans, I felt blessed to spend most of my weekends and summers with my aunt, who the neighbors were sure was a witch. She practiced the art of Divine Sacred Feminine spirituality and was a psychic clairvoyant who performed seances for her clients and friends when she wasn't busy working her normal job as a nurse at the VA hospital. My father was also clairvoyant and a natural healer, so it was not to anyone's surprise when one of my gifts came through at eight years old: my hands got hot, and I was empathic to the energies of my family and our animals. Knowing the shamanic healing power that runs in my family, my aunt had me start practicing "healing" the cats with my hot hands. Soon came heightened awareness of my gifts of premonition and my clairsentience evolved quickly as I approached puberty. Luckily in my family, our gifts were nurtured and spoken about openly. After all, Jesus was a healer and miracle worker, so to be gifted was divine.

My aunt not only took me to church and believed in and loved a Christian God, but we also went to powwow and honored The Great Spirit in everything. We loved to sing along to spiritual music and gospel at church on Sundays. My aunt had the most beautiful voice, and I thought, *If I could sing like her, I'd never stop singing.* I was about twelve years old and dealing with asthma when my aunt had me sing as loud and full as possible to open my lungs. Out came a big, full voice just like hers, and immediately my asthma disappeared. God had healed me with that voice; it was up to me to use it to bless others.

My fear engulfed me as thick as the fog, and I had to question, *"Where was God?"* I had slowed only a little bit, driving forty-five miles per hour staring straight into a brick wall of white vapor, when abruptly, I called out in a panic, "God help me! What should I do?."

The desperation, the confusion: it was like spring of 1991. A friend of mine introduced me to his parents, the pastors of a local Baptist church. They invited me to come to sing the upcoming Sunday, and I was overjoyed to share my voice for God. I'd been a shy child, but here at this new church, I made friends and felt safe singing and showing my magic, thinking that they loved God and Jesus like my family and me. I was wrong.

It was a cloudy afternoon when a few of my church friends came to find me and invited me to come over to the pastor's house. I had an uncomfortable feeling about it, but I brushed it aside because I had grown to love and trust them over that year I'd been attending and singing at their church. As soon as I came in the door, I was grabbed and thrown on a bed; the pastor and his wife began spraying me with water and speaking in "tongues," shouting for the devil to get out of me as they held me down. I was in shock — a sixteen-year-old girl without parental supervision or consent, being held down by two adults on a bed being spoken to like I had evil inside of me. This was so frightening, looking into the faces of people I trusted and loved and seeing only hate looking back at me. The friends who had come to collect me were standing around watching while the pastor held me down and his wife flicked holy water upon me. I was so terrified by the experience of this spiritual violation that I finally just let go. I closed my eyes and surrendered. Not in the way they thought, but instead to a loving, peaceful God that would see me through this violation of my spiritual sovereignty.

Just as I relaxed into the peace of God, they stopped the attrition to pull me up into a hug. Smothering me with smiles and congratulating themselves, they decided the evil within me had been exorcized. I stood shaking, as I smiled uneasily at their joy and quickly made my way towards the door. I cried the entire walk home, in disbelief that they thought my gifts were anything less than the miracles Jesus performed. *Why did they punish me while worshiping him?*

Luckily, my gifts remained, as did my love for God. The only thing *cast out* was my belief in others' ability to love and accept me for who I was. I never wanted to go back to church or see those people again. I called out to God, "What do I do?"

On that winding, fog-ensconced road I began calling out again to God, terrified as I stared blindly, desperate for help. Suddenly, I heard within my spirit, "Let go."

I'd hear those words again. One day in 2016, I was suddenly inspired to watch a famous pastor's sermon when the program cut off abruptly. I went online to see if it was streaming. The website had a banner displayed at the top for a *Pastor and Leadership* conference in Orlando, Florida. Everything inside me jumped up and shouted *"Go!"* but I argued with myself. Since the exorcism incident, I hadn't been to church in over twenty years, and I wasn't sure if I would be safe. I couldn't sleep until I bought the ticket, booked my flight, and reserved a hotel. I had no idea what I was doing or why, but God was not asking; I was being called.

Orlando was gorgeous in the sunshine. The conference was a startling sixteen-hour, three-day commitment, and I was all fired up. Of course, I loved the sermons, the gospel, and even the church atmosphere I'd missed so much. Every day was a full day of feeling called to a bigger purpose and a need to share God's message through me. I'd evolved so much as a person and in my spirituality, my gifts, and beliefs since last attending church, but the energy and excitement was intoxicating, and I loved it!

On the last day of the conference, I came out of the final sermon absolutely on fire from the music, excitement, and the fervent request for financial donations. I was all lit up and out of cash as I had given my last dollar to donate to the church. As I stood in front of the Orlando conference center in high heels and a dress, I realized it would be quite a long walk without the trolley money! I was about to start trekking several blocks to my hotel when a rickshaw driver rode up to me, asking if I'd like to hire him. *I certainly would, but I had just given away the last of my money!*

He asked if I had come from the *Pastor and Leadership* conference, and I told him I had. As we struck up a conversation, he said he'd been eager to go himself but couldn't afford it. Then he offered me a ride to my hotel, free of charge, which I gratefully accepted. As we were riding through the streets on the warm summer night, I learned he was nineteen years old and saving up his money to go to New York City to work with an at-risk youth ministry to answer a calling God put on his life. I encouraged him to listen to that inner voice and follow his dreams.

Finally, we arrived at my hotel, and as I got out of the buggy, I looked up at the beautiful full moon basking its glow upon us. With a smile, I offered to pay him with a hug. He accepted and then became a little shy and uncomfortable. I was afraid I had embarrassed him, but he said that God had something to tell me, and would I mind if he shared it with me? I could feel the truth in his words and became shy myself. Despite my hesitancy, I let go and said, "Sure," smiling up at him.

He looked me right in the eyes and said, "You don't have to know how, but God will use your music and voice to spread the ministry. You don't have to worry about how it's going to happen. God will speak through you. You just have to let Him."

In that moment, I could hear God whisper, "Let go." I was scared, yet I completely believed in the truth and sincerity of this young man ministering to me.

I stood there astounded because I was feeling that very thing in my heart: God would use my voice to share the ministry through me. I knew it was a prophecy whose time had come. I thanked this rickshaw prophet with my heartfelt gratitude. What an angel he was — gifted to me; clearly, the reason I felt I had to fly 3,000 miles to a conference for ministers. I was put there to hear God's message delivered by this angelic young man. He smiled at me and rode away into the summer night as I walked to my hotel room.

Those words have stayed with me and showed me that since God doesn't get it wrong, I needed to trust. Weaving through that foggy night, I called out loud, "God, what do I do?" I heard within my spirit to *let go*.

Let go? Really!? As in the steering wheel? What!?

Panic was followed by a sudden sense of peace; a knowing to let go and let God. My hands were still on the steering wheel, but I was no longer driving. No longer trying desperately to see out the window into the thick fog, no longer looking for tail lights or the white line of the road. I simply became present. One hundred percent present. All of my senses were heightened, and I was aware but ridiculously calm. *If this was it, okay.* I surrendered to God. I let God take the wheel, so to speak. And as I did, just as suddenly as it had come on, the fog lifted. It was gone completely. Immediately, as if it was never there.

For the rest of the trip, I made sure to find a place to stay before the sunset, so I could enjoy each place and see the beautiful scenery passing by. I indulged in the mystery of where I would end up at the end of the day. It was a magical, spiritual journey and divine experience of letting go, trusting God's got me and doesn't get it wrong.

I saw all 21 Missions in those three weeks. Each one was uniquely beautiful in its own right. I sat in the sunshine on a rock at St. Luis Rey, overlooking the glistening pond near the lifesize sculpture of Jesus, basking because my trip wasn't about getting anywhere but about *BEing* in the moment, with God.

Since then, my road has taken me to many places. I have worked with teenagers and adults in workshops, teaching meditation, love, and healing. I've been singing and sharing my voice on stage and as a public speaker. I've been making my "ministry" about giving God back to the world and putting God back into our miracles, magic, and ministry. I have come full circle. I came back to church after twenty years, yet it was outside that I met someone to minister to me. It was outside that I was seen for the anointing upon my life as a blessing, not a curse.

I came through the fog of some of the most terrifying trials of my life, and so will you. You won't always be able to see what's around the next corner, but God has you. God is there even in the thickest fog, the hardest situations, and the biggest disappointments. Let go, and let God guide you through it all. I believe everyone is an instrument , a voice of God to share. Your magic is your ministry; let God reveal that to you.

IGNITE ACTION STEPS

I AM

I: Immersion. Immerse in books like this, positive spiritual beliefs that reveal the truth of you, lift you up, and keep you immersed in the greatness of God we're all meant to be in this world.

A: Alignment. Align with God, your higher self, to strengthen your confidence in yourself. Align with other successful, positive (God-centered) people, places, and experiences, and your life will be an ongoing blessing.

M: Meditation. Spend time in meditation daily. It is one of the most profound spiritual practices that allows for both immersion and alignment. If prayer is speaking to God, meditation is listening. This time feeds your soul, your heart, and your mind. It allows for more tolerance, patience, and expansion of the deep well of awareness within you that brings you peace despite whatever trials may be happening in the external world.

I Am = Me. The healthy "Me" is taking care of ourselves, so we have love to give to others. This is not selfish, it is the most important thing we can do so that we can have an overflowing reservoir in which to bless others because we ourselves are blessed.

Malissia Woodall — United States
Filmmaker, Screenwriter, Author, Singer/Songwriter, Performer, Healer,
Therapist, and Coach
www.malissiawoodall.com
malissiawoodall, malissiamusic, malissiasmusic
angeloflightproductions, malissiawoodall

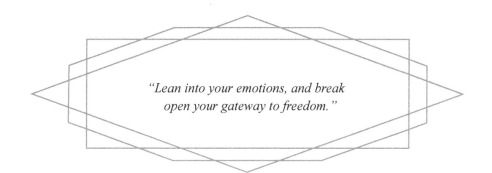

"Lean into your emotions, and break open your gateway to freedom."

PANDORA'S TREASURE BOX

BY TISH MEEHAN

It is my intention for this story to help you uncover the hidden wisdom that lies in your deepest wounds. Life's experiences are peppered with both darkness and light — positive and negative lessons — but *you* get to choose how *you* want to show up. When you touch into those places within you that evoke emotion and resistance, know that there is deep wisdom and truth waiting to be brought into the light. Your own struggles, grief, and despair hold the keys to your transformation, for they help you see all parts of yourself, from the brightest sparks to the darkest shadows. They teach you how to embody your truest, most authentic self. Lean into your emotions and let them flow, digging up the buried treasures within you. For without the dark, we cannot know the light.

When I woke up that dark Tuesday morning in November, I didn't know much, other than the fact it was way too early to be up yet. The sounds of my father whispering quietly had beaten my alarm clock and roused me from my bed. I walked out of my bedroom towards the sound of his voice, and half-asleep, I asked, "What's wrong?"

Then he told me, "Your mother is dead." A simple statement of fact. And I screamed.

When I was fourteen, I lost my mom suddenly. She had a massive heart attack in the middle of the night when she got up to use the bathroom. No one heard her. She was alone when she left this world. Those seconds when my dad told me that my mother was gone, my heart shattered into a million pieces. This was not just a life-changing moment for me — something in me died with my mom. I am not sure I can even name that part of me, only describing it as a cross between one day having my innocence, youth, faith, and love and the next day feeling it was gone. I *am* sure that I have been searching for these pieces of me ever since that moment.

My mom wasn't the huggy type of parent (that's my dad; still is). My mom was the one who made things happen. She was always there, physically, in our house. She was there every morning when I was eating breakfast and every afternoon when I got home from school. She would be lying on the couch watching her afternoon show, and I would climb into the space behind her legs and watch along with her. That had been my favorite place to lie as a kid. I called it my little house; it made me feel safe and secure. As I got too big to lie there, I would often sit at her feet, or on the floor in front of the couch.

The last day that I was able to lie in that special place was the day before she died. I knew that my mom needed me that day because I could see her falling to pieces in her own world. My mom, who was never one to cry, was weeping as she nursed a broken heart. Her mom, her best friend, my grandmother, had died the day before, and my mom was overwhelmed with grief. I had never seen her so vulnerable and broken. It was so jarring that I stayed home that day to be with her, to give her some comfort and love while she was in so much pain. When she lay down on our comfortable couch to rest, I sensed she needed extra comfort, so I squeezed behind my mom's legs once more, even though I could barely fit. It had been a long time since I had lain there, but I knew that she needed me. We lay there and cried, and then let the lull of the television calm us. We stayed that way for a long while, our breath in sync, her warm hand on my head. That was a special moment with my mom, helping her through her pain and loss as she held me through mine. I was grateful for that day. That *last* day, with my mom.

I remember that night when I was in bed; she came to tuck me in, something she had stopped doing as I was now a teen. As she left the room, she said goodbye, not goodnight. I distinctly remember that moment, seeing her shadow silhouetted by the doorway. That was my last memory of her being alive.

I was traumatized; my heart shattered into a million pieces. My body and mind were both completely numb, and the only thing I could do was breathe. I walked through my days that way. The numbness was followed by waves of grief, uncontrollable tears, anger, and a heavy sadness that I can still feel at the very depths of my soul to this very day. I was barely a teenager in my first months of high school, now navigating this new world without the most important person in my life. I was unable to eat or sleep properly. I constantly worried that something bad would happen to my dad or sisters. I cried so much at home, but locked my tears away at school, afraid of being set off in front of friends.

I had spent much of my early years learning how to suppress my emotions so that I could be in control. But what I felt and experienced over the days, weeks, and months after my mom died is beyond words. *How could she leave me when I needed her?* I would wonder with extreme anger. Then came the feeling of guilt for being angry at someone I loved so much. I even thought that perhaps the way I was — sensitive and emotional — caused my mom so much stress that her heart couldn't take it anymore. I felt so much regret and shame, but I didn't know what to do with it. This is the cycle that I lived in for much of my teen years. It's a blur, yet so clear at the same time, like part of it is still happening inside me at this moment. I am sure it still is.

My family was a hot mess, and although we had each other to lean on, I didn't want to be a burden to them. Instead, I invested my time in my small group of friends, holding on tightly, hoping I could pretend to be like them. But that didn't work either, and before I knew it, they decided not to be my friends anymore. I walked to my locker and saw them standing in a circle down the hall, near the girls' washroom, whispering. They would look towards me and then go back to their whispering. I felt sick to my stomach. Tears sprung into my eyes, but I wouldn't let them see. I mentally ran through everything that had happened over the past weeks to see what I could have done to upset them, but came up empty. I walked past that group with my head held high, but it felt like the floor was dropping out from under me. One of the girls, the mouthpiece for the group, decided to share with me the reason for everyone turning on me. She said coldly, "Tish, you have so many problems, and you blame everything on your mom dying." It was a punch to the stomach, and just another reason to shut down. I felt like I wasn't good enough, like something was wrong with me. I became a victim in my own life.

After that, I did anything and everything to be liked. I stopped saying how I felt or what I wanted. I looked to my new friends and family to guide me and help me make decisions. The part of me that used to be fiery, courageous, assertive, and connected was gone.

When I was a little kid, I was feisty. I knew what I wanted, and I wasn't afraid to say it. If my family didn't go where I wanted to go, I would make sure it was known that I was very unhappy. "I'm tired, I'm hungry, I'm thirsty, and I want my blankie!" were my favorite words. My aunt loves to recall the time when we were on an outing, and I threw my socks at my mom because I was done with the day and wanted to go home. I stubbornly fought to have my needs met. My sensitivity and emotional range caused chaos and frustration to my parents and sisters. Somehow I was nicknamed *Little Thunder Cloud* and *Mona* because I moaned and complained... a lot. I didn't understand why I felt the way that I did and often thought there was something wrong with me.

My dad and sisters would tease me at dinner sometimes, and I can't even recall what about. I can see now, looking back, that I felt exposed, embarrassed, and like there was something not right about me. I would get so upset that I would storm off enraged. That usually happened at dinnertime. I remember white-hot tears burning in my eyes as I locked myself in the bathroom. I sat on the floor to calm myself, but living in a small house meant I could hear them laughing at me through the vent. It broke me more than I wanted them to know. I felt shame over my anger, and rage, and the tears that I couldn't keep locked inside. There are pieces of me that I left behind in those moments — my confidence, assertiveness, and fire. This was the start of my self-imposed emotional lockdown, and coping was an impossible task.

My parents didn't know how to share and talk about my emotions with me. Instead, after an outburst, I would be sent to my room to deal with my overwhelming anger alone. I would sit there, fuming, pounding my fists and forehead into the wall, screaming in my pillow. When that wore me out, the tears would come, followed by the guilt and shame of what I had said and done. This was the cycle of my childhood. I feared the outbursts; told I was too emotional and too sensitive. *There must be something wrong with me.* I didn't want to be seen, shutting myself in my room or the safety and peace of my dark closet. I felt unloved and unlovable.

My fear and insecurity began to weave its way into other areas of my life. I would scooch down low in my seat in class so that I would not get called on, convinced that I wasn't smart enough. I followed the crowd at school. I ignored my gut instincts when something didn't feel right. I had friends but didn't show them the real me as I was so uncomfortable in my own skin.

After losing those friends that day at the lockers, I wore masks of who I thought I should be, and pushed my sorrow deeper. Drinking brought confidence, but that was followed by shame and depression. I had a lot of dark thoughts and wondered whether I could manage to live this life anymore. I thought about how merciful it would be to die and join my mother on the other side, but I couldn't do that to my dad and sisters. I got really good at pretending. Pretending to be okay. Pretending to be happy. Pretending that I wasn't being crushed by everything that I shoved down inside. The truth is, I felt like the walls were closing in on me and that I was being dragged under, into the darkness of a deep depression. I felt like I was dying on the inside.

Then there came a flicker of hope, of light. I met a man when I was seventeen, and married him at twenty-nine. I thought that all of my problems were finally behind me. He made me feel like the world was right-side up again. Things became predictable and stable. I focused on creating a life that would fill the hole in my heart. I had done it! I was a successful adult! I was married to a great guy, a homeowner, had a career as a teacher, and eventually, we had three amazing kids. My focus shifted between the roles of wife, mother, and teacher, and it fulfilled me for a while. I let my husband lead the way and make most of our big decisions because it felt good to be cared for. Becoming a mother brought so much love and joy, but it also made me aware of the cracks in my foundation. I loved my husband and children, but my unhappiness began to spread through me. I turned inwards to try and heal the darkness of my loss and grief so that I could finally be myself and live the life that I yearned to live — one of joy, unconditional love, and passion, and to be an equal partner in my relationship.

I was my own Pandora's box and I was scared to open myself up. The real me was lost somewhere in there, amid my former pieces: the four-year-old feisty kid, the lost and broken teenager, and the newly awakened adult, all longing to be seen and shown. I became miserable, angry, lost, and sad all over again.

That is when I found my spirituality. I dove deep into the sea of self-healing and learning in the hopes that I could shed those burdens and begin to feel alive again. I studied energy healing, yoga, and coaching which lit up the darkness in me. I found myself in a community of loving, supportive people, and I felt at home for the first time. I also unlocked all the emotions I had suppressed. The more I tried to heal myself and be who I needed to be for my family, the wider *my* personal Pandora's box was opened. My husband and I grew further apart the more I leaned into being myself. I struggled with an internal battle between the old me, who didn't want to shake the foundation I had created for my kids, and the real me who knew that the foundation was an illusion. I stayed in that place for many years, always choosing to stay.

One day, I could no longer deny it. I remember feeling completely lost in an emotional wasteland, stressed from a job I no longer loved, and angry and resentful for not listening to my own needs. There was a moment that I felt my breath leave me, and I sat on the floor of my kitchen, head in my hands, silent tears running down my cheeks. My children were home with me. I could see their little feet on the cold, white floor of my kitchen as they approached to ask if I was okay. One of them hugged me; I am not even sure who. I sat there for minutes, then hours, frozen. I remember hearing my husband arrive home. The garage door closed behind him, with the cold air rushing through the room as he came in. I couldn't get up or find the words to tell him that I was lost. He kicked my foot and said, "What's wrong with you? Get up." No emotion in his voice. The unconditional love and care that I needed in that moment didn't come. And just like the day my mom passed, my heart shattered into a million pieces. That was the moment I knew I had to leave.

A year and a half after that day on the floor, I told my husband that we needed to separate. I had thought long and hard about it, changing my mind and trying harder to make it work, but I could no longer be that person that was a heap on the kitchen floor. We sat at our dining room table, my heart racing with fear and guilt. I found the strength to hold myself up. The moment I told my kids their dad and I were separating, I felt all of the oxygen leave my lungs. I looked into their innocent eyes and told them we would not be living together anymore. I could see the pain and confusion on their faces. I felt as if I had just shattered their world.

It took me a few months to move out, find a place, and create some semblance of living my life on my own. I started journaling, meditating, and devouring every book I could find on growth, self-worth, and self-love. I began finding little ways to show up, be present, fully open, and vulnerable. I had to do all the hard things that I had taught myself not to do. I leaned on a new community of like-minded individuals to help me stay centered and to follow my heart. I found unconditional love and those closest to me helped me see that I hadn't been fully living. I had been a shadow of myself for many years, and I finally discovered what it felt like to be alive.

I am still working through all the moments of my past. There are days and weeks that the darkness starts to weave its way through my energetic field, into my mind, and becomes a weight on me. I am right back at that moment when my mom died, and all of the pain and sadness comes flooding back in. My old insecurities and conditionings from childhood begin to creep in, and my inner critic becomes so loud it drowns out the truth that my heart and soul wish to share. I work with the tools I have learned and allow myself the grace to feel the darkness and move through it instead of trying to bypass it as I have done in the past. I pray. I pull cards and meditate. I talk to my guides and angels, and even to my mom. I ask for help. I ask again. I surrender. I surrender again.

Sometimes it feels like the tide will pull me under, and I will be drowning again, just as I was when I was fourteen. Sometimes I let myself go there, but I have the awareness now and I ask for help. I do the hard things. I slip and fall, but I get back up again. I show my kids the power of emotional intelligence, of being vulnerable, and how important it is to be who you are and feel what you are feeling no matter what. I shower them with true unconditional love. I finally have a sense of peace, knowing that what I have been through has taught me that I am enough just as I am.

You have an important purpose in this lifetime and part of that is learning to use your experiences and life lessons to uncover all parts of your beautiful, divine Being. I encourage you to learn to trust your gut and your emotions, and allow yourself to embrace all that you have experienced so that you can shine as brightly as a star in the dark, velvety night sky. It is not easy to open Pandora's box of emotions and experiences. In fact, it takes a lot to keep it locked up tight. It's through the opening and revealing that you get to experience the wholeness of yourself and see yourself through the eyes of the Divine — perfect, whole, complete, and wise. Your inner child needs you. Your family, friends, and children need you. The world needs you. It is time to let all of you shine bright and let the world see you.

Ignite Action Steps

Never settle. Keep doing the hard work. Listen to your inner wisdom and trust your heart. You know what is right and true for you. Set your boundaries; speak your truth with love and compassion. Cry when you need to cry. Use your journal when it is all stuck in your head. Get out in nature, and feel the wind on your face. Be present and live into the Now.

Ask for help. Advocate for yourself. It is okay for people to see you being vulnerable. Find a coach, mentor, spiritual healer, or whomever you resonate with. Even if it is having a coffee with a good friend. Be open. Talk about how you're feeling. When you share with heart and intention, you'll find beautiful things inside your Pandora's box.

Tish Meehan — Canada
Transformational Soul Coach and Spiritual Teacher
www.tishmeehan.com
tishmeehanspiritualhealer | tishmeehan1111

Janine Marek

"Live life while you're alive."

LIFE IN THE PAST LANE

BY JANINE MAREK

Wisdom, gathered while traversing life's trials and tribulations, often comes from loss. Grief, a result of this loss, is a sensory process; an emotional journey where a sight, smell, or sound can trigger memories, sending you reeling once again. Be patient and kind to yourself; working through loss can be exhausting, yet also transforming. The most effective way to get through grief is with awareness and talking. Loss is part of life, be mindful of that. With loss you can learn to appreciate life, seeing it as a joyous treasure.

The door slamming behind me sent a familiar echo throughout the stairwell. Climbing the stairs, I heard the hospital PA system announcing, "Over Capacity Protocol Level Two." Translation: "Standing room only. Get ready to run around!" My final shift as a porter was not going to be calm or easy. Nothing could ruin my mood though. I had my belongings packed, and was moving to live and work in Canada's beautiful Banff National Park. At fifty-eight, it was going to be the first day of my newest adventure. The journey from disconnect to reconnect had been long and hard. But with life, you can't wait until it isn't hard before you choose to make it happy. Happiness is a choice, not a result.

I got my first taste of "hard" in my teens. Chaos. Not the kind that comes with adolescent hormones, but chaos coming on the heels of gut-wrenching grief. My first time experiencing death was at fourteen, a toddler cousin was killed in a farming accident. He'd been under my grandpa's supervision at the time, and we not only lost the little guy, but witnessed firsthand what intense grief could do to a man and how it could destroy a young family. Accompanying my dad and his brothers to the graveyard, I watched the strong men in my world digging a tiny little grave. The reality became unbearable when the boy's grieving father insisted on taking his turn. The intense anguish of the situation proved too much, and these once hardy pillars of strength crumbled. Looking back, I'm in awe of the emotional courage and tenacity this digging required; an unbearable, yet beautiful display of brotherly love and solidarity. The heartbreaking days that followed left me forever feeling numb and disconnected.

Death was uncomfortable — almost taboo — something we didn't understand and for sure didn't talk about. Instead, from that day forward, we went about life not knowing how to grieve, feeling somewhat confused but pretending all would be well. As a family we got good at this. We navigated the minefields of loss and grief the only way we knew how: staying busy, working hard, and finding little things we could laugh about. I was grateful for my family's aptitude for optimism; it became our life source through the ensuing years, while our community was immersed in a black cloud of tragedy. After we buried our tiny cousin, we laid to rest an infant, mourned the loss of our young grandma from cancer, and bid farewell to two young cousins, aged twelve and thirteen, all within a five-year time frame.

Not knowing at the time what empathy was, I didn't understand how I could sense the pain of those around me. I felt physically sick and had a hard time catching my breath, churning in what felt like a life-sucking vortex. Grief, at times, became all-consuming. But our family simply wouldn't give up, and that kept me getting up and showing up as well. We were great at helping in the community, making our time count. By this time, I was in high school, going through the motions, becoming a master of emotional hide-n-seek. I felt permanently off-kilter, pretending strength in person, but crying behind closed doors.

After graduation, I thought it would be great to travel. Nowhere in particular, just anywhere away from the turmoil associated with my small community and its ongoing losses. At nineteen, even though I was well versed in death, I wasn't proficient at handling it, having only the examples of my gritty and determined family members to follow. We simply stayed outwardly strong and smiled through the pain. Autopilot became my new norm as there seemed to be no end to the waves of grief that kept washing over me. I'd show up physically, seldom be there emotionally, and was always preoccupied mentally. I knew not to talk about our deceased. Instead, I thought about them continually, because in my youthful ignorance, I irrationally believed I could take the pain away from the grieving parents or, better yet, magically wake up from our ongoing nightmare. But life doesn't work that way, and neither does grief.

With time, things settled down again, laughter returned, and positive memories were made. Our family's fun, quick wit, and humor were great coping skills. Lacing comments with irony and sarcasm created a split second of laughter, which might be all the time needed to keep from falling apart. We were adept at pretending though; behind smiles remained tears, and under laughter, souls could be heard ripping apart. Life had been cruel. But life isn't fair, and it certainly wasn't going to stop just because we needed a break from it.

Going through past trauma, I realized grief was a journey, a long drawn-out process where you don't ever really "get over" a loss, but with time, you can learn to get "through" it. Life had been tough, but we were proving to be tougher — you have no choice. That is how you build resiliency. What I know now, of course, wasn't apparent to my younger self. At the time, I was simply swallowing my grief and letting it eat at my soul, showing up to validate myself where needed, using whatever strength I could muster at the time, all while subconsciously bracing for the next death.

To cope, I got busy. *Really* busy. It wasn't a conscious thought process, but if you don't have time to think, you won't have time to feel either. Busyness got me through and kept me buoyed as life's clock kept ticking. I married Prince Charming and was thrilled to be a farm wife. We got to work making a living. It didn't take long to realize growing up on a farm was a different scenario than making a living from it. True, there are many wonderful blessings to be had on the farm, and it's a great place to raise a family, but farming is hard work and endless toil. The theme of death is big on the farm; it comes with the territory of raising food for consumption. But by this time, my skin had thickened, and I could handle life without much thought or emotion. Staying busy and laughing often seemed like efficient coping tools at the time, not realizing that my inner peace was disappearing with all the busyness as well.

It's a good thing I was born with stamina though, because our hectic lifestyle was about to be ramped up. We welcomed twins to our busy world, three days before our youngest's second birthday. Math was never my strength and I'd just proven that by having four kids in three and a half years. It's a good rate of return in the farming world, but needless to say the subsequent years became an endurance test amongst a blur of craziness. We dealt with the ensuing madness, tending to the workload of the farm, and caring for litters both inside and outside the home. Staying busy was the only thing I knew.

That was until grief, in all its ugliness, returned this time taking my dad in its wake. His death honestly broke me. He was a larger than life personality and had the unique ability to carry sunshine in his back pocket. We needed that sunshine and it was gone. We had plans — so many plans for life — all pointing us in one direction, but reality was taking us off course, without a roadmap. With our built in busyness, life didn't wait for us to recover. There was no time to think, let alone grieve. I just got up and did the same thing over and over and over again as the days of our lives ticked away. I negotiated life with steel walls around my heart and a survivor's mentality firmly set in place. These new additions helped me mindlessly get through any task at hand.

Life wasn't easy, but for the children, I stayed strong, alive, and engaged. I loved those kids. I wanted each to know how special they were but found it challenging to divide myself in so many ways. They needed the energy of a strong, playful mother. I was resilient but overprotective, coming across intense at times. I saw my kids as the only perfect part of my husband's and my world; I was so proud of our self-made creations. Yet, I know my anxiety and fearfulness robbed them of the ability to be fun-loving thrill seekers. I couldn't dare trust that my family's experiences wouldn't be repeated. Years passed, and just like that, my job was over. The empty nest hit hard. I'd stayed strong, too long for too many, and didn't know how to live for me. My heart ached as I realized I was detaching from the farm and its lifestyle, slowly being nudged into independence. I'd been pretending for years and was tired of the façade. I felt a hunger to explore the world on my own. Bitterness was seeping in, chasing away our happiness. I wanted to get better, not bitter. I felt drained and emotionally out of control.

A quote from a wellness seminar I attended inadvertently became an action step which drove me forward. "If you always do what you've always done, you'll always get what you've always got. If nothing changes, nothing changes." I wrote that down, and as I re-read the words, I felt them hitting my core. Something needed to change. *Everything* needed to change. I'd been stuck, consistently repeating old habits, now viewing them as daily doses of craziness. Something simply had to change. From my marriage to my mentality, I had been doing life on cruise control. I'd fought hard for so long to avoid feeling grief, that in doing so, I disconnected from what happiness could feel like. Yet now, this new mantra was igniting a glimmer of hope, offering up tiny morsels of courage towards change. With no more excuses, and that infamous clock ticking, I said "Yes!" to living life on my terms, setting out to chase a few dreams beyond my back door.

That transition didn't happen instantly. Leaving my lifestyle was incredibly daunting. Nevertheless I focused forward, manifesting what I thought adventure could look like for me. I felt the fear and did it anyway. Thankfully, my inner child had survived the years of chaos and I hadn't lost the ability to see life through eyes of wonder, curiosity, and playfulness. Thanks to my inner child, I've enjoyed countless adventures near and far. I've hiked and biked many miles, enjoying cycling adventures where my mom drove the pace car beside my bike. I was camping at night, relishing in roadside picnics, and getting up close and personal with Mother Nature and beautiful people while cycling throughout the western provinces of Canada, down the Oregon coast of the United States, and through the California, Napa Wine Valley.

Once I was told that "if you've got a pulse you've got a purpose," so I found my purpose by attaching adventure to humanitarian work. This has taken me to Guatemala several times, allowing for extensive travel throughout Central America. Africa, though, was a monumental life achievement. Prior to my fifty-first birthday, a group of kindred spirits and I built a school in rural Tanzania, allowing 553 children to attend school through fundraising. Once the school, home stays, and safaris were complete, we challenged ourselves to climb Mount Kilimanjaro, because, "Why not?" An insanely hard, worthwhile life experience; another time where simply saying, "Yes!" created some of the most beautiful memories.

Prior to Africa, my first big adventure of independence was a cross-Canada trek that challenged me physically and mentally, and was the catalyst for my spiritual transformation. I met God while cycling across my country to the farthest point east in the northern hemisphere. To add to that blessing, I was able to manifest a "perfect for me" job while driving home. I began working as a porter at the local hospital, ushering in a wonderful new chapter of my life. Porters, a unique bunch, transport anything and everything within the hospital walls, walking nearly twenty kilometers per shift. When receiving my service pin, they stated that in the ten years I had been working, I'd trekked the entire circumference of the earth!

I loved portering. It was fun and physical, but came with a daily dose of hard reality, too; celebrating birth one minute, transporting death the next. I handled this well, as my life's theme had death and painful experiences weaved throughout. At the hospital, I was privy to grief. My experiences from the past were in stark contrast, though, to what I witnessed on the front lines — seeing shock and grief in its rawest form. Emotions could turn to anger, occasionally upgrading to violence. Panic can do this when reality hits; loved ones realize it's too late to have important conversations. This last-minute panic brings forth uncharted emotions, and grief can get messy. There is no right or wrong way to maneuver through loss, but I feel that it's an important topic to talk about in advance. It's not fun to broach, but it may help with understanding emotions. Being proactive isn't morbid; it's mindful… a selfless act done on behalf of others. Initiating uncomfortable conversations in advance, when calm, can bring understanding and awareness, helping to lessen the emotional minefield. You can't fix grief. It's a hard, slow process, but you can move through it in small, mindful increments of time.

With being immersed in death, I've awakened to life. Mortals don't control their timeline, like we think we do, so I encourage you to be grateful for your days. The reality is not "if" but "when" there will be loss. An attitude of gratitude goes a long way in finding joy and wisdom throughout your trials. Don't wait for the "right time" to have fun or be happy. Time is a thief that waits for no one. This knowledge helped shape my mindset, and the years at the hospital drove that fact home. As a result, I'm determined to do as much as I can with my allotted time. Be open to conversations and resist the urge to shut them down when they get uncomfortable. Grief is a process, something you won't get *over* but with time you will work *through*. Pretending it won't happen is fruitless; accepting death as part of life can help you live passionately, with purpose and focus. Laughter comes after the darkness and light returns to your world, but you'll need to give time… some time.

The cliché rings true: "Life is what you make it." I'm encouraging you to take the wheel, get out of the "past" lane, and set your sights on life's next beautiful horizon.

IGNITE ACTION STEPS

Take a hike: It costs nothing, yet the benefits are immeasurable. Learn to take care of your body; it's your forever home, the only one you get. Try to understand it, respect it, and maintain it. Good health isn't only what you eat, it's what you watch, see, feel, and think as well, so be mindful of what you're putting in. Be proactive instead of reactive with your health. Don't wait until there's a diagnosis to start taking your health seriously.

Bond with nature: Get outside, it's therapy for the senses. Hug a tree, better yet, plant one. Trees are amazing producers of oxygen, literally our life force. Life lessons can be learned from trees. They will withstand the winds of change, enduring outside forces as they get wounded, scared, and threatened.

If well-grounded, they'll stand firm. If broken, they refuse to quit and will transform their wounds into beauty in a different way. Mother Nature is amazing and necessary, but she needs our help. Try to leave nature better than you found it. You can't fix it all, but future generations will appreciate any TLC given. Be mindful of the long-term results of the choices you're making now.

Hug your inner child: It's okay to cry. Life hurts at times. Get it out, then get up off the floor; you don't belong there. Play. It's necessary and needed. Make your time here fun; it's fleeting. Try to turn mundane trips into an adventure; explore your world through the eyes of a child. Be kind to yourself! Kindness counts in a cruel world. Laugh. Don't underestimate the power of laughter, especially when life hurts. Walk your pets. Better yet, try talking to them, sharing yourself with something that won't judge, diminish, or reject you can be a saving grace. No pets? House plants or photos also work.

Keep it real: Don't hide or conceal your sadness or grief. Tears are messengers saying everything our words can't. Cry, scream, yell if you must, let it out. Learn to say what you mean and mean what you say. Volunteering is a wonderful thing, because with giving you receive. It's uplifting, especially when intentions come from the heart. Kindness is a language deaf people can hear and blind people can see. Dare to dream. Don't wait until life isn't HARD to be happy. Life happens whether you're engaged or not. Practice your passions. Dreaming costs nothing but will sow many seeds. Focus on intention: try being brave enough to take that first step. Visualize "what if" scenarios with a "why not" mentality. Blaze a trail down the road less traveled. Never say, "I can't." Say "I'll try," because the reality is, whether you think you can or you can't, you're right.

Not "if" but "when":

Janine Marek
May, 1961– ….

What are you filling your "dash" with? Experiences? Memories? Acts of kindness? Materialism doesn't fit on a headstone.

Janine Marek — Canada
Adventurer, Mom, Grandma, Lover of Nature
ifci.janine@yahoo.ca
@janine.marek.9

Barb Lilley

"When we enter into silence, wisdom magically appears."

FINALLY FREE TO FLY

BY BARB LILLEY

My desire is to empower you to live the rest of your life for your highest and best good and help you identify and release behaviors that no longer serve you. I wish to help you get in touch with your intuition, that inner voice, or Divine Wisdom. It doesn't matter what you call it. I believe it's all the same. I want to show you by example that guidance is always available. The only requirement is that you listen.

My story began over forty years ago. The ending is still in progress, but my steps have been guided along the way.

As a young child, I received guidance from an invisible source. Sometimes it was a voice in my head; other times, it was just a sense of knowing. I didn't know where it came from or what it was. I just knew I could trust it. My dreams often foretold events that later occurred. I sometimes felt a warning, and my awareness was heightened when things were about to go wrong, like a family member becoming sick or an accident ready to occur. I felt the pain of others. I knew where they were hurting. As much as I could, I relied on my intuition to guide me without becoming scared. My intuition kept me safe, even though I often chose to ignore it.

Parts of this story are known by only a few people. I hid it from most. I felt shame that I allowed it to happen to me, fear that I no longer knew how to trust, and guilt because I didn't listen to my intuition. Here, I'm telling it in its entirety for the first time because my dreams and meditations were calling out, saying to tell this story NOW. This time, I chose to listen.

In the late 1970s, at twenty years old, I dreamed about saving the world and helping everyone in need. I was that girl who ran onto a busy road to rescue a stunned mallard duck that had collided with a vehicle. I was that girl who always cleared the snow for the elderly couple next door. I was that girl who was a friend to everyone who needed a friendly face or a caring ear to hear them.

While studying at the University of Toronto, I became friends with a classmate. I found him very quiet, calm, and sensitive, similar to myself. He seemed lonely, keeping mostly to himself and focusing instead on his studies. Yet, whenever I saw him, he was always smiling, and his smile was contagious.

After we'd known each other for a while, he told me he noticed me on the first day of school. He'd made a point of sitting next to me, copied my name from the class roster, and looked up my address and phone number that first day. My stomach felt a bit queasy when I heard this, as I thought it bordered on creepy. But I quickly dismissed it. He told me he wasn't in a relationship and wasn't looking for one. I told him I had a boyfriend because I wanted to make it clear I wasn't looking for a relationship with *him*. He didn't seem too happy when he heard this — but perhaps I was reading too much into his facial expressions.

Out of nowhere, one day, while we were talking about homework, he told me he loved me. I guessed he could tell by the worried look on my face that I wasn't comfortable hearing those words from him. He quickly retracted his confession of love and told me what he meant was that he loved me like a sister. That made more sense. I felt somewhat better, or at least that's what I told myself.

Summer break was coming in a couple of weeks. I was going to Florida with a girl from my French class. I was so excited. This would be my first time on a plane. When I shared my excitement with my friend, he proudly told me he had his pilot's license and offered to take me flying before my trip.

A man of his word, later that week we went flying. It was a dreary day. The air was very dense and heavy, the temperature cool and clammy. The sky was filled with dark clouds and isolated patches of fog. We didn't stay out very long because flying was restricted. Despite the conditions, I found it exciting. Flying was a sensation I had never felt before, a feeling of freedom and exhilaration.

A few days before my trip to Florida, on a perfect day in May, he called to ask if I wanted to go flying again. It was mid-morning; that ideal time of day when it wasn't too hot. The sky was crystal clear; the sun was shining. As we taxied down the runway, picking up speed, he turned toward me and smiled that contagious smile. I smiled back.

After a smooth take-off, we were over a small lake. It was so peaceful, and there were no ripples as the sun reflected on the sparkling indigo water like diamonds. The towering trees that enveloped the lake were a palette of every shade of green imaginable: forest green, emerald green, moss green. It was a picture-perfect moment. Watching out the side window, I turned to look at the front windshield. We were headed toward a dark and dense forest, away from that luminous, picture-perfect scene. The trees appeared almost threatening. They were packed so tightly together, competing for sunlight and air to survive, an ominous sight.

Suddenly, I felt a sick feeling in my stomach. I instantly recognized it as my intuition warning me. I was preoccupied with trying to get my bearings when I felt something on my left thigh. I glanced down at my leg, startled to see his hand there. *This can't be happening!* It was totally out of character; he had always been a gentleman before. I was confused and trying to process the sight of his hand when I heard, "Now I've got you all to myself."

My entire body became stiff, and I was on high alert. At the same time, I felt a violent downward thrust of the plane. I grabbed the strap at my window with both hands. My body was no longer upright in the seat as we careened downward. My stomach was in my throat as a horrible cry of pain from my own mouth pierced my ears. I saw nothing but darkness. I remember thinking, *This is it! I'm going to die! I'll never get to Florida! I'm not ready to die!*

After I stopped screaming, I noticed the plane had miraculously leveled off. But for how long, I wondered? I listened to the sound of silence. I took a couple of breaths, and it brought my awareness back. Shocked I was still alive, I slowly opened my eyes, expecting to wake from the nightmare. But I was still trapped in my reality. I thanked God I was still alive. Yet, instinctively, I knew that it could change any minute.

I turned toward the seat beside me. I was staring in the face of a monster. His face and ears were scarlet red. The veins in his neck were fiercely pulsing. His eyes were protruding from their sockets; his pupils were dilated like pools of black oil. It scared me even more when I looked into those eyes and was unable to find the person I knew. My friend wasn't there, and I wondered if he'd ever return. Intense anger radiated from his being — anger toward me and me alone.

My intuition told me it was up to me to try to take control and create a positive outcome. I had only one chance. He said nothing. He just stared at me. The plane remained level, thank God. My knees trembled uncontrollably as I draped my purse over them. I didn't want him to see my fear. Thoughts and emotions started to take over my body. I wanted to cry. I wanted to scream and yell at him. I wanted to slap him on the side of the head and ask if he was out of his mind, but my intuition already knew the answer to that question. I felt like a helplessly trapped animal as he continued to stare at me, anticipating my every move while watching me squirm.

The passing seconds seemed like an eternity. Then, a sudden wave of calm slowly encased my body. I heard and trusted that inner voice, that Divine Wisdom that I felt within me, and I knew I was no longer alone. I took a couple of slow breaths and opened my mouth. I didn't have a clue what would come out, but I knew I could trust that it would be the right thing.

In a steady and quiet voice, I asked him about his plans for the next week. Somehow I knew that if he answered me about his plans, then that meant there would be a next week for both of us. I waited and wondered what he would do. My prayers were answered when he responded in his normal voice. Cautiously, without turning my head very far, I glanced in his direction. The monster had retreated, and my friend was back.

I was very anxious to get back on the ground, though I tried to conceal those feelings. I made up an excuse about needing to be somewhere soon. Moments later, we touched down with another smooth landing. I opened my door, grateful to be back on solid ground. At that moment, I made a series of vows to myself, repeating them over and over: *I will never fly in a plane with this man again. I will never travel in a car with this man again. I will never be alone with this man again. I will do everything in my power to distance myself from this man.*

I mentioned nothing to my parents and kept the experience to myself. I didn't think anyone would believe me; I didn't want to believe it. I felt ashamed for ending up in that situation and believed it was my fault. My friend never mentioned the incident either. I often wondered if he even remembered it. I contemplated asking him about it but decided to keep quiet.

When thoughts and emotions came up around the event, I would push them away. When I got on a bus at night, I would scan the passengers, making sure he wasn't one of them. At home, I was always triple-checking whether the doors were locked. I was paranoid, highly aware of my surroundings. My new normal was fear and shame.

After Florida, I enrolled in a summer night class at the university. The second night of class, he showed up and sat beside me. I have no idea how he knew I was in that class. I never told him. One evening, at school, he asked about my boyfriend. This was the first time he acknowledged him. Next, he proceeded to tell me that he knew how to kill someone by breaking their nose and pushing it up into their brain. As I write these words, I am still horrified by that remark. I think he said things like that just to see my reaction. To scare me. To watch me squirm.

On the way out of class one night, he talked about committing suicide. It was not the first occasion where he had mentioned it, and I wasn't sympathetic. In a rather stern voice, I told him he needed professional help as I distanced myself and turned away.

He didn't respond. I knew right away I shouldn't have said anything. Anger consumed him. Once again, for a fleeting moment, I saw that monster. He yelled at me, demanding to know if I had told anyone about his suicidal thoughts. This time, I wasn't as scared, because we were on the school grounds surrounded by students, not alone one thousand meters up in the air. Plus, my feet were on the ground, and I could outrun him.

The last time I heard from him was just before the start of the fall semester. He called me to ask if I wanted to go flying "one more time." I thanked him and said, "No." The next day I was in my sister's kitchen helping her make cherry jam. I noticed my feet were sticking to the floor and thought, *This floor needs to be washed when we're finished*. The radio was on. We were chatting and half-listening when the news started. I heard the announcer say my friend's name. I blocked all other thoughts and sounds to listen. "Taken a plane and was missing… " were the words I heard. I intuitively knew what had happened to him. My knees weakened as I grabbed the sink for support.

I felt a tremendous amount of guilt around the death of my friend. I asked myself, "Why didn't I help him, and why didn't I get him the help he deserved?" I wondered if I was partially responsible for his death. If I was, how could I ever live with myself? All these thoughts and more were racing through my mind. I told my dad that I wanted to go to the police and tell them what I knew. Although I hadn't told my parents the entire story, I *had* mentioned the talk of suicide. Dad told me not to go to the police because I didn't know anything for sure. He was just trying to protect me. But my intuition knew differently.

After the incident, I changed. On the one hand, I felt grateful to be alive. On the other, I struggled with trust and feelings of guilt and remorse. I questioned my own intelligence and character judgment, wondering how I could have been so stupid. There were plenty of signs along the way that identified his mental state. I chose to ignore them.

Several weeks later, the police phoned the house looking for me. They found a piece of paper with my name at the crash site. Shortly afterward, an investigator from the Ministry of Transport called to set up an interview. Both gentlemen were very supportive and sympathetic. A professional character analysis of my friend's handwriting was read to me by the investigator. I learned a lot from that report. That happy, always smiling young man was not who he portrayed himself to be. When the interview concluded, the investigator told me there was nothing anyone could have done to save him.

I left the interview knowing nothing about the process I would have to go through to resolve my feelings. I felt broken and was looking for a quick fix in order to heal. I hoped someone would say something and instantly, everything would be better. Once again, I chose to hide my emotions, as it seemed to be working thus far. That's what I thought and continued to think for forty-four years.

Then, the time came to write my chapter for this book. I had an idea in place to tell a different story, but my inner knowing told me my idea was off. Instinctively, every cell in my body knew it was time to finally acknowledge and process what had happened. While writing, I have allowed some of my feelings to surface, realizing that I no longer wanted to carry the burden with me.

While writing this story, I began the process of grieving the loss of my friend. I remembered some of our conversations, his intelligence, and his infectious smile. The gentler side of him made me realize I needed to forgive him — something I had never even considered. I found it relatively easy to forgive my friend but didn't know how to forgive the monster. I struggled, trying to reconcile that they were one and the same. My intuition told me I had to acknowledge him as that troubled soul outlined in his psychological profile. By understanding his condition and acknowledging his illness, then and only then, was I able to forgive him completely. I pray that my friend has also forgiven himself and that he is free.

After I finished writing my story, intuitively, I knew that wasn't the end. Writing this story was just the starting point. Divine Wisdom told me much more had to happen. The final and most important step was: I needed to forgive myself. I needed to release the feelings that I had been harboring.

As an older woman now, I found it difficult to relate to that younger version of me and her trauma. Until I pictured that naive twenty-year-old girl, the one who thought she could save the world. The one who always trusted others. The one wanting to help whoever she could. The girl who tried to fix him. I finally forgave her.

After more than forty years, I ask myself: "Why am I finally ready to deal with this?" Perhaps it's the writing, meditating, and soul searching I've been doing. It really doesn't matter. I believe my intuition was telling me, *Enough is enough; you need to deal with this and move on.* I can honestly say I do feel lighter as if a burden has been lifted. I recognize this as a process that will continue to unfold as long as I allow it.

I continue to receive guidance and work with my Divine Wisdom daily. When I listen, it serves me well. I feel the words of Anais Nin, a writer whose words I have written on a piece of paper and have been carrying with me for years. What she shares resonates within my soul and offers healing: *"And the day came when the risk it took to remain tightly closed in a bud was more painful than the risk it took to bloom."*

If you are holding on to unprocessed grief or hiding away from the lessons your intuition has already taught you, let my story prove to you that it is never too late to start healing. I hope it inspires you to open yourself up to your intuition and trust that inner voice and Divine Wisdom. It is there for each and every one of us, and it can set you free. You deserve to LIVE the rest of your life for your highest and best self. It's never too late to make changes. All you have to do is listen.

Ignite Action Steps

- Unplug all distractions from your daily life. Enter into the silence by clearing your mind in order to allow your senses to receive. Hiking, biking, and kayaking can be very therapeutic. The constant movement will calm your mind and open you up to allow your intuition to come through.
- Guided meditation or silent meditation are both effective ways to develop your intuition. Experiment with various types of meditation and figure out what works for you. If your mind is active, practice walking meditation. Go out in nature, smell, hear, see, and be at one with the beauty of the outdoors and simply listen.
- Take development classes to enhance your intuitive abilities, the possibilities are endless. You may also take advanced studies such as medical intuition and mediumship. When you tune into your inner voice and awaken your intuitive spirit, you connect with yourself and get to know the *real* you.

Barb Lilley — Canada
C.G.A, C.P.A. (retired)
farmgirl623@gmail.com
 Barb Lilley

Sharon Eistetter

"Retirement is your chance for rebirth!"

RETIRING INTO REBIRTH

BY SHARON EISTETTER

Many people enjoy a long, rewarding career, then retire and move on to the next stage of life. It can be scary, or it can be exciting. It is your chance for rebirth: take it! I want you to be aware you can become whoever you want to be and do whatever you want to do! You are free! You now have the freedom to explore, learn, rest, rejuvenate, work, create, and discover everything that is possible.

I walked out of my office building for the last time to a still, cloudy sky that matched my mood. If there were sounds, I didn't hear them, because I was inside myself. It was the end of my thirty-eight-year career as a senior director in a financial organization. I was retired. I should have felt elated, joyous, relieved, and free; but instead felt sad, lonely, and oddly hollow.

How I felt was no surprise, given how I dreaded the ending of my career for many months and even years. My last year had been difficult, dealing with a boss that was constantly pressuring me to retire. It was hard to forget the ageist comments he made to me long after our meetings or phone calls were over.

My time with that company, the entirety of my career, had been rewarding. I worked really hard, starting with the company as a twenty-one-year-old, and climbed the ladder with excitement and vigor! I dedicated my life to the company's demands, moving from place to place as requested, even to cities that weren't my ideal choice. Of course, not every relocation was bad, as I met my second husband through one of them. My family came along as I relocated, and I willingly sacrificed much of my personal and family time to be successful, hoping to live up to the expectations of the job.

I was raised to have a good work ethic: Work hard, and you can achieve whatever you want. I was a tomboy, raised on a farm, and a fiery little girl who excelled at school. In retrospect, I was an achiever. I did well at university, funding myself on scholarships. The more I accomplished, the more confident I felt. It only made sense that as soon as I graduated, I would jump right away into an environment of achievement.

Work was the place I felt validated and rewarded. It had been an experience with a cherished company I loved, and the feeling of belonging to a work "family" for thirty-eight years was incredible! My career became my identity and provided me with opportunities to excel and build my self-esteem.

All throughout my thirty-eight years of work, despite being financially comfortable enough to retire, I knew I would have a difficult time when the day arrived for me to exit. I hadn't developed a lot of passionate hobbies. My work-life balance was off, but I thought I could adapt, as millions before me did. *How hard could it be to have no work obligations for the rest of my life?* For me… difficult. Little did I know I would embark on a journey of the mind, body, and soul that would take me into boredom, fear, illness, solitude, and finally into a place of contentment and new excitement.

The first few months of retirement were frustratingly boring. I kept wondering when my sense of freedom would show up! I felt so unfulfilled that within four months, I gave in and accepted a one-year term position similar to my old job, except it was a work-from-home gig. I didn't enjoy it, feeling like I was having to prove myself at fifty-nine. I didn't get a spark from it or the sense of belonging I desperately craved. I developed a bleeding hernia and resigned after five months. I was starting to realize work wasn't going to fill this big hole in me that had revealed itself.

I then took on a marriage commissioner role and quickly mastered it, but again, didn't find joy or belonging in the experience. I enjoyed working with the couples and performing the ceremony, but I still felt inexplicably unfulfilled. I had all the time in the world. I had financial security. My kids were grown and onto their own lives. My husband, Brad, was supportive and patient. I had all this but didn't know what activities I could do to fill me up or inspire me. It was that same hollow feeling from the day I retired. I just felt more empty.

I read everything I could get a hold of on the topic of retirement. I discovered there aren't a lot of books out there. Most of the resources covered financial planning, but none gave me the rich ideas that I was craving on how to *succeed* at this stage of my life. I didn't want to become a TV watcher. I wanted to thrive; to flourish as a person with something on the horizon.

Guilt and shame engulfed me. I wasn't enjoying my life more; I was having trouble feeling grateful for my life. It was all so weird and upsetting. I couldn't find anyone in my circle that felt like I did about retirement. The isolation I felt only made the hollowness darker. For more than two years, I tried and struggled to fill the void on my own terms. I didn't want to find a job again; I wanted to find myself, my true self.

Two and a half years after I'd walked out those company doors, I went to England to visit family. I got sick toward the end of our time there, and when we returned, I got more and more tired, lost my appetite entirely, and suffered from cold sweats whenever I would fall asleep. The pandemic was just being discovered, and by the time I went to a walk-in clinic, the medical system was completely shifting. I ended up going for blood test after blood test and telephone appointment after appointment with specialist after specialist. It was four months of unending questions with no answers. Of course, I'd already had a couple of years of wondering what was wrong with me, but this was different.

I had become so fatigued and weak, Brad had to help me up from the bed, recliner, or wherever I was for the day. I started to think about death, and we talked extensively about what he should plan for if I passed. It scared the hell out of him and he cried, but I was just numb and couldn't muster the tears. It just pissed me off that I wasn't going to enjoy that wonderful pension I had worked so damn hard for all those years!

After four months of every test imaginable, I got a diagnosis of an auto-immune disease called Adult Onset Still Disease (AOSD) that causes severe inflammation in the body. I was honestly skeptical about my diagnosis but accepted it for the sake of forward momentum. After a month of resisting, I started to take the prednisone my specialist prescribed, and my symptoms *did* disappear almost immediately. But I knew there was something deeper involved.

A couple of days after starting my treatment, when my eyes opened in the morning, I realized I had energy in my body. I didn't have the crushing fatigue and body pain. My throat felt a little dry and scratchy. I looked at Frankie, my cat, who was sleeping beside me and thought, *I am so thrilled he is here with me, and I can pet his soft fur coat*. I was startled by the new sensation that was overtaking me, as my years of doubt and emptiness were replaced in an instant with one feeling: I was 100% grateful to be alive.

I had had many thoughts of gratitude in my life, but this was the first time I felt it to my soul. I got full body shivers thinking, *Thank you, Universe, for another day I get to walk on this earth.* This was the beginning of my new beginning, my rebirth.

The next two years of my retirement journey involved looking inward. The more I learned about *dis-ease*, the more I believed it is more than a medical issue. It's based in spiritual and emotional blockages. I am a science person by education, and I am committed to many of its teachings. I am also a meta-physically spiritual person by passion. I started to study spiritual topics, and I joined online communities that gave me a sense of belonging. I took courses that piqued my interest. I have been a life-long seeker of knowledge and discovered I had the time and interest to dive deep.

My technological skills had not been strong for many years and were even weaker since I retired. I was a woman who could barely operate her IPhone™ and had developed the idea I couldn't keep up. Well, that wasn't true at all! I started on a journey of self-guided learning to brush up on those skills. I not only overcame my fear of learning technology but actually enjoyed it and continue to stay on top of the latest changes!

I started to work one day a week in a ladies' clothing boutique and really enjoyed it. The pay was low, but the activity was very rewarding! I would get dressed up, help women with their clothing purchases, and formed friendships. I even helped the owner get a marketing program up and running with my newly minted tech skills!

Most importantly, I started to take care of who I was as a human being. I realized that throughout my long corporate career, I had become stifled and constricted in so many ways. I was a good employee, a loyal employee, but I had lost who I was in my quest to succeed.

I began defining my success differently. I developed a strong morning routine that got my day going in the right direction. I practiced gratitude and discovered that the more grateful I was for everything in my life, the more enriching my life became. I was starting to change as a person. Previously, when I was so focused on a career-based achievement, I was competitive as our company rewarded results, and I was a results-oriented person. Once I shed the corporate garment after retirement, I discovered that my competitive nature very much softened. I could see that enjoying the moments of life rather than excelling at externally set standards, was the true reward.

I spent many days at home with my books, online communities, and my thoughts. At first, it felt like I was unproductive and wasting my time. The timing of COVID-19, and the restrictions it placed on travel and life in general, actually helped me focus on myself. Honestly, the timing was divine. I had always gotten my sense of achievement and worth out of long to-do lists and checking those off. I was now living a life of many days of quiet introspection and learning. And I came to love it! As months passed, I became more and more comfortable in my own skin and my own life. I realized that I was truly enjoying this alone time to THINK; time I really hadn't had while raising five children and having a very active social life. It took retirement, a sobering dis-ease that dropped me to my knees, and a COVID-19 enforced solitude to really process my thoughts and ideas and learn to love myself.

The old saying that we need to "find" ourselves rang true, and I liked what I found. I found a kind, funny, clear-headed, generous woman who has a lot to give and a lot of knowledge and wisdom to share! I found a woman who is not defined by a career, the size of her clothes, or the size of her annual bonus. I found me, and I liked me. I was finding joy in simple conversations with my husband, children, and grandchildren that were like none in the past!

Despite having a long career in science and management, I had always been fascinated and curious about metaphysical topics like astrology and crystals. It was time to dig deeper. I learned about quantum physics and energy, being the fiery Aries that I am! I began to shift my field of consciousness and raise my vibration. I was *feeling* a new me.

I studied Feng Shui and learned how energy affects everything we are, do, and experience. I "Feng Shuied" the house, much to the puzzlement of my husband. But we are both enjoying the beautiful energy of our home. Our home is filled with joy and laughter — even Brad sees the difference!

I was finally starting to feel happy and free. It took me nearly five years after retiring to understand that I had autonomy over my schedule and thoughts. I found the Sharon that was missing and began to fall in love with her.

That promoted my journey to continue on a path of rebirth and self-exploration.

A person has to have a pause, despite the difficulty it brings. I couldn't go from what I did before to total bliss without all the pain and boredom in between. We sometimes need to be broken before we can rebuild. There is no such thing as ageism to me anymore when we have so much to share with others, to give humanity, and to grow within ourselves. When I did the work on myself, enjoyed working on the stillness, and let go of the busy life I once had, I found that there is so much right here inside of me. There are endless experiences to appreciate in life. Once I started recognizing them, I found all the treasures they had to give.

Currently, I am working on a book about how to flourish in retirement after a long, dedicated, focused career. Writing this book is filling a gap that I discovered when I retired. I'll be sharing information on how to develop daily routines, staying current on technology, side hustles, social connections, and volunteering. More importantly, I will address the emotional importance of health and longevity, rewarding hobbies, a freeing lifestyle, a heart-centered mindset, a soul-centered purpose, and birthing your life in such a way it creates a legacy.

It will be the book that I needed to read when I was preparing for retirement in those first weeks, months, and years! It excites me to know this book will help so many other people and start them on a fulfilling next chapter of their lives. What's perhaps more exciting is knowing that I'm passing on the wisdom I gained on my journey.

I want you to be thrilled and feel excited every day when your eyes open! Let immense gratitude fill your heart, and allow the Universe to provide space and time for you to discover who you are. Plan what you want to do with your time and make it joyous. Embrace your rebirth as a human *being*, not a human *doing*. You get to decide, so map out the most epic journey possible for your life!

IGNITE ACTION STEPS

Set up a daily routine and follow it

Make a simple to-do list the night before of activities you plan to do. Ensure it includes a mindset aspect (gratitude, meditation, a walk, reading inspirational material, etc.), and do something different once a day (or once a week at minimum). This will start your day on the right note and carry you through with a high vibe!

Own your health

Get a family doctor or other health practitioner such as a naturopath if feasible and available. Get regular blood tests to determine cholesterol, inflammation, and blood glucose markers, and monitor if they change yearly. Move your body for at least thirty minutes a day, and cut down or eliminate alcohol, cigarettes, and other harmful substances that our bodies just can't process as we get older.

Stay in touch with family and friends

Text, call, or email a family member or friend regularly, and try to set up coffee dates and lunches with folks to stay connected. Join a meet-up in your area to meet new friends with similar interests. Get active on Facebook™, Instagram™, or some other social media platform. Even if you don't actively post, it's a great way to remain aware.

Technology is your friend!

It is really important to be able to navigate your phone/laptop/tablet and to comfortably utilize the digital world. Anything you want to know can be searched and found on Youtube™ or Google™, and all you need to do is check the upload date to make sure the information is current. Anyone can learn. The first step is overcoming the fear of making mistakes and messing something up. Reach out to a techy friend or grandchild for support, ask questions, and stay curious.

Learn, learn, learn

Give yourself permission to learn and study whatever in the world interests you. If you aren't sure where to start, think about something that interested you as a child that will indicate a lifelong interest!

Side hustles — earn some extra $$

Consider a casual or part-time job, in something totally different than your career. Turn your hobby into a side hustle and sell your wares on Etsy™, Facebook Marketplace™, etc. Become a secret shopper. Become a personal shopper. Day trade. Take up dog walking. The possibilities are endless. You can earn a little extra cash and, at the same time, have fun!

Sharon Eistetter — Canada
Author, Speaker, Coach
www.sharoneistetter.com
 Sharon Eistetter
 Flourishing in Retirement
 Sharon Eistetter
 Sharon Eistetter

Mary Streeter

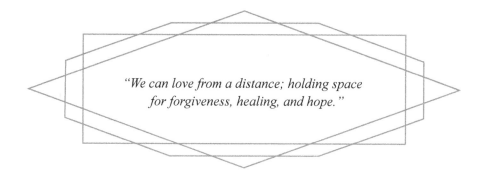

*"We can love from a distance; holding space
for forgiveness, healing, and hope."*

LEARNING TO LOVE WHAT IS

BY MARY STREETER

I hope to remind you of the resilience you have to ride the waves of struggle, and continue to feel hope and find joy. When we step out of our shame and allow ourselves to be real and vulnerable with our experiences — the pain, emotions, and struggle — we begin to realize we are not alone. It becomes a gateway to healing. I share my story with the hope of touching a tender place in your heart that opens the lens of compassion and understanding for your own journey. I believe the purpose of life is to be happy, and despite it all, to learn and to share.

Life had shifted so quickly; I felt as if I was stepping back to admire a beautiful sandcastle I had spent a lifetime creating, sculpting so perfectly and loving into life, when suddenly, it was like a wave came and swept it away as if it never existed.

I was just coming up for air. My youngest was in high school, and I had finished my graduate degree, was doing work I loved, and became a volunteer for an organization doing global health work in Africa. I had even done a deep dive on my relationship of twenty-five years — healing and growing back together after years of parenting, getting lost in the journey, and growing apart. I had learned how to take care of myself; practiced yoga, meditation, and mindfulness. That summer, I felt like a younger version of myself, reuniting and playing with my husband again after years of hard work and responsibility. Life was good. I look back at this and realize this was preparing us, making us stronger, for the next leg of our journey.

It was late fall. I came home from a long shift at the hospital to find my oldest daughter lying rather listless on the couch while her four young children ran around the house. I remember this feeling of scattered, untamed energy hitting me as I walked in the door. Kneeling down, I reached out to receive the armful of children barrelling toward me. Lifting my gaze, I noticed things scattered about; empty cereal bowls on the counter. Clearly, they had been there for a while. My daughter, barely able to pull herself up over the back of the couch, lifted heavy eyes my way as she said weakly, desperately, "Mom, I need help." This was followed by a low and faint, "I know you know what's going on."

I did not. The words that followed, "I'm a heroin addict," felt like an arrow being launched into a space in my heart. Her words vibrated through me, a sucker punch to my gut, taking my breath away as I stood there in disbelief. I'd never felt so many emotions occurring in parallel. I wanted to scream, cry, and vomit all at once. But I did none of these things, as some deep inner calm let me simply whisper, "What do I need to do?"

I began to follow my daughter's guidance as she listed the few recovery centers in our small state. I kept dialing the phone: no luck. My heart got heavier with each call. I felt like sand was slipping through my hands with each rejection. Her suffering felt so intimate, and every cell in my body was driven by desperation as I pleaded through the phone on my daughter's behalf. I was simultaneously trying to maintain a sense of calm, while getting the kids snacks and addressing their needs, to cultivate a false sense of well-being. It was an act that I would continue to perfect as a means of survival; protecting my grandchildren and armoring my heart.

Someone on the other end of the phone finally said yes, their center would have an opening the next day. I half exhaled before I realized she had to survive until tomorrow. Gazing her way, she was like a wounded animal. I had no experience with this, and I felt horrified and helpless. We ended up in the emergency room of the university hospital where I worked. I was hoping to get her something that would get her through until the next day. I had worked in the ED (Emergency Department) and knew all about drug seekers, and here I was begging for help. We got none. Late that night, after exhausting all *legal* options, my daughter took the phone and made a call. I drove her to buy a street drug to get her through. I was an accomplice to a drug deal. This would be the first of many times I found myself in an unimaginable situation, trying to help save the life of a loved one. I did what I never thought I would do, as she deeply struggled with a demon that would continue to plague her and our family. I felt ashamed, overwhelmed, and like I had failed as a parent.

We got through the night, and the next morning, I tucked her into my car and made the two-hour trip to the recovery center. It was a long ride, and she was barely holding on. Or was that me? I am not sure I was even breathing as I gripped the steering wheel, holding on tightly to each precious moment, so fragile, like a piece of glass that could shatter at any moment.

As we entered the treatment center, the door locked behind us. It felt cold, institutional, and smelled like vomit. The intake was excruciatingly long. She was sick and it seemed ridiculous to be asking her these questions. Couldn't they help her first and deal with the details later? My logic apparently, not theirs. *Finally* complete, it was time for me to leave. I held her tight, and as I let go, I felt a piece of me and the life I had known slip away with her.

Rain pounded down as I slumped over the steering wheel, needing to rest and be held while I fell apart. But there was no one and no time, because I felt an urgency to get home and hold onto my grandchildren, whose world had just been turned upside down. This time, when I walked into the house, I met my husband's tired gaze. We looked at each other and silently acknowledged a slight sense of relief that we had gotten our daughter to relative safety. Although overwhelmed with suddenly having a house full of children, this was at least familiar territory for us. Besides, rehab was what, twenty-eight days? We fell into bed each night, completely exhausted but convinced we could carry the baton for a few weeks. Yet, in three days our hopes melted to fear when we learned she had left the recovery center. This fear would turn to horror with each passing day that we didn't hear from her, not knowing if she was dead or alive and fearing the worst. She was such a wonderful, caring mother — she couldn't possibly be alive and not have rushed home to her babies. Could she?

I felt like I was walking through fire while hearing the insistent echoing of my daughter's words, "I'm a heroin addict." It reverberated in my head as I tended to the children, giving them baths, and finding them beds, clean clothes, and some toys. We told them stories, went for walks, made them food, tucked them in at night… and prayed. In moments of stillness, between the inhale and the exhale, I wondered how this happened. *How did I not know? A good mother would not have raised a daughter who would end up a heroin addict. What did I do wrong?* Uncertainty and blame danced around in my mind; my heart was raw as I grasped for answers.

Things became more overwhelming really fast. We scrambled to find day-care and after-school programs for the kids. The reality was that this was not temporary. We would soon find ourselves in a family courtroom testifying about the truth of our daughter's addiction, and over the course of a few days, we'd become foster parents. Then two years later, on my fiftieth birthday, we'd adopted our grandchildren.

I could fill these pages with the struggles my daughter continues to have as she travels through recovery and relapse, but that is her story to tell. What I can share is the story of how we started to piece together a new life while mourning the life we had lost. My love for my daughter is unwavering, but when in the grips of addiction, she is less my daughter and more an addict: that is the honest, painful truth. As she becomes more and more distant from who she was, she becomes more and more unfamiliar to me.

This has taken years for me to see clearly, learning how to set loving boundaries to safely walk beside her and stay hopeful.

We were a couple of months into the journey, and I felt overwhelmed with all the tasks of daily life, rushing to keep up while I felt like a perpetual rolling boulder would crush me at any moment if I paused to take a breath. I was still experiencing every emotion possible on a daily basis and holding it all in as I kept my story close, only sharing it with family and a few friends. Filled with shame, I was certain that we must be the only ones on this journey. I couldn't deal with the questions, or having to explain something I didn't understand myself. Additionally, the stress had exacerbated my hormonal imbalance of peri-menopause, and my iron had bottomed out. I was hitting my rock bottom with no time to care for myself, because I was dripping with children to care for and bills to pay. Life felt impossible, and the day came when I found myself sitting outside the courtroom for the custody hearing, on a bench alone, crying. A social worker approached me and touched me on the shoulder, "You don't have to do this," she consoled me. Without hesitation, I responded, "I *absolutely* do have to do this."

As I left the courthouse that day, I felt a sudden release within. The finality caused a shift within me, birthing something new. It was January in Vermont, and as the bitter wind swirled around me, I felt a warm rush of calmness sweep over me and settle in. It stayed present through the next morning's chaos and still hovered inside when I was dropping the kids off at school. As they scrambled out of the car, my attention lingered on a woman walking kids to school; a foster parent like I'd once been. She looked wretchedly unhappy. My heart softened as I took in her presence and thought, *Why is she doing this if she is so unhappy? She doesn't have to. She has a choice... I have a choice.* I let that thought melt into me. I did not want to be a mirror of this person beaten down by life, full of fear and resentment. In that moment, I realized that while I may not have control over the circumstances in my life, I could choose how I was going to respond to them.

With the shift in perspective, I began to see the many gifts of our family's journey unfold. In our community I couldn't really hide what was happening: I suddenly had four young children in tow. I was forced to open up, be seen, and let people help. When people offered sneakers, boots, and jackets, I accepted. When meals started showing up, I said, "Thank you." When my sister's book club offered to take the kids' Christmas lists and buy, wrap, and deliver the gifts, I was moved and incredibly grateful. It still brings me to tears — the generosity, human compassion, and caring that we received. Our village showed up when we desperately needed them, without us even asking. This fueled the light of hope in me, and although nothing felt like enough in the beginning, it was humbling and one of the many ways that I began to see grace showing up at our doorstep.

Through this grace came the reigniting of my inner light. I began to delve into the tools of resilience I had gathered over the years: practices of gratitude, breath, and mindfulness. This didn't require me to set aside time I didn't have, but I'd weave these practices into moments, and over time it began to change my days. I found myself responding with more patience. I felt less overwhelmed and was gaining more clarity. Some days, practicing gratitude might have been simply being grateful that I was breathing, the sun was shining, and we had a warm home. Regardless, the benefits still came. I might have still been standing in mud, but I began to feel the fresh air and sunshine. I could finally breathe again, and life began to look more welcoming; it was the first step of healing.

I've shared my story of the first days of this journey and the painful emotions I experienced while getting my daughter help. I carried her pain and struggle as if it was my own. I continued this kind of deep engagement in her journey for years and endured many arrows to my heart until I finally realized that I did not have to walk into the darkness with her every time. It didn't save her, and it continued to open wounds in me, leaving little room for healing.

Publicly exposing my heart created a vulnerability hangover each time, and I sometimes wondered if I could keep speaking the truth of my story around addiction. Except that the more I did, the more people would start to seek me out in the hallways, school parking lots, the sidelines of sports games, or linger at my office door, thanking me for sharing with them, and saying, "Yes, me too." They would reveal their story, I would listen, and we would feel all the feelings together. I began to realize the power of stories to heal, and to speak our truth so that it loses some of its control over us. I also began to appreciate the beauty of community and connection. We need to be seen and heard. We need a sense of belonging, for it helps us to step out from our shame, and it makes us feel worthy of the journey.

Many of us have our stories of addiction, or walking the path with someone we love struggling with addiction. Our stories are of struggle and hope; they are powerful, and they connect us. My daughter's struggles are not mine, but they are an important part of my story. I can love from a distance, holding space for forgiveness, healing, and hope. Letting go and creating this space allowed me to embrace the unfolding of *my* journey and the most meaningful work I am doing in the world today, raising my grandchildren and staying resilient so I can keep my light bright, shining it on the path for others.

"Loving what is" takes courage and tenacity. We are born into a world that leads us to believe our lives are a series of events with matched outcomes based on our behavior, choices, and luck. This holds some truth, but the bigger truth is that life is an invitation, a call to service, for our own and collective evolution. It is not random; it is up to us to decide how to ride out this journey. The events of our lives and the choices we make as we face them, become a road map, like whispers of divine guidance, showing us the way forward through the gateway of healing and into the light.

If you find yourself on a similar journey, I say to you, first and foremost, take care of yourself. This is warrior work, and you will be challenged. It will bring out the worst and the best in you. When it arrives at your doorstep, you have choices. Take care of you. Be gentle. Only you can control your outcomes, so hold space for love. My wisdom is: "Welcome what shows up." Choose to handle things "wisely." Set healthy boundaries as they are a sign of love. Be willing to let go and choose acceptance as a doorway to finding your own wisdom. You are worthy of this journey, and the gifts will be many. Discover the light within, nurture it, and allow it to guide you. You have everything inside of you to heal and be whole. You are light, and you are loved.

IGNITE ACTION STEPS

I offer some simple practices to guide you:

Gentleness: Be gentle with yourself. Nurture and nourish yourself with healthy food and things that feel soft and create ease (baths, walks, journaling, music, and tea; simple pleasures). This will help ground you, building your strength and resilience.

Allow: Get still and feel all the feelings, even if it means falling apart. This is fearlessness; our heart needs to process difficult emotions so that we can find our way to the other side, bringing healing and clarity. This practice can help guide you:

R.A.I.N: **R**ecognize what you feel, **A**llow it to be there (it belongs), **I**nvestigate where you feel this in your body, **N**urture by breathing, long and slow, while relaxing your body. I share a guided practice on my website in the resource section if you would like to learn this practice.

Receive: Practice the art of receiving: from healers, friends, and neighbors. Try to notice all the ways that life is supporting you; from serendipitous encounters to moments of awe. Drink them in as the elixirs of life.

Trust: Ask for help from your higher power. When you feel like you're holding up eighty percent of the sky, let go, surrender, and allow grace to show up. It is so hard AND completely necessary for your well-being. We can't control the outcome; we can take care of ourselves, love, and hold space for health and healing.

Be Present: Practice mindfulness, a simple but difficult practice when life feels hard. The harder life feels, the more we need to bring our bodies, minds, and souls into the present moment. It allows the chaos to fall away so we can ground and find our center. Drop inside and listen to your heart. It will never misguide you. Find a link to a simple mindfulness practice in the resource section.

Light: Dip into and nurture the light you have within. Visualize a bright light in the center of your chest. Breath life into that light and let it fill you and remind you of the true essence of who you are. Hold that light as sacred, and let it remind you of the unconditional love inside you. You have everything inside of you to heal and be whole. You are light, and you are loved ♥.

Mary Streeter — United States
Speaker, Author, Podcast Host, Holistic Life Coach
https://www.marystreeter.co
🅵 *marystreeter*
🅞 *@marystreeter.co*

Stephanie Fabela

"Believing in our own goodness is how wisdom grows; it's an act of kindness that heals our deepest wounds."

THE REAL BULLY

BY STEPHANIE FABELA

This is a story about bullying, the breakdown of connection and community, and the impact of separation and isolation during adolescence. It's about the quiet anguish that needs to be noticed and the safety it requires to be spoken. This chapter looks at what we do with our pain and how we can foster the resilience to move toward each other in the face of suffering rather than apart. I pray that my journey will open up courageous conversations amongst people who are committed to loving each other, because this is how we recover from hardship: *by pulling together.* This is how grace is made *real.*

My body is pulsing with electricity as I begin to put these words onto paper. I am daring to make visible something that I have locked away until now. Writing this story demands that I dig deep into my psyche with a prayer that I will find the buried treasure of my wisdom hidden inside my most "unhealable" pain.

If we were meeting in person, you would see a woman who is capable and friendly, with a bright smile that shines out from a cascade of silver curls. I have a natural stability that encourages others to seek me out for help. What you wouldn't easily recognize is the burden I carry, that, for forty-three years, I haven't known how to resolve. Even though I've emerged strong from this tragic time, it has left a hole in my heart that keeps me constantly aching to feel held by an unshakable love that would never give up on me.

Given all I've learned, it has felt hard, even shameful, to accept that I haven't been able to lay down this burden of anguish and sorrow for so many years. Memories of silent torment live inside me like a fresh wound, constantly reminding me that a younger part of me is still frozen in terror, believing she isn't safe and never will be. My young world was hit, at twelve years old, by a tidal wave of sexual shame, gossip, and humiliation.

It all started with what was supposed to be a dream week away from home with my church youth group. I was excited to finally learn how to ski and have the chance to be on a proper adventure. Thirty kids from my church and school piled onto the tour bus that would transport us from Oklahoma to Colorado. The atmosphere was lit up with a buzz of silliness and banter as we got settled in for the long fifteen-hour journey.

What happened on that overnight bus ride is still a muddle in my mind. Rumors were started, provoked by jealousy over some attention that two boys were giving me. A girl, who I thought was a friend, made up the story that I was already having sex at twelve, letting boys do things to me that a "good Christian girl" wouldn't allow. Even though the accusations weren't true, they got twisted up in the tangle of fear and confusion I was holding around my sexuality. As the chaos of my secret world felt exposed, everything in me froze: no voice, no fight, no rebuttal. My silence was taken as my agreement of guilt.

This was a time in my life when I was wrestling with desires, fantasies, and curiosities that deserved the privacy of my own reflection and reckoning. Instead of knowing that my questioning was a natural part of growing up, I was riddled with worry about potentially discovering that my sexuality was wrong. My family, culture, and religion had already warned me about my sinful nature, and these messages were hitting me hard. It all became a "perfect storm" of input that caused me to be suspicious and doubtful of my own innocence.

The adventure of this trip turned into a nightmare of rejection and isolation, all based on the flood of fear that was unleashed through these rumors. The connection field around me went instantly cold. Everyone was talking about me, but no one was talking *to* me. Kids I had known since I was eight, who I had grown up with in church, who had been baptized alongside me, were acting as if they didn't know me and couldn't see me suffering. The core values that had guided us — the empathy of standing in someone else's shoes, the compassion of caring about another's pain, and "doing unto others as you would have them do unto you" — had all disappeared.

Once I was back home, I couldn't find the emotional safety to tell my parents about what had happened. Although I know they loved me deeply, we had been in a power struggle for years. My transition into adolescence had only intensified the strain in our connection. There was very little trust between us, so it was easy for me to assume that they would think it was all my fault.

Back at school, the drama continued as the rumors spread to my classmates. Kids from another school, who had been on the trip, passed on the rancid gossip to their peers. Not only was I losing the friends I had, but I was also losing the potential friends that I would never make. Why would they bother being my friend, given the "kind of girl" they had heard I was: branded a disgusting whore and slut.

I crashed into an invisible wall of contradiction: the community and trust that I thought was real had vanished when it mattered most. I couldn't make sense of it. I had all the "right" resources — parents, grandparents, aunts, teachers, coaches, a church community, pastor, youth group leader, teammates, friends. Yet, *no one* was daring to say anything to help me, support me, or stand up in my defense. Although the rumors themselves were horrible to endure, it was the experience of being left alone in it all that broke my heart the most.

Survival was all that mattered, so I withdrew and tried to make my suffering invisible. As a way to keep swallowing my failure day after day, I started sneaking alcohol whenever I could to dull the agony that was becoming unbearable. I began judging my body and rejecting my sexuality. Secrecy and self-reliance felt more trustworthy than the volatile world of needing others who weren't there.

Unable to let the pain out, my overwhelmed nervous system became my new bully. In the same way that I couldn't "digest" my experience, my gut became unable to digest food. Numbness was taking over me, except for the searing migraines and stomach pain that would force me back into my body. I had turned the outer harshness inward onto myself.

I began eating over-the-counter painkillers from morning to night to suppress my anxiety and the rage that was burning up my body. A year went by, and I ended up in the hospital. My gut was rejecting food of any kind. My body was failing. My identity was crumbling. The people in my life were constantly angry and disappointed in me. It was clear that I was failing at life.

I couldn't keep holding my breath in this shame storm that seemed to have no end. I decided that if I wasn't worthy of being protected, then my life must not be that important. Desperate for the agony to stop, I planned my exit from life. I didn't actually want to kill myself, but I was collapsing under the weight of carrying this burden of blame. I decided that a bottle of pain pills would be my way out. I just needed to wait in my bedroom until the early morning hours, when everyone in my family would be asleep.

The house was silent and still, and I knew it was time to decide if I still had the nerve to jump off this cliff. I poured the small white tablets into a pile on the floor, not knowing how much was enough. Even though I was terrified, I reminded myself that my pain would end soon as I drifted out of my body. I scooped up a handful of pills and stared at them: *Was I really going to do this? Was there no other way through?*

I must have been praying right up to that moment for something to save me, to redirect the pain that was destroying my soul. And then it came: a loud, thrashing aliveness rose up in me to fight against the madness. The obsessive loop of *"I'll never be good enough"* suddenly was overridden with an out-raged voice inside me, screaming, *"THIS — this horrible smell of shame and hopelessness — THIS is what's not good enough!"* The armor around my heart cracked open. I dropped the pills and broke down sobbing. I was somehow, in that moment, "granted" the resilience to live.

From that point forward, the Fighter in me woke up. I grew more defiant as the bullying continued. On the inside, I was trying to toughen up so that I wouldn't break any further. This armor helped me to weather the storm of the next few years as the rumors started up again and again. Fighting kept me guarded and suspicious of support, but it also gave me the resourcefulness to keep breaking through my fears until I could find my way into adulthood.

As I sit here now, putting these words on the page and working through this story that I've never said aloud, I am flooded with anxiety and dread all over again. A barrage of old emotions, the putrid smell of fear, the tightness in my gut that makes me feel like I can't breathe – it's all coming alive as this frozen part of me is reawakening. But, instead of the path I took before, this time, I am surrendering to the grief that my heart and mind could not process back then.

I am ready now to grow stronger from this pain and make time to unwind the deep freeze of trauma from my body. It feels like emptying out an old stor-age locker filled with bad-smelling memories and broken shards of suffering. Symptoms that plagued me as a child are active again: headaches, gut pain, rage, despair. Even though this experience is difficult to relive, it's so import-ant that I have this chance to relate to my young world with the empathy and understanding that was missing in the past. I now can recognize how scary it must have been for the twelve-year-old me to have her body breaking down alongside her heart falling apart.

My heart is full of compassion and love for how innocent she always was through all of it. I see how she took on all the blame and stored up the pain in her body and spirit. I understand now how to hold her so that she's not facing life alone and can guide her in the ways that will help her to grow stronger.

Today, I am a momma-bear who knows how to navigate the death and rebirth that tragedy brings. I am the caring presence that is needed to make this time new — compassionately steering myself down this river of grief without making anything wrong. Even though there's still an echo of ache in my heart, every day, something new opens up and eases inside me. My combative stance has shifted into a steady, kind embrace that is making my Fighter stand down and guiding me off this battlefield.

Another essential element to completing this rite of passage is You, being here with me. Your presence, as a witness to my story, is confirmation that I'm not alone, and my silence is no longer needed.

I'm seeing a vital puzzle piece that has been in my blindspot until now. Everyone involved in this tragic play was innocent. We were all being bullied, and *the real bully was fear*. Fear of failing at life, of not belonging, of being a bad parent or a bad person, of being inadequate or too much. We were all struggling on our own, traversing the tightrope of shame without a safety net of secure connection and acceptance.

As I unwrap these long-overdue gifts of gratitude and forgiveness, I keep remembering that I cannot truly, deeply accept myself as long as I continue "making wrong" the experiences that shaped me. To blame or resent them, or wish for them to have been different, would be a wish for me to be different. I am *exactly* who I need to be: someone who is ready to bear my scars and proudly serve from the deep well of wisdom that was hewn from my tragedy.

Letting go of the certainty that someone else has wronged us: this is our work. Blame forms a wall that keeps us separate from our suffering. As we take that barrier down, brick by brick, *forgiveness floods in.* It is a gift that's been ours all along, a birthright of grace and goodness that is waiting for us to realize that division and separation are no longer needed.

Shame is fueled by three ingredients: silence, secrecy, and judgment. Changing any one of these is what gives us the power to create a new outcome. Silence requires bravery to break through and be honest about what we are going through, now or in the past. Secrecy needs the resolve of presence: to listen without opinion or disapproval. Judgment will always be there, but its authority to bully us is disabled when we dare to care more about ourselves and each other, than needing to determine what and who has wronged us.

Bringing my story out of silence, secrecy, and judgment has given me the safety to open up to life without needing to defend against the past. My heart is holding hope again, with more certainty than ever before, that *believing in our own goodness* is how we grow stronger and wiser from tragedy and loss. It is an act of kindness that heals our deepest wounds.

I want you to know you have the capacity to grow from *everything* that has happened in your life. I hope that my story has opened you to the wisdom of *who you can become* from what you have been through. Know that there is no wrongness that will *ever* have more power than the goodness that lives within you. Protect and feed this fire of goodness within you. Cause it to flourish in others. The things that have happened in the past are the fuel to Ignite your future.

Believe in your goodness.
Treat it as though it's irrefutable evidence of your success.

IGNITE ACTION STEPS

Practice Ownership Rather Than Blame

This practice challenges us to *seek goodness* rather than lashing out from a place of fear and blame. Taking ownership sets the stage for our mutual success. When you are disappointed or in conflict and need to reset your hurt feelings, take the time to use the following exercise to help you fortify your connection and encourage the vulnerability and honesty that your special bond deserves.

Do this practice with your partner, children, and friends — one-to-one or in a small group. Go back and forth, each person taking a turn to share at each step, before moving on to the next step. No matter how it goes, make it a priority to appreciate each other for the effort that's been made. And remember that you're exercising new muscles of awareness and emotional vulnerability, so be gentle as you learn, and keep practicing!

CELEBRATE where growth is happening and trust is building. Sitting in conservation and looking at one another, use the following statements as you share whatever is true for you at each step:

Step 1: "One thing you've done this week/today that has helped us to build trust was…" End with appreciation: "I'm grateful to you for that!"

LISTEN without opinion or questions. Simply receive.

Step 2: "One thing I've done this week/today that has helped us to build trust was…" End with appreciation: "I'm grateful to myself for that!"

Before going to the next step, take a few moments to let yourselves feel good about how you both are growing and contributing to the trust between you.

RECOGNIZE where growth and trust need to be strengthened.

Step 3: "One thing I did this week/today that was challenging/hurtful to our trust was… and I want to keep learning how we can build more trust together because you are/we are important to me."

BE GRATEFUL for the time and attention that was given, and the honesty of what was shared.

Stephanie Fabela — United Kingdom
Speaker, Author, Intuitive Coach, Intimacy Specialist
www.stephaniefabela.com
All About Intimacy www.allaboutintimacy.com
allaboutintimacy

Stacie Shifflett

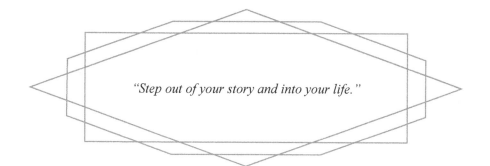

"Step out of your story and into your life."

RAISE YOUR AWARENESS, ELEVATE YOUR LIFE™

BY STACIE SHIFFLETT

My hope is that my chapter Ignites in you the desire to evaluate the life you are currently living and inspires you to move into a life consciously created, one in which joy and inner peace are the defining characteristics. We tend to live our lives on autopilot; doing the same things, having the same thoughts, and experiencing the same emotions day after day. I want you to know that we aren't "stuck" with the lives we currently have, particularly our internal lives. We each have the full power to elevate ourselves and, more importantly, our inner peace through conscious living. Know that, whatever your story is, it can be enhanced or replaced with an even better one.

"You're still in your story."

I remember when those words were spoken to me, rather harshly, after I opened up to someone with tears welling up in my eyes. Their words stung me; the moment made even more dramatic for me as the person turned away, abruptly ending the conversation. Clearly, there was no willingness on their part to meet me at my level and gently pull me forward. Not that it was their responsibility to do so, but I was at an event with hundreds of others who were all working consciously to change the stories of their lives. This group typically held space for others, especially when tears were involved. But not today. Not for me anyway. At least not at that moment with that person.

If only that person knew how far I had already stepped out of my story. If only that person understood how much resolution and resolve I had already shown. If only that person realized that I had already grieved and risen from unimaginable anguish as I had survived the loss of a child years earlier.

I cannot even begin to describe the pain of losing a child. It was unexpected, since by all accounts, everything was going well with my pregnancy. Then, at seven months, my water broke, which created a cascade of unanticipated issues. The hospital I'd planned on for the birth and the doctor, wouldn't accept me as I was classified as high risk. The baby was breech, necessitating an immediate Cesarean delivery. Then, the biggest surprise of all: the baby had several serious birth defects that remained hidden during routine prenatal care. Multiple surgeries, including an open heart, would be required for him to live a "normal" life. The doctors remained optimistic throughout his month-long stay at the neonatal intensive care unit, and I did too, following their lead. I visited the hospital for hours and hours each day to be with him, filled with love and hope that he would play sports someday, just like the doctors told me. After about thirty days, however, they rushed him into emergency open-heart surgery as he was turning blue from lack of oxygen. They were hoping he would grow a bit before that surgery was needed, but his little heart could not do its job. I remember them keeping me up to date throughout the hours-long surgery, assuring me each step of the way that everything was fine. But the last time I saw them walking toward me in the waiting room, I knew something was dreadfully wrong before they uttered a word. And it was. They lost him.

I quite naturally and expectedly slipped into depression. Time seemed to slow. I retreated into the safety of my home and wouldn't answer the door, certain it would be yet another delivery of flowers from sympathetic friends or associates. I didn't want flowers. I wanted my son back. I didn't want to return to work or resume social activities as I couldn't bear the thought of the conversations I would have to endure. People were offering their condolences and concern, saying things like, "God only gives us what we can handle," or "Maybe it's a blessing in disguise." Not helpful. Equally unhelpful were declarations that I simply needed to jump back into my life and move on. How was I to do that when I was so filled with sadness that I could barely get dressed each day?

My doctor recommended a grief support group for bereaved parents, and, despite my reluctance, I attended. There were many people at that meeting.

They had all lost children of varying ages to different tragic circumstances. I realized, hearing them speak, that these parents had experienced a lifetime, albeit a short one, with their children. Somehow, in that moment, instead of feeling I had been robbed of cherished and joyful moments with my child, I reasoned internally that not having those memories would somehow make it easier for me to heal. I wasn't surrounded by constant reminders of my little one, as he had never come home to create those memories in my heart. I was jolted back to the group's conversation when one of the men attending the meeting — and I remember this so profoundly — shared his wife's inability, years after the death of their child, to leave their home. Not even to go to the grocery store. This shocked me. I felt such deep compassion for this family who was struggling to put some sort of normalcy back into their lives, and then, as my thoughts turned back to my situation, I realized this could easily be me. I decided right then and there that I did not want to be imprisoned by my grief, forfeiting my future to it. That was the one and only grief support meeting I attended.

My realization did not mean, however, that my journey out of this personal hell was easy. It was not. It simply meant that I made the decision to no longer be a victim of this dreadful circumstance. I was consciously willing to make the effort required to move toward re-engaging in my life, which I began to do with the support of my family, step by step, day by day.

"You're still in your story."

I had enough awareness within me to understand that the person who said this to me likely had good intentions, even though it felt poorly timed and ill-placed from my perspective. Their response may have resulted from a hundred different things, and none of them likely had anything to do with me. Perhaps they were trying to jolt me out of my story, or they just sought to turn their attention back to the speaker on stage. But at that moment, I realized what they said was true. I *was* speaking from within my story. I had made a lot of progress, but anger, grief, and unanswered questions were still deeply embedded within me. I was still grasping to understand my situation. And what was wrong with that? Nothing! The manner and pace of creating change in our lives, and the depth of that journey, are determined by *us*. Don't let anyone tell you otherwise. Don't feel ashamed if you struggle to move forward and are unable to "act" as if nothing ever happened. It's not about recovering *fast*; it's about recovering *fully and deeply.*

Why do we lean into our stories? Because it's natural for us to do so. Our brains are wired for consistency and routine in both actions and thought. We brush our teeth the same way every time, using the same hand and the same strokes. Our thoughts are no different. According to a 2005 article published by the National Science Foundation, out of the tens of thousands of thoughts we have each day, 95 percent of those are the same thoughts we had the day before, and 80 percent of those are negative. And we do this unconsciously! As in without our awareness!

That is why most of us march forward in our lives doing the things we've always done, thinking the things we've always thought (or became accustomed to thinking) without much deliberate thought about why. Many of us, at some point, begin to wonder, even briefly, *Is this all there is?* We tend to sweep thoughts like these, our innermost feelings, quickly under the proverbial rug, often feeling guilty for even considering them, since, for all intents and purposes, life is good. From the outside, anyway. But what about our internal lives? In my life, my inner voice and outer experiences amplify until I pause to truly listen to what my higher self, my soul, is telling me. It is trying to share life's greatest lesson: to seek and find spiritual calm within, and embrace loving myself, just as I am. Everything else flows from there.

Our stories, and our beliefs are powerful. They can fuel us or bind us. They can lead us toward great achievements, or they can keep us mired in an unhealthy situation for far too long. We all have personal stories that demonstrate both sides of this spectrum. And, probably like you, my story of tragedy and loss was not the only thing to shape me. I have experiences full of light, courage, and achievements and have lived fully immersed in happy stories. For instance, I once executed the acquisition of a company worth tens of millions of dollars with no financial investment on my part. How did I do this? Belief.

The idea to acquire that business came to me in an instant and filled me with an all-consuming passion. It was in an industry in which I was dubbed a "subject matter expert," and I had a lot of experience with, and relationships within, this particular company. Obviously, my idea was divinely timed, because when I approached one of the business owners, I was told they had just listed it for sale with a broker. I initially thought this would not work in my favor. As a "cashless investor," which the business broker called me, I thought my chances would be further limited if I couldn't rely on my relationships inside the company. But, as it turned out, the Universe knew best. I persevered with faith and a deep internal knowing that it would happen. I never doubted the outcome. I rallied and enrolled a partner who had experience that I did not, and, after nine months of effort, the deal was made. I cashed out when the original investor sold the company five years later, thereby creating financial security for my future.

I fully embraced all of the beliefs necessary for a positive outcome throughout that acquisition process — I lived that story. There was no place for doubt within me, and, when others said it couldn't be done, I stayed the course, achieving my desired result. This is a great example in my life of how positive thoughts and beliefs create or manifest successful outcomes.

It's important to know that in our lives, happy stories can come full circle from sad ones. About two years after the loss of my first son, I was blessed with a healthy baby boy, who I love and cherish deeply. He is the child I was meant to raise to adulthood. How do I know this with absolute certainty? Because my deceased son walked into my bedroom one night, years after the birth of my second, awakening me from my sleep. I saw him so clearly standing by the door, appearing to me at the age he would've been at that time. His message was simple: he was fine; his life continued in another realm; he had achieved what he came to do; and the child intended for me to raise was sleeping peacefully in the other room. I haven't recalled that memory in a long time, but I have to tell you that tears are flowing as I write this now. What a beautiful reminder that all is exactly as it should be in the grander scheme, even when heartache is involved.

We all have moments that forever change our lives, and within these moments lies the opportunity to propel ourselves forward more deliberately. *If* we heed the call. Sometimes these moments are like an explosion that results, almost instantly, in adopting a new outlook, behavior, or belief that ignites us to move forward. Other times, they evolve more gently, like an ember slowly burning that seemingly goes out yet rekindles a fire we thought we had long ago extinguished, urging us to heal what has remained unhealed.

A few years ago, I fully embraced my journey to better understand my internal life. Like so many of us, when faced with a personal challenge, I hurried through many books and classes and seminars, collecting knowledge like nuggets of gold, oohing and ahhing over each new discovery. I stashed everything I learned into my pouch of precious possessions as I quickly moved on to the next, continuing to search for *the* secret to eternal happiness. I gained quite a lot of knowledge along the way as I absorbed and tried to consciously put the soundbites of personal development into action. "Energy flows where intention goes." "Success is 20 percent effort and 80 percent mindset." "Nothing is impossible as the word itself says, 'I'm possible.'" And a lengthy one, attributed to Lao Tzu, reminds us: our thoughts become words, which become actions, which turn to habits, which become the character that becomes our destiny.

As much as I tried to bring these teachings into my life, fully appreciating and understanding their meaning as well as their truth, how to actually integrate them into my existence as a means of deep personal change was challenging. Those nuggets of truth remained like pieces of impure ore; the value is hidden inside. They required transformation, much like the smelting process which removes crude matter to reveal the cherished material within, like gold. Only after the impurities are removed, can it be molded into something precious. So it goes with our internal lives.

We must first become fully aware of and then address that which holds us back — most notably our beliefs — to begin creating beautiful artistry in our lives. But how do we do that? How do we interrupt the cycles in which the same emotions and same feelings re-emerge in our lives bringing us back to our internal reality? The truth is it takes consistent effort, an extraordinary amount of personal awareness (which needs to be learned), and a strong desire for change. In my experience, it's an ongoing process. Often, just when I think I've got it, my next lesson is revealed as the Universe presents me — presents all of us — with unending opportunities to refine ourselves as she deepens the lessons that lead us toward self-mastery and inner peace. To me, inner peace is sacred and achieving it is the secret sauce to a life well-lived. I have learned it is not something that can be left to simply manifest itself. It doesn't just organically evolve. It requires effort and it must be learned. And, in many cases, we are compelled to learn only as a result of a life in crisis. Why? Because we didn't step out of our situation, our story, to listen when it began whispering to us.

Let me ask you these questions. On a daily basis, are you living your problems or creating a life that aligns with your heart and the true desires of your soul? Are you setting aside time to listen to your still small voice? Your soul's voice? The voice of Spirit? Can you even *hear* that voice? Are you still in your story?

I invite you to step off of the treadmill of your life and pay attention to what calls to you from deep within. In times of stillness, nuggets of truth will joyfully reveal themselves to you, grateful that you have stopped to listen. Learn to gently set aside the constantly running dialog of your thoughts. Trust me. Whatever your story is, it can be enhanced or replaced with an even better one. Accept yourself with loving compassion, and rest comfortably in the knowledge that where you are today is exactly where you should be. You will be led toward the lessons meant for you to learn, which can ultimately guide you to your best life; however *you* define that. Don't let anyone else define that for you. That's between you and your Soul.

IGNITE ACTION STEPS

If you feel powerless over the future direction of your life or desire to step out of your current "story" and into your future, here are some strategies to support you:

- Seek stillness to quiet the noise in your head so you can hear the still small voice of your higher self. Release yourself fully into these moments of peace to calm both your mind and your nervous system.
- Spark curiosity about and then question your beliefs. We live in the context of what we've been taught. You have every right to challenge your beliefs and replace them with ones that support the life you wish to create.
- Quit seeking outside validation that you are "right," which doesn't serve you in stepping outside of your story — it only keeps you entrenched within it. Instead, seek connection with your inner self.
- Invite a trusted advisor or mentor into your life who is a few steps ahead of your journey and exemplifies traits you aspire. You can learn from their experience.
- Honor the great accomplishments in your life and your positive traits; something we often don't allow ourselves to embrace for more than a fleeting moment.
- Gain clarity of what you want and what you don't want in your life. It's helpful to know both when charting a path into something more desirable.
- Release what doesn't serve your highest and best. This may be a belief, a habit, a job, or a relationship.
- Devote time to yourself each day. We become so accustomed to tending to the needs of others that we often forget to support ourselves in a loving, compassionate way. Spend a little time each day focusing on what is good in your life and telling yourself that you love you!

Stacie Shifflett — United States
Owner & Founder Modern Consciousness™, Certified ThetaHealer®
Certified Free-mE Emotional Freedom Technique (EFT) Practitioner™
Master Practitioner of Neuro-linguistic Programming
Professional Neuro-Shine Technology Coach™
Certified High Performance Coach™
www.ModernConsciousness.com
Email: Empower@aware.life
🄵 *ModernConsciousness* | 🄾 *modernconsciousness/*

Michelle Norlin

"Freedom is on the other side of our fear."

A JOURNEY OF SURRENDER AND TRANSFORMATION

BY MICHELLE NORLIN

As you read my story, I want you to believe that no depth of depression, shame, or grief can derail you from finding your truth, freedom, identity, and self-love. Allow the dreams you hold deepest in your heart to propel you forward until you reach your fullest potential. If you can capture the belief that you are worthy, valuable, and your magnificent place in life is right in front of you, waiting to embrace you, and show you who you really are, freedom will come. Anchor yourself to what inspires you and brings you freedom. Freedom is your strength.

I was born on a beautiful day in July 1958, and unknown to our mom, there were two special blessings that day, two twin daughters, Michelle and Melissa. We shared a special bond being in each other's company daily. We learned from one another, and always found comfort in our friendship. We were quite mischievous and kept our parents busy. No matter what challenges we faced, we had each other. As we grew, we excelled and enjoyed many sports in our school years. Even though we both were competitive, we celebrated each other's wins. We challenged each other and supported our talents for athletics. We tried all the competition-level sports that our school offered and found tennis, volleyball, track and field, and softball to be our favorites. In our high school years, we enjoyed switching classes and dressing the same just for fun, with no one knowing except for a few close friends.

We had family getaways, weekend picnics, and hikes with our parents. There were lots of sleepovers with our friends, pool parties, and a full life with great friendships that molded us. Melissa married three years after high school, and I did the same two years later. Melissa had two daughters and I, two daughters and one son. Of course, all the cousins were best friends just like their moms.

I worked in the years prior to my marriage and then became a stay-at-home mom who cared for our kids and also oversaw the business administration of my husband's construction company. Volunteering at their schools, attending their activities, sleepovers and pool parties, connecting with them during their highs and lows, across life's challenging journey, was my honor as a stay-at-home mom.

Melissa became a career woman, a pharmacy technician at a local hospital, where she worked for twenty-two amazing years. Life was full and happy. We loved hearing each other's voices daily and being a part of each other's lives. It was a family joke that when the telephone rang after dinner, someone would say, "I bet that is Auntie Melissa." And of course, it always was.

The only thing we twins did not share was a faith in God. As my faith grew, I experienced all sorts of new emotions and insights. My faith was leading me joyfully into finding my quiet place whenever the storms of life were too overpowering. I found comfort knowing I could lean into my Creator, who I had been learning so much about. I could tell Him all my sorrows and hurtful moments and thanked Him for how He guided me through each day to feel peace.

Yet every time I shared the joy of my new faith, Melissa was resistant. One weekend, I decided to attend a women's retreat, organized through the church, and invited Melissa to come. To my surprise, Melissa accepted. There were two days of amazing teachings and worship, quiet walks, coffee breaks, lunch with our friends, reflection, and just sharing what we both got out of the program. On the last day, the invitation went out to anyone who wanted to accept the Lord into their lives, and Melissa stepped forward. It was a precious moment we shared; another bond forged between us. On a quiet walk after lunch, the wind blowing through the trees, the sun shining, Melissa said to me, "Thank you for never giving up on me and always giving me an opportunity." Together, and with our families, we grew in our faith and discovered new truths of love, companionship, and freedom.

The faith we shared was tested several years later. Melissa called, and it caught me by surprise. She asked if she could come over. She and her husband arrived and shared the heartbreaking news that she had kidney cancer. My heart sank. The thought of losing my best friend was more than I could imagine. But I kept it together for Melissa's sake, refusing to show my fear and concern. We were both forty-one-years-old, and still had so much learning and growing to do: families to raise, trips to take. Her doctor recommended surgery, and I supported her decision. She underwent an operation to fight the aggressive disease. After surgery, she was told by her doctors that they "felt hopeful they got it all," and she came home. She needed assistance and attention, and I was blessed with the opportunity to be by her side, and care for her while her family was at school or work. We shared so many moments, discussing how grateful we were for the many wonderful years ahead with family and each other. Through this very challenging experience, we braved the storm; our special bond never weakened.

Life regained a sense of normalcy, and we were very grateful that God delivered Melissa through. But a year later, a re-test showed the cancer was back. It was a sad day for all of us as we prepared to fight again, put on our happy faces, and support Melissa however we could. The cancer was in her adrenal glands and spreading. We were told to prepare for her to leave us, and we tried to enjoy every minute we had together. We all shared helping her, visiting, and loving on her. Soon, a hospice was called in. I was finding the strength, yet hanging on by a thread and doing my best to support her.

I sat by her side daily, while she slept due to the medication that kept her from feeling all the pain in her body. I knew life would never be the same without her. Her body was shutting down, and I realized it was time to accept that she was letting go; it was coming faster than I wanted. God was calling her home as she shared seeing mom and grandma, who had already passed, waiting lovingly for her arrival. I pondered all the memories and the close bond we shared: her wedding day and mine, our youth, our children's births, our adult life, our loving pets, and how we made such an impact on each other's lives through good and bad, from childhood into our forties. Our connection was so deep and close, one of total trust and union. How fortunate I was to have a twin sister who shared all my challenging times and the triumphs in my life. Since the day she was gifted to me, our love and faith in each other was solid. Ours was that special twin bond; a union formed in the womb and never severed until death.

Melissa confided in me during her waking moments, "Michelle, take care of them; they will need you." I assured her it would be my honor to care for her family. In hearing these words, I was forced to realize I was facing the day I would lose her. My heart was pulling in every way possible with fear, grief, loss, and uncertainty. How would her passing affect her family and all those she touched? How would it be to live without having this amazing woman in our lives? What would it mean to hear the phone ring and realize it wasn't my sister? Some days I couldn't cope; it was like half of me was taken away. I was broken inside because we had been joined at the hip since birth. I was with her the night before she passed. The next morning, she was gone.

I had no choice but to pick up the pieces as best I could. As I started to heal, minutes turned to days and eventually years. I was doing my best to move forward without forgetting. Yet, as the years passed, my identity was shaken by all the transitions that arose in my life. Lots of change was happening in our family, and my confidence was wavering. I questioned, *What am I really here for? What is my purpose?*

I sought the answers in my faith. I reached out to God and listened to His words: "You will be shaken to your very core. Your identity as you once knew it will be lost, but do not fear." His plan was about to begin, and as I leaned in to walk with God daily, he started peeling away layers of me that did not build me up, bring truth, understanding, or contribute to my growth. Learning to hear His voice and make the changes was my new direction and purpose. The beauty of God is He is always in charge and willing to rearrange our lives when we are willing to give Him the driver's seat. But we must relinquish control, or we may aimlessly stumble around till we do.

A few years later, having sold our home, our motorhome became our new residence. I was struggling not being able to put my feet down and organize our lives. I found myself falling deeper into despair, hopelessness, and trying to make sense of it all. I became fearful and broken. It felt like I was living in a shoebox. There was no room to spread out, have my own space, or retreat to my own safe place. Life felt closed in, and it was all I could do to climb out of bed and manage my daily affairs. With no real direction, I stumbled, searching for truth, purpose, and the reason *why* life was so hard on me. Seeking understanding, I took long walks talking to God, trying to find my focus and not lose myself in fear and doubt. He knew I needed to be grounded to something, so he told me to take care of my family and the affairs of life. This gave me a sense of normalcy and purpose, even though my life did not feel *normal* at all.

Months of overwhelming emptiness filled my mind, but God was drawing me to Him, holding His hand out for me to grasp in my darkness. I desired to know Him deeply, to help me find freedom from my worries and the confidence I needed. I asked Him to give me clarity and heal my hurting heart. I permitted Him to show me the wisdom for my life and the truths I so deeply wanted. I found myself praying, trying to control the fear, desperately listening to hear His voice, afraid of losing my faith, and making sure I did not slip into the abyss of despair. I sought thankfulness every day, looking for the good, being grateful for my life, and my healthy mind, body, and spirit. Even though I was not walking in my freedom, I was on a journey to overcome everything that had held me back from being who I knew I could be. I finally came to the realization, letting go of all that had held me captive, and declared, "NONE of this will defeat ME."

My faith started to rise; I was making strides in believing in me, and my new identity was changing. I proclaimed words of affirmations to build confidence. I was facing those giants that I once thought I could never overcome by saying, "YOU DON'T HAVE POWER OVER ME ANY MORE!" Yet, the dark voices returned, and boy were they determined to carry out their job. The vacant hole they were pulling my mind down into was always there. The waves of doubt that crashed over me were more than I could bear. I even contemplated death some days, because death would silence all the pain. I agonized with fear, unworthiness, shame, guilt, and hopelessness, and there I stayed, bound to that jail cell, out in the deep, and the waves kept coming.

In those desperate moments, I forced myself to claw up the sides of that black hole of fear and despair. With everything inside me, I persevered, fought back, and reached the top. That was a wonderful moment. I was never going to go back there again regardless of how my mind lied to me with, *You're a failure; nobody will miss you if you're gone. You are unworthy.* I cried out to God, "HELP ME!" He spoke back to me in the sweet voice, "Quit dancing with the lies; it's go time." I had to either believe my limitations or embrace His truths.

I knew I needed to anchor myself to Him. I had to have that lifeline. I imagined the largest three-strand steel anchor, like the ones on huge naval carriers, and envisioned myself throwing it from where I was, to my Heavenly Father. That vision was so strong it helped me stay connected to Him, because my life depended on it. He WAS my lifeline.

My journey of learning to stand when I was broken and felt helpless had started, and the hope of joy and peace was all I reached for. Days of fear and hopelessness still swarmed around me, and my mind was in a battle for *life*. But I pushed past that to grasp the life I knew was mine that God had promised when I received Him into my life. I challenged myself to speak positive thoughts and believe in a greater purpose. I sought truth on my path to the very freedom I desired as I read books to fill my soul. I studied peace, and joy. I was going to have victory over depression at all costs; no "jail cell" was going to hold me captive, no matter how many battles I had to endure.

I had come to a place of real surrender. I was still learning, as surrendering was a new place for me, but I was finding comfort in His presence, and it was becoming my new normal. I came to know that though trials may always be around us, they don't own us; we choose our paths in life. We are empowered to see them as part of our growth and lessons we take away from our life. We can say, "Today I find peace with you. I'm grateful for what you have taught me to this point, but from here forward, I'm in charge." God was removing all things that did not serve me well, renewing my mind to trust Him alone and discover the purpose He had for me.I surrendered to God daily, and His promises became my hope. His truths became my freedoms, and His freedoms my transformation. He taught me patience in the moments when I faltered. He taught me grace, urging me to be kind to myself as I shared my pain and sorrows with Him.

It's a choice of what we believe to think. God shared with me, "The battle has already been won. I give you the keys to life and freedom; choose life. Remember, you're a fighter. I've got your back, and I will hold you up when you cannot see. You are stronger than you know. I am your best friend; there is no judgment. I'm your strength; I'm with you in the valley, fire, and storm. My mercy is enough, and it comes with healing."

I took those keys of life, confessed my freedom, stood on the promises in His word, and asked God to remove the chains I had allowed on me. Only God can remove those chains and place us on a path of freedom, bring us out of darkness, and fill us with peace. I leaned in deeply to my best friend: God. We shared long talks, and I discovered my new identity and liked who I was becoming. My faith was growing stronger, and I was finding confidence in who I was. When I had released all the areas of my life that I put before God — my desires, wants, needs, and plans — God started to heal me. I discovered self-love, honored myself first each day, practiced affirmations and freedom of choice for my thoughts, and believed that with His help, I would find the true happiness He provided.

Today, I thank God that he used my sister's death, my depression, and my fears, all towards a greater purpose. He told me: "Your journey is a story you are going to use to touch many women's lives. If you can't work through the victories and stand up under the pressures of life; pass my tests on every side, as I lead you to do; let go of everything I ask you to; choose my ways over yours, knowing my plan is the best one; how will you use what you have learned to touch other lives? What I'm teaching you, you will teach them."

Loneliness and brokenness are a gift to help us understand we need the infilling of a power greater than ourselves to cleanse our souls and find peace. Whatever the vehicle was to get you to your transformation, God is there in the darkness waiting for you to anchor to Him. To be your guide, counselor, and best friend. Life is a precious gift; it's what we take away from all the lessons and what we choose to think and believe that make it so divine. Always think the best of everyone, encourage, speak life, and practice joy, followed by lots of new adventures.

My special bond started the day God gave me my twin sister. As we walked together all those years, I see the significance of sharing life with the person that fills you, supports you, won't break faith with you, and will be that anchor for you to stand strong and believe in you. God is that truth for me. Find your truth, and it will steer you to the most unimaginable places your heart longs for.

Ignite Action Steps

- Choose to face your challenges straight on. Deal with each one, one at a time. Find resolve and peace with them, and then let them go.
- Develop habits that keep you centered on peace and moving forward. Let go of old belief systems and start believing the NEW YOU is possible. Join a self-development class, a yoga class, and a coffee group to develop new strong relationships that pour into you and your strengths.
- Realize you are a work in progress. Extend grace to yourself daily. Praise yourself for the growth and lessons learned. Dream big, go for it, you've got this!
- Reward yourself for all the hard work with praise, and start today reconditioning your mind to say, "GOOD THINGS ARE COMING MY WAY."
- Set boundaries for your soul. Guard your heart with the utmost caution. Check your love tank daily. Care for it with an appreciation for self and gratitude, and be mindful of your true authentic self. You have found yourself; now never let YOU go. Cherish freedom, love, and peace; they will guide you on your journey.

Michelle Norlin — United States
Truth Seeker, Mom, Wife, Author and Relationship Coach
twin_blonde@hotmail.com
 Relationship & Marriage Coaching by Michelle
 @coachingbyMichelle

Alessandra C.L. Pasut

"The way you engage with the present moment is the way you choose to engage with life."

DIVINELY PROTECTED

BY ALESSANDRA C.L. PASUT

Become best friends with the present moment; this is where your power lies — with you, here, *now*. Allow my story to show you that you can take back your power no matter where you are on your path. Be firm in who you are *and* keep an open mind. Life is not black or white. It's a process, a discovery, a journey. What do you want your path to be?

As paradoxical as it sounds, death has been a major theme in my life. At twenty-six years old, I've had six near-death experiences. I've seen my life flash before my eyes; every moment laid out in order, taken in all at once. I can't even begin to recall the image or understand how I could have witnessed the entirety of my life in a fraction of a second. Still, I remember the sensation of complete understanding. My whole life, I grew up learning about my family's familiarity with the supernatural, from ghostly to angelic encounters, to out-of-body, to knowing the future, and I experienced these myself.

Water is the source of life, and yet it has taken multiple lives from me and almost taken my life three times. My mother's father drowned after being wrongly medicated for depression seven years after his first-born child, Arthur, drowned at the age of four. My father's father came to Canada to help build a better life. As his family was on the boat from Italy to Canada to reunite with him, he fell off a bridge on his way to work to the shallow river below, 16 Mile Creek, where he perished. I almost fell to my death in this exact same river, tumbling down a massive slope head first before a tree branch pierced the sleeve of my sweater and was strong enough to support me. I honestly believe it was my grandfather who intervened and saved my life.

The two grandparents who I had the privilege of knowing were like the salt of the earth — my maternal and paternal grandmothers; my Grandma and my Nonna. My Grandma lived with me growing up, playing a significant role in how I was raised. My Nonna, the matriarch on my dad's side, honored family traditions and kept us all connected. My Nonna passed away when I was four. She was a bright light on earth whose spirit I can remember as vividly as ever; even at a young age, I felt the hole that her loss created. My Grandma passed away from a stroke when I was fifteen. I was able to be by her side with my mom and aunts, holding her hand as she took her last breath. It was when my mom told her she could let go, and she did, that I realized she knew we were there. As hard as it was to watch her slip away, I feel blessed that I was able to be there for her in her last moments. As she slipped away, I slipped into numbness.

One day, I noticed my natural brown hair growing in and realized my dyed blonde hair did not suit me. The hazel of my eyes looked more vibrant, the tone of my skin livelier against my natural hair. I thought to myself, *Anything we do to change nature just fucks it up,* simultaneously crying tears of sadness and joy in a moment of awareness. Then all of a sudden, I felt my grandmother standing beside me. I froze, stunned for a long second before I slowly turned. "Grandma?" I said hesitantly. I couldn't see her, I couldn't hear her or smell her perfume, but as if she was standing right there, I could feel her. She stepped towards me, placed her hands on my face, and said, "Ma, belle puce" (my little bug), her term of endearment for me. I didn't feel her physical touch on my skin, I didn't hear her words pass through my ears, but I felt the exact specific sentiment behind those words and actions like they were downloaded into me telepathically. Before I could move or react, she disappeared. It had been hard losing her, moving into a new house, and changing schools at the same time, so it meant the world to me that she visited. I know, with every fiber of my being, that her spirit remains intact and that she, and all my loved ones, are always loving and protecting me.

At the same time, I was also dealing with the immense weight of hiding a relationship from my parents. On New Year's Eve of 2011, almost a year after my Grandma passed, my partner's father was shot in his chest with his own gun and it was ruled a suicide. In this horrific time and with all that I was carrying,

I didn't know how to be there for him. I still feel deep remorse and wish I could have done more. We were high school sweethearts who were as in love as two fifteen-year-olds could be, yet slipped apart so easily. I felt like *I* slipped apart. That triggered a depression that made me feel totally numb. I couldn't feel the grief anymore from feeling it all the time and began to self-harm just to feel anything. I felt like I understood life to be cruel and scary and was not interested in continuing. I considered ending it but wanted to try everything I could to save myself first. Except I had no energy and almost no desire.

One night when I was seventeen, I was lying awake in bed trying to sleep and considered meditation; it was the simplest thing I could do. It didn't involve me putting myself out there or even moving and I felt like, in my numbness, I could easily slip into a mindless state. I started by trying not to think, which made me think more, then I just tried to become aware. I used my breath to steady my heart rate (a technique my mother first showed me when I was young and unable to sleep), which felt like tuning a radio, adjusting my frequency, trying to find a clear channel. The first few times I tried meditating, I got nothing perceivable from it and could have stopped there thinking *this isn't working* or *I can't do it* as most people do, but because my energy was so low, I felt like this was the only thing I could manage. A few more nights went on like that until one night, just for a fraction of a second, like a breath of fresh air, I felt *pure peace.*

That was the spark that reignited my flame. As soon as I recognized it, I lit up, lost my focus, and the feeling slipped away. I tried to get back to that place, but my mind was buzzing, analyzing what that feeling was and how I got there. I began meditating for longer periods, multiple times a day and started my deep dive into esoteric practices, ancient sciences, and philosophy. Bridging the gap between biology and spirituality became my passion as I found myself particularly interested in the power of the heart and its link to Spirit.

As I felt myself healing, I came to believe that if everyone meditated, it would be a cure for all mental and physical illnesses. I was able to reach such a deep meditative state that I stopped feeling gravity holding me to the surface I was on. Like I was the nucleus of a cell, in the center of it all and connected to everything — completely at one with life itself, floating in infinite peace. At this point, I was meditating three times a day every day for fifteen to twenty minutes and started dabbling in lucid dreaming and astral projection. I also practiced seeing with my eyes closed, a sight beyond the imagination that sits in the same place — the mind's eye. I felt amazingly empowered and radiant.

That is when I started practicing energy work. I was eighteen, commuting to and from Toronto on crowded trains and buses to go to school at Ontario College of Arts and Design University. I practiced extending my energy field to be inclusive and would find people being friendlier with me, once even handing me twenty dollars out of nowhere. I also practiced protecting my energy, casting a bubble of white light around me. I would set the intention and believe, "I am protected and any energy that comes my way, goes back to the sender as love," and people would respectfully give me space. In my personal practice, I would use my breath to charge my heart and send that energy to my palms where I could channel it outwards in any way I wished, guided by my intention.

It was a powerfully transformative, healing, and uplifting time, and at the same time, I was doing a lot of spiritual bypassing. That is when we use spiritual practices to mask or separate us from the material world instead of helping us integrate with it. While breathwork, meditation, and energy work helped me get over my depression, I still hadn't faced what made me depressed. I hadn't unpacked my subconsciously stored trauma — I hadn't done the shadow work.

At nineteen years old, I felt ready to participate in the world again, and found myself in a toxic relationship, stuck in a cycle of trying to get a narcissist to see the error of his ways. I lost touch with my spiritual practice and fell into a violent depression, coupled with crippling anxiety. I began obsessively and compulsively picking at my face, leaving me with scars to this day. I felt the urge to take my life again, as in the darkest times of our lives, fear tells us *this is how it is now*. For almost four years, I stayed in that relationship, subconsciously working through issues of loss and abandonment.

I felt like I was at a rock bottom I had never known before. I didn't feel numb. I felt everything — oversensitive, overstimulated, anxious, panicked, and depressed all at once, constantly. Even the setting sun would set me off into a panic for no logical reason. I went to a therapist and was diagnosed with chronic depression and generalized anxiety disorder. It was too expensive for me to continue regular treatment even with the generous discount the therapist provided, so I did it on my own. I had the know-how to heal myself; I was just starting from a wildly different place. This time it was much harder to stop engaging with my thoughts — I had spent so long identifying with them.

Then, at twenty-two, I had the opportunity to watch a Neuro Linguistic Programming (NLP) practitioner work on a woman live, in person. NLP is a form of hypnotherapy that focuses on the language we use to encode meaning in our minds. After watching a woman's life-altering healing moment and sobbing with her, the practitioner asked if anyone had a quick *"this-or-that"* problem they would like to solve and I volunteered.

He coached me into a semi-subconscious lull. I became aware of my subconscious on a palpable level as it slipped into the foreground and my conscious mind into the background. When he asked me to visualize something to represent each side of the issue in each of my hands, it was my subconscious that did the work. In my left hand was a void. In the other was a black blob, like The Blob or No Face, an all-consuming entity. The practitioner then said, "Now both your hands will start coming together," and they did! When my palms merged, he asked, "Now what do you see?" I looked into my palms and answered, "A pink blob," which at the time meant nothing to me.

I came out of the hypnotic state and went back to my seat when someone asked me, "So, how's your problem? Is it solved?" I paused for a moment and thought deeply about it. I knew what issue I had gone up with: I was still in that toxic relationship and wanted to leave, but something kept me there. I knew the void represented the massive hole that would be left in my life if I were to leave, and that the black blob represented staying in the relationship and how it would be like an entity was sucking the life from me—*him*. As much as I remembered these things, the only thing that could come out of my mouth was, "What problem?"

I didn't see it as a problem anymore. Yes, the issue was still plaguing my life and nothing had yet been resolved, but it was different now. There wasn't this separation between two ideologies anymore. The situation wasn't black or white; it was one shade of gray. I was unhappy and abused and struggling to leave. I realized that things are not *this-or-that,* and all we can do is our best in each moment. I stayed in that relationship another year, experiencing a slower, more traumatic near-death than I had ever known.

I finally left the relationship at twenty-three, filled with pain and resentment. I felt like years of my beautiful youth had been stolen from me and left me with PTSD and physical scars as reminders I wear on my face. But slowly, I began to feel relief. I didn't forgive him for what he had done to me. I instead came to accept the reality that it happened rather than seek to control it by trying to create a different outcome, or reject it ever for having happened. Being positive is not about negating the negative or pretending it doesn't exist; it's looking at the glass and acknowledging that it is, in fact, half empty, and it is also half full. I get to choose which I focus on.

As much as that relationship tore me apart, it taught me I could put myself back together again…again. All those years of putting someone else first brought me to a place where I can now be compassionate to others and *still* always put myself first. It taught me there is strength in holding my ground and there is strength in surrender. Though it led to more trauma, I don't regret having stayed. I am not ashamed because though I knew I deserved better, something bigger was playing out. I had to get over my need to save people and I now know that is not my responsibility. As hard as it was watching someone I loved hurt himself and others, even me; I learned that we have to respect people's right to make their own decisions. Now, I have boundaries that protect me when I am not respected, or my needs aren't being met, and I surround myself with people who honor me.

I took the lessons from the pain and began to take action towards my healing. A year after leaving that toxic relationship, when I had just started getting my feet back on the ground, I tragically lost two of my uncles and a dear friend. A lesson that healing is not a linear process; as life peddles on, there's always more to grow from. Grief can be both a depleting force *and* an opportunity to meet the rawest versions of ourselves so we can grow into who we really want to be. I've learned that when we release expectations about how anything *should* be and have gratitude for what *is*, we are able to truly honor the blessings we receive and trust that we are divinely protected through it all.

Now, at twenty-six, I am literally closing the chapter that has been the last eleven years of my life by releasing this small fraction of my story. I became a certified yoga teacher and Reiki energy healer. I now practice and teach shadow work (uncovering the subconscious) and use divination tools and practices as a means to continue my own healing as I help others on their healing journeys. It was *because* of my trauma that I gained the connection to the healing modalities I use now, not in spite of it. Though trauma held me back in many ways, when I release myself from carrying it, I propel myself forward in my healing journey.

Acceptance is a major part of the never-ending healing journey that we are all on, exploring the path back to the purity of our true essence that we came to this earth with. The ups and downs of life, the Spanda, are like variations of notes playing together, producing a melody. No matter where you are in the depths of it all, when you step back and listen, it's a beautiful song, and you have the power to heal your heart by unapologetically singing it. When we allow ourselves to flow with all the elements of life, we give ourselves the ability to alchemize a harmonious existence. The way you engage with the present moment, is the way you choose to engage with life. Choose what brings you towards your heart and soul's desires.

IGNITE ACTION STEPS:

Create Space: Right now, whenever and wherever you are, relax your face, strengthen your posture with open body language, become aware of your breath. This is your home. Where your power resides.

Receive: Pay attention to signs, symbols, and coincidences. Feel into your emotions fully, listening to the sensations of your body. Nature/randomness is an intelligent force that is always expressing itself. Wisdom is all around us and within us always.

Protect: Set clear boundaries with yourself and stay firm in what you feel is right for you. Simultaneously remain open to other perspectives, so you're not limiting your options to only what you already know.

Choose Love: Choose love over fear. Worry is a prayer for what you don't want. Hope is a sent request for what you do want. Look at both sides, respecting all the variations that life has manifested, and focus your energy on what brings you towards your dream life. When fear comes up, start thinking of what the best-case scenario is and how you can act through love rather than respond to fear.

Enjoy: Laugh often, be silly, be curious, explore. Release shame. Don't be afraid to look like a fool. You're worth the full experience of each moment. Fall into your desires, knowing you are divinely protected.

Alessandra C.L. Pasut — Canada
Spiritual Guide, Reiki Energy Healer, Yoga teacher, CEO of Biorhythm
Holistic Wellness https://linktr.ee/biorhythmHW
  BiorhythmHolistic
  BiorhythmHolistic
  BiorhythmHW

Katherine Davidson

*"Journey the path from regret and dependence,
to joy and healthy self-love."*

FIND YOUR TRUE LOVE

BY KATHERINE DAVIDSON

**I want you to feel hope when you read my story and know that you are
not alone. I want to be with you and acknowledge that betrayal can be
agonizing, and I understand the overwhelming pain and heartache it causes.
I have been there and it has turned out to be a catalyst for change in my
life. My desire for you is that you leave the past behind and travel the
path to hope and healing. I wish that love, encouragement, empathy, and
compassion surround you and help you believe in yourself and your future.**

That December day is seared into my mind forever. The laughing and shouting of my fourth-grade students faded as the children scrambled and pushed to
get out of the school. The end of each school day was like a tsunami moving
back to sea, leaving destruction in its wake. I glanced at the winter artwork
drying on the desks and the glitter everywhere. A soft smile settled on my lips,
and a sigh of relief swept over me as I collapsed into a chair, surveying the
tasks at hand. I began tidying up the chaos and looking at plans for the next
day's challenges.

I was jarred from my thoughts as I looked up and saw my husband appear in
the doorway. Having my husband unexpectedly show up at work was never a
good thing, and it told me something was wrong. His usual confident, cheerful

demeanor had been replaced with a look of dread. A wave of fear washed over my body. *Why was he here?* He was supposed to be in Florida at an executive business meeting. I stared at him in disbelief, waiting for an explanation. With an edge in his voice, he announced, "I need to talk to you." He said nothing more, and an uncomfortable, anxious silence persisted as we walked to the car.

What could the terrible news possibly be? *Had there been an accident? Did someone die?* As we left the school, I grasped his hand. *Don't worry, we can handle this,* I thought, though I was afraid to break the tension by saying it out loud. He looked at me and said, with pain in his eyes, "I will always remember your kindness." My heart hammered in my chest, my stomach tightened, and I felt weak.

We slid into the car and he blurted out. "I have ruined us." His first words confused me. *What could he possibly be talking about?* I looked at him in disbelief. "I have been fired for having affairs at work." My heart pounded harder, and I fought the rising alarm. I felt something squeezing my chest. Panic paralyzed me and terror mounted in the silence.

It couldn't be true. Yet, inside I felt a buried dread rising and gripping me. A voice within wanted to scream at me: "You knew! You KNEW! You aren't surprised!*"* Despite my daily positive outward face and our congenial relationship, I had been aching inside about how our marriage had evolved over the years. He came to bed late, after I was asleep, and left before I was awake, always working and expressing overwhelm with his crises at the office. Now, I understood that the way he had pushed me away sexually meant something much more serious than I imagined. It wasn't a high-stress job like the counselor had suggested that caused his lack of interest in sex. He was having sex with other women. Deep inside the voices shouted, "Your gut told you something was wrong! Why didn't you listen to your heart?"

We drove home in silence. My head was pulsing and tight. Stomach-churning sensations turned to nausea. My hands throbbed as my heart beat faster. The uncomfortable prickling physical sensations were sweeping over me. The panic was in full control. He turned to me and said, "I have packed a few things, and I will leave."

I was sitting inside my grief and the confusion he had created, but my lifetime of concern for him did not just evaporate. I felt pity rising. He was in a terrible crisis. He had just lost the job he loved, returned to our city publicly humiliated, lost the security of a lifetime of work and the respectable career he had been building. Some part of me wanted to support him and help him through this crisis, but the new knowledge was devastating. In the following days, I bounced between empathy, rage, uncontrolled sobbing, and everything in between. My body racked with nausea and fear, and my interrogations of him left us both devastated. I couldn't eat or sleep, realizing we were dealing with his sexual addiction, compounded with gambling. Going to school, focusing on my students and work was my only escape.

My husband and I had been through so much together in the last forty-five years, much of it fulfilling and rewarding as we raised six children of our own. I had watched this man create a highly successful career and provide leadership in our church. He gave our children blessings and attended church with me every Sunday. We enjoyed each other's company and attentively cared for our family together.

Now I had to ask the question: *Who is this person? How could he keep this secret life going undetected by his family?* He said he wanted to recover and heal our marriage, and I wanted to believe him. I felt desperate to find a path forward because I couldn't imagine us not being together. I had longed for emotional connection and vulnerability in our marriage, and now that his secret was out, I thought I understood what had been in our way. We could fix this, and maybe if I stood by him, he could finally love me in a more complete way.

My expectations from youth had focused on the hope of the fulfillment and joy an eternal marriage would bring; two lives uniting in love and shared dreams. But in the early months of our married lives, I began to feel uneasy. *Why am I unhappy?* I would wonder, questioning whether I had made a mistake. I was told that marriage was hard when two people come together from different backgrounds. We had made eternal covenants to each other, and as I saw it, my only option was to uncover what was wrong so we could be comfortable together. I started the practice of reading and studying human behavior and the habits of healthy relationships. Within our marriage, there was a frequent, comfortable sex life, but there was constant pressure for more, and I wanted to feel appreciated and loved outside of the sexual relationship. The reality was that sexual addiction from my husband's youth had created walls and defense mechanisms that prevented emotional connection and honesty. I kept struggling to understand why, despite all our efforts to read and talk about intimacy, nothing ever changed.

With this disclosure of betrayal, I sank to a low beyond anything I could have ever imagined. I felt that everything I had worked my entire life for lay in ashes. Though I was told over and over the addiction was not my fault, and I could not fix it, I went straight to work, trying anyway. How could he not love me after all the fun we had together and the support I had given to his career?

I'd moved away from friends and family and worked tirelessly to raise a loving, kind family. I proceeded to search for counselors and programs but therein lies the issue. This problem, HIS problem, was not mine to solve. Following the familiar pattern in our life together, I assumed the responsibility of healing our marriage and his challenges. I could not yet see that my sense of self was tied up in my bond to him.

His cold, matter-of-fact admission filled me with rage, and I wondered how I could have so completely deceived myself. The effort I had exerted; the concern I had for his recovery and for the well-being of our family sickened me with shame. For years, my heart had ached for him, for me, and for the children. No more! I felt only bitterness. How could I have been such a fool? He demonstrated no compassion or remorse in his harsh words and made no effort to mitigate the devastation of what he was saying. There was no empathy for how those words would land with me as he told me that he didn't care about our marriage and his heart left our marriage 25 years ago, at the time that he began having affairs.

I didn't say much or linger. I cried all the way home. How could he stand there and say those words with no emotion? I had spent those twenty-five years trying to love, support, and accept him. We had an active sexual relationship for much of that time. Now he tells me this. I spent the last ten years with grief and sadness, trying to live with the fact that he claimed he was unable to have sex. I endured four years of recovery programs, and this was how he felt.

I had been told by therapists that there were characteristics that I might not enjoy dealing with around this kind of addiction, such as narcissism, lack of conscience, and antisocial behaviors, and I didn't want to believe it. I found encouragement in the fun of being together — camping, golfing, eating out, hiking — and I thought maybe we could move beyond this trauma. Maybe everything wasn't lost. I had fallen prey to my unrealistic fantasies and his cowardice in being totally honest, apparently for twenty-five years!. I realized that I had been unwilling to see the signs and accept the reality. They call it betrayal blindness. *Abuse no more.* I needed a divorce.

There was a period of great anguish and loss. Anger and resentment followed, but there began to be a shift in my thinking. I realized that I had not been facing the reality of my situation and that the only person I had control over was me. My questions intensified with an openness that was new and directed inward. *What was it about me that caused me to struggle for so long to save an abusive marriage? Why did I cling to a person who had betrayed me emotionally and abandoned me? I had never felt deeply and emotionally loved as a person. Why did I think that would change?* I saw the glaring fact that I was willing to suppress my needs and wants for the continuation of the marriage. Religion had taught me that marriage was forever. I felt I had made a promise, which influenced my inability to let go; I needed to stand by him and see this through. I believed that his religious values would empower him toward recovery. I had been encouraged by couples who had overcome these same issues. Until I realized, that was not going to be my story. Divorce was my answer. I was facing the terrifying thought of being alone. I was not able to see or embrace the freedom that divorce would bring.

Understanding myself and eliminating unhealthy behaviors became my intention. After years of being mad at God, my prayers became more frequent, and I pleaded to find a way forward that would bring peace. I was guided by my need for answers, read books, and took courses on recovering from betrayal. The psychologist, Vicki Tidwell Palmer, has become a crucial voice in my recovery, once saying: "Women are taught from a very young age to look to a partner/spouse/husband for completeness and wholeness….and this search for wholeness without, rather than wholeness within, leads to a multi-layered web of self-betrayal." When I read this statement, my chest immediately tightened, and my stomach knotted, and a familiar wave of anxiety washed over me. She was talking to me. She was talking *about* me.

I had to dissect why I had been clinging to someone so toxic. Michelle Mays' course, *Braving Hope after Betrayal,* helped open my eyes to my blindness, and I was surprised to learn that science shows that the attachment I was feeling was in the very cells of my body. The irrational draw to an unhealthy relationship was real and explained by biology. I knew I was holding onto a connection that was harmful to me, and I needed to stop carrying the shame of a failed marriage. That shame was not mine. I had to focus on loving and accepting myself. It wasn't easy because my mind often slipped back to blame and bitterness. My thoughts could quickly drift onto the unfairness of my plight and the abandonment by the one person who should have had my back. Loneliness and heartache were frequent visitors. I realized that kind of backward-looking, and regret kept me stuck in the past, focusing on a person I had no control over.

I grew up lacking confidence, feeling inadequate, and shy, so it was a major paradigm shift to quiet the self-blame, the feelings of failure, and work toward seeing that this was not my fault. The consequences of a life of addiction were severe and harsh. A focus on self-compassion and a positive sense of self became my priority. Numerous books and courses contributed to my understanding of my situation and emotions, but the exposure to Family of Origin concepts began to bring it all together. I desired to nurture the shy, self-conscious child from my past and began directing my energies toward loving her. I understood the origins of self-doubt and the feelings of being less than others. I was aware of the critical voice inside. I knew that self-love was my responsibility and that looking outside would never be the solution. But how could I integrate this self-love into my heart and feel it?

One practice that I used to nurture the wounded child was introduced to me early in counseling by my psychologist. During our sessions, I closed my eyes and used deep breathing to assist my body to relax and connect with the subconscious. I brought up agonizing images of Kathy from the past. I couldn't believe the images that my subconscious showed me. I attempted to provide comfort and compassion for this hurting child and wounded woman. This deep inner work helped me recognize that my positive face was covering deep emotional damage.

I began using that technique again after doing Family of Origin work. I went back to an image my therapist and I had uncovered in our sessions: little Kathy being dropped off in the evening, at an elementary concert with no one staying to watch. I felt her sadness as she looked out and knew no one was there to cheer for her. After some deep breathing, I returned to the memory of the concert of my childhood, only this time adult Kathy was present — excited, waving, and celebrating after the concert. I felt a tremendous peace flow into my body on those occasions as I told her I loved her. Returning to my childhood memories, recognizing the deficiencies, and nurturing the inner child were crucial. I frequently visited the adult Kathy, embraced her, and provided comfort. I am not sure I can identify exactly one time, but there are many little experiences of meditation: visualizing Kathy, putting my arms around her, encouraging her, and challenging her self-criticism. Caring for her has made a change in me.

On a daily basis, I needed strategies to push away the uncertainty I was experiencing. Mindfulness, the ability to be in the present, to recognize the voice inside, has been invaluable in helping me monitor thoughts and feelings. Learning to recognize harmful ruminations, taking a few deep breaths, and staying with the grief or self-doubt, helps to dissipate the uncomfortable sentiments. As undesirable emotions or self-doubts arise, I ask: "Am I in the victim role? Am I taking responsibility for my life? Is that a critical inner voice from the past?" Once musings come to the surface, I can modify my thinking patterns.

I had to learn to cope with critical voices from the outside, also. It is hurtful when I hear people say, "Well, it takes two, and there are always two sides to marital problems." But I can now disregard those comments as ill-informed.

Sexual addiction is a disease. Sexually addicted persons have issues that require outward support and self-introspection. No one can pinpoint the exact cause or solution of addiction; therefore no one should cast any blame. It took me a long time to gain that wisdom.

I like the new me, and I am beginning to be able to say the gut-wrenching heartache that brought me to my knees, also lifted me up toward freedom. As I reflect, I see the way, so many little things aligned to lay the path I ultimately walked. Moving my focus to the present me, and comforting the Kathy of the past, has shaped the future I build for myself. As I find the true source of love within me, I delight much more in daily living and the world around me. Anger at God has been replaced with humility and gratitude, as I take in the lessons of the myriad books, family, friends, counselors, and blessings that have found me at just the right time. Now my connections are genuinely sweet and tender, with no pressure, nothing to hide, or forced promises. It took letting go of my matrimonial bonds to finally find the truest love of all. The love of self.

IGNITE ACTION STEPS

- Open your mind to introspection, and be willing to face behaviors that are not building your best self.
- Use meditation or journaling to embrace your feelings in tough times. Deep breathing and staying with uncomfortable emotions can help them dissipate. Writing is an effective way to transfer ruminations from the mind to the page.
- Realize that a partner's addiction has nothing to do with you. It is not your fault, and you have no ability to fix it.
- Extend compassion to yourself. You are doing your best and that is enough.
- Take a few seconds, many times a day, to see the good and let it settle in your mind: a beautiful sky, a warm wind, the beauty in nature, acts of random kindness. In the midst of the worst days, the sun still shines.
- Before going to sleep, reflect on the moments in the day you were grateful for.
- Plead with God for his help and little miracles will appear.

Katherine Davidson — Canada
Teacher, BA, Education
www.katherinedavidson.net

Jameece D. Pinckney

"Faith over fear will take you beyond your limits!"

THE OTHER SIDE OF THE WINDOW

BY JAMEECE D. PINCKNEY, JD, M.ED.

This story is written to share my journey of courage. I hope it stirs up the audacity in you to move beyond the pain of your past and become present with your passion. I wish for you to be inspired, encouraged, and empowered by my ability to overcome fear with faith. I pray your heart becomes nimble, igniting endless possibilities to soar beyond your own boundaries, reaching limitless heights.

The pane is cracked in the window and it's slightly ajar. I notice it every time I stand, gazing through the glass when I have to wash dishes. I see birds perched on the power lines behind my house as the water runs over each plate and cup. It's as if they are watching me. I've gathered everything from the table and the stove and stacked all the pots, pans, and plates in one place to make it easy for me to reach them all. Despite all the times I have done the dishes before, this time was different. My legs are weak, and I am trembling as the sound of his voice travels by me. What should only take me twenty minutes seems like an eternity because I'm afraid of what's happening around me. My birthday was yesterday, and I should still be basking in the glow of turning nine years old. After all, I was so happy to receive my very first bible as a birthday gift from my mom. Standing at that window, even as I felt a belt strike my back, I refused to let one teardrop fall. It was a pinnacle moment. It was there that I showed the audacity to stand in faith for myself, siblings, and family. I could barely see over the ledge, but I continued to look up into the calm blue sky. Within my heart, I said, *Lord, there has to be a better place for me and a bigger world out there to see, on the other side of this window.*

You see, my life at that point had been shattered, and no one knew but me. *If only I were eighteen,* I often wished, so that I could escape the challenges I faced daily — challenges that no child my age should ever have to endure. I knew, however, that as the oldest of five children born to my mother, I had to hang in there for the protection of my siblings. While I often had to succumb to the intrusions I faced, I carried within me the strength of my faith. Even at nine years old, I believed that no matter what I went through, my faith allowed me to hope for a brighter future. I thought, *If only I could become older faster, become my own person, and see what the Lord had in store for me on the other side of that window.*

When I was in sixth grade, all the students in my grade level were brought to our elementary school auditorium for a special presentation. Our guests were the Pulaski Middle School band. I was sitting in the second row, in front of the stage, which gave me a complete, up-close view of the entire ensemble. I sat in awe and amazement at the students as they held all their shiny instruments. As they began to play, my heart started pounding as it joined in sync with each drumbeat. The melodic sounds were in such unison, and when one student stood up to play a solo, all I could see was myself up there on that stage, playing my own instrument. Before the band director could say the names of each section, I had already decided that upon entering seventh grade, my instrument would be the one shaped like the first letter of my name — the saxophone.

That moment set me on fire. All the pain I had experienced in my childhood to that point suddenly dissipated when my eyes were opened to the possibility of doing some*thing* new that could take me some*where* new. I was creative, eager, filled with potential, and that moment gave me the courage to say "yes" to a passion I didn't even know existed, a purpose bigger than myself. I had faith that even though my circumstances at home left me fearful and afraid to move forward, music could make me fearless. I felt I had something optimistic to look forward to as I transitioned into middle school.

My seventh-grade band teacher became my first mentor. He saw that I had something to give to the world and cultivated the gift he saw. He encouraged my mom to buy me a saxophone, which in 1983 was $800. For a poor family, that $800 might as well have been a million. But he was able to work out a deal for us to buy the instrument for $40 a month. It was still a hardship, but one my mother was willing to bear for my audacious dream. I walked two or three miles to school at that time, and I carried that saxophone with me as if I were a queen and it was my crown. When someone makes you feel like you are worth something, like you are someone special, it has an unbelievable impact on your life. The instructors and my mother validated my faith and helped me blossom from a shy little bird to a bold, confident girl who could hold her head high. The more my talent grew, the more recognition I received, and the more my life's path changed.

I used that momentum to excel in academics, becoming an unstoppable force in spite of all the fear I had grown up with. I was transitioning from looking through that window to walking toward whatever great things were on the other side. By the time I graduated from middle school, I was already known by the teachers in my new high school because of my musical talents.

My home situation was still bad; we were living in a condemned house. I shopped at the Salvation Army for my clothes. My mother had to nail the lids from our canned goods to the floor, patching the holes to protect us from the rodents running rampant. My classmates were not aware of my living conditions, but it didn't matter because I came to school and carried myself like I lived in a two-story home with marble floors. When I was inducted into the National Honor Society, I wore my gold sweater and white honor society sash with such pride. At school, I always had the support I needed to keep from folding under the pressures of my home life. My high school biology teacher, guidance counselor, and dean became my new mentors. They paid for me to do the things other kids did so I could excel in high school on an equal footing. As a junior in high school, I was invited to go on an exclusive scholastic trip to Washington, D.C., one of only a few students selected in our city. My desire to see what was beyond that window piqued my curiosity. We had no money, and my mom said we couldn't afford the trip, so several teachers, along with my dean, paid for me to go. While I was fearful that I might not have food to eat the entire trip, the chaperones made sure I did.

At the conclusion of our trip, I remember taking a picture with all the students and our state representative from Indiana. On our ride home, I reflected on every little detail from the moment the dean's office told me I was selected to go, to the incredibly long ride home. I thought to myself, *I am worth it, and this trip for me was a validation.* It validated my faith in people and the remarkable way they step up in love. It validated that God's favor was upon my life and the way He carried me through my difficulties into the path of those supportive people. It was a validation that I actually meant something to others because of how they cared for me and understood that although there was trauma, their support could bring triumph.

As I headed into my senior year, my guidance counselor made sure I applied for all the scholarships for which I was eligible. I was elated to leave high school and embark on a new journey with five scholarships and an acceptance letter to Tennessee State University. I could finally feel what it was like to be on the other side of the window.

After matriculating through college and years of working my way up the corporate ladder, I was edified by the lessons I had learned along the way and the successes. But there were new hurdles for my confidence to jump. I had a complex about the way I looked: the size of my feet, the shape of my body, and, yes, the color of my skin. At times I felt I would never fit in, so I pushed hard to go *beyond* fitting in instead, to stand out in an exemplary way. Attaining the status quo never seemed to be enough. I was determined to be more and do more with myself. Many people along my journey, particularly those I worked for, had a way of making me feel they controlled my career. I translated that into feeling like they were controlling me. That's not what I wanted beyond the window. In fact, in those moments, I felt like I was still nine years old, staring out the smudged glass. That is when I decided that I wanted to work for myself and be a woman in control of her own destiny. I didn't know what being my own boss would look like, but I knew as long as the Lord was on my side, nothing was impossible to achieve.

The Lord gave me the name of my company one night, as I was driving home from bible study a year after I finished law school. It was very dark on the road, and there were no streetlights. The darkness gave me pause, but it was perfect for me to hear His voice. The name He dropped in my spirit was HyQuest — a name that means always on a quest for more, seeking higher; it means elevation. As I explored the name, and its potential, I saw the vision of a company start to take shape. I had been working in law, but there was an audacity percolating within me that said it wasn't my path. Just as I had chosen the saxophone before knowing how to play it, I knew the Holy Spirit would tell me what direction my life would take and if starting a business truly aligned with God's purpose for my life. I kept faith that just as He had before, God would put me in the presence of the people who could show me the way and support me in my journey. Then it hit me like a ton of bricks, it's time for me to move to D.C.

In an unthinkable leap of faith, I got a one way ticket to D.C., leaving everything behind, and just *went*. This would be where my new beginning would take shape and I'd find success building a business called HyQuest. But not so fast. There was a long windy road ahead of me, before I could win my first contract, let alone start a business which took over ten years after my arrival in D.C.

The night I landed in D.C., I had butterflies and didn't know what to expect. My sister picked me up from the airport and as we drove around Crystal City, VA. It felt right and I knew that's where I wanted to live. She lived in Maryland which was where I would be staying and she told me we couldn't afford to live in Crystal City because it was a high rent area. I told her if the Lord landed me in D.C., he had also prepared a place for both of us, since we would be roommates. The next morning I hit the ground running. I asked the Lord for vision, and to introduce opportunities that would give me work to make money and experiences that would help me learn the world of government contracting. He did just that. I also prayed that he would open a door for us to find a place to live in Crystal City because it would allow me easy access to the metro train in and out of D.C.

God did not disappoint. He opened a door for me to get some consulting work with the Navy in D.C., and he allowed us to get a $2,600 a month, two-bedroom apartment on our $1,500 a month budget. While shopping at Walmart, the resident leasing agent called my sister and told her he had some good news. She ran over to me and said, "I think we got the apartment." I told my sister, "That's why I told you to apply because the bible tells us that faith without work is dead." We were both smiling ear to ear, and once he knew both of us were listening, he said, "You won't believe it, but there is also a move-in special, and I can lease the apartment to you for $1399 for the first year." Tears started rolling down my face, and all I could say was thank you, Lord. You had already prepared a place for me, knowing my leap of faith, but me not knowing your plan.

I lived in Crystal City for two years before I met my husband. When I got married to Gilbert "Gil" Pinckney, I decided to move forward with HyQuest Consulting Solutions, LLC™, so that I could also capitalize on my husband's similar background in government contracting. HyQuest became my side hustle while I worked a full-time job, and the decision to join in business with him made me think combining forces to maximize knowledge, talent, expertise, and business contacts was invaluable. This decision, coupled with his similar experience and military background led to numerous opportunities. I developed a plan to build my consulting "side hustle" into a full-time business that would enable both of us to work in business together. I had carefully laid the groundwork for launching HyQuest. I was ready for the opportunities. I was mentored by many senior-level businessmen and businesswomen over the years and honed my leadership skills from position to position as I climbed the corporate ladder.

After thirteen years in the corporate world, I decided to leave my job and work my business full-time. I was certain I knew exactly what I was getting into. However, I realized that leadership was not easy; having the right skills and experience was critical. I ultimately decided to take the leap of faith to leave my job because I had planned for it. I even remember when the Lord spoke to me and said, "Today is the day." It was a scary and daring move to make, but I realized I had hit a glass ceiling and was ready to make the move to becoming a small business owner. I knew, at that point, I had what it takes to be successful and was confident in the equity I brought to my own table to achieve the goal. When I had considered every possibility and planned for every known contingency, I courageously took the leap, left my job, and officially became a president and chief executive officer (CEO). Having my husband as my chief operating officer (COO) has been a phenomenal benefit as we've grown the business and advanced our synergy.

My road to CEO was not an easy one. I had to come through fear, step into faith, and find the courage and confidence to see what was possible for me. I had to say "YES" to my life and be a CEO: Courage, Equity, Opportunity. I had to fight fires, climb to the mountaintop, and watch my step all along the way. Every step I had to take brought me to this moment and ignited my life, woke me up and solidified my faith. I learned that any crack in the glass only makes room for the light to guide us to the other side of the window.

My childhood left me begging to live beyond the window. My life matriculating as a college and professional student kept me determined to beat the odds. My career goals kept me striving to be the best, despite my obstacles. In spite of every surprise, and because of them, I can say with pride that for nearly six years, I've been firmly entrenched as the president and CEO of a successful minority- and woman-owned small business. I've relied on persistence, adaptability, audacity, and flexibility to keep me moving forward.

As I stand in reflection looking back inside the window, I see the nine-year-old girl peering at me. The window is ajar, and I hear her quivering voice ask, "Is there a bigger life for me on the other side of this window?" With tears streaming down my face, I tell her that our journey has been imaginatively inspirational, audacious. Our life has been transformed by overcoming fear with faith, and by walking boldly with our courage and raising our own bar. We faced challenges, of course, but by God's grace, we not only made it to the other side of that window, but we also achieved extraordinary things.

I shared with you a message of Courage, Equity, and Opportunity. I pray my story resonated in a way that stirred up the audacity in you to move beyond your pain of the past and become present with your passion. I hope that you were inspired, encouraged, and empowered by my ability to overcome fear with faith. I pray your heart is now nimble, and you take away nuggets that will Ignite endless possibilities so that you soar beyond your own boundaries reaching limitless heights.

IGNITE ACTION STEPS

Let your reflections move you forward. Don't stay in the mirror of reflection too long. You drive from the front seat, not from the rear. In other words, it's okay to reflect on the past because there are lessons learned, and oftentimes, there's refuge in reflection. But to see progress, you must keep your journey moving forward.

Pain can inspire your passion. Acknowledge your pain, press in, push through, and let it Ignite your passion. You can't bypass your pain, but you can use it for your good. Pain can fuel your purpose and will open doors beyond your imagination. Know that the depth of your situation is an indication of the height of your future.

Know your worth; you're kind of a BIG deal. People will place no more value on you than you place on yourself. Celebrate the big wins. Celebrate the small wins. Sit in the chair at the head of your table. Then write your name on the table. You add value to everything you do, so yes… you are a big deal!

Have the audacity to be intentional. Go for what you know and be intentional about getting it done. Don't let failure be your obstacle or worry be your defeat. Tackle each day and continue to raise your BAR achieving… *Believable… Attainable… Results.*

Pay it forward by HELPing others and the community. Nothing is more gratifying than your success, except when you help others. Always remember to pay it forward. Find a dynamic nonprofit that you can connect with, like the OPHELIA Foundation, which I founded and established on the principle of Helping Others.

Jameece D. Pinckney, JD, M.Ed. — United States
Visionary, Leader, Author, President & CEO, HyQuest Consulting Solutions, LLC
www.hyquestconsulting.com | www.businessbosscollection.com
www.opheliafoundation.org
@hyquestconsult | @hyquestconsult

Nicole Mixdorf

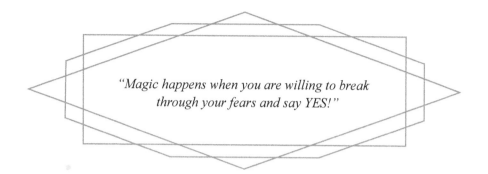

"Magic happens when you are willing to break through your fears and say YES!"

THE POWER OF PURPOSE

BY NICOLE MIXDORF

We all have those moments we can pinpoint that totally changed our lives. In this story, you'll walk through several of them. My hope is that by the end, you will feel inspired to uncover the truth of who *you* are meant to be, so you can stand in your power, overcome your obstacles, and shine your precious light into the world.

I was tired. Really tired. That bone aching, soul-crushing kind of tired. The pressure from my high-paying corporate job as a successful sales executive for a large global firm was wearing on me. But it was my sweet daddy's battle with cancer that was weighing on my heart more than anything. He was my best friend, my confidant, and I was watching him wither away. His doctors stood by, doing nothing for him, as he suffered unnecessarily at their hands. I remember the roller coaster of emotions so clearly: anger to sadness, frustration to helplessness, love to fear. I was the rock of our tight-knit and loving family, doing my best to hold it all together for my dad, my mom, and for everyone else, which didn't leave much for me. It's no wonder that all that stress started making me sick.

Stress affects everyone differently. For me, the stress manifested in my gut and immune system. I developed a debilitating condition called ulcerative colitis, the same illness that plagued my dad when he was younger. It caused bleeding ulcers in my intestines that ravished my body and left me feeling so exhausted. I discovered that when you don't feel well, it makes everything in your life so much harder. You can't give one hundred percent of your energy or attention to anything. At the time, I didn't know how to slow down, so I did the thing that most corporate professionals do: keep going, pop a few pills, and hope the problem goes away. But that was not sustainable.

I did my best to push through the pain, illness, and fear for the better part of a year until my body couldn't take it anymore. The constant bleeding and immediate urge to rush to the bathroom (up to twenty times per day) left me completely depleted and was interfering with my ability to do my job. I could barely function. My doctor had been begging me for months to take some time off work to heal my body, which I, of course, resisted, as I was "too busy" and had "too many responsibilities" on my plate. The truth was that I was in rough shape and was no good to anyone, least of all myself. I finally gave in and agreed to take one month off work, even though the doctor wrote up the order for three.

The moment I told my dear friend about my leave of absence, she immediately told me to pick out a retreat for the two of us to attend together. As destiny would have it, I discovered that Deepak Chopra was hosting a retreat the following week at his magnificent wellness center near the beach in Carlsbad, California, which was just a short drive from my home in Los Angeles.

Upon arrival, we were greeted by the scents of vibrant blooming flowers of the richest colors of deep purple, gold, blue, and magenta. A gentle breeze blew through the palm trees overhead as we savored the warmth of the sun on our skin. I remember feeling a complete shift in energy the moment we arrived. The hustle and bustle of my busy life — hopping on and off planes, managing a growing team, and leading international training — no longer felt important. It was the first time I truly permitted myself to slow down and to feel safe doing so. What a deep exhale I took, opening myself up to the possibility of the powerful inner change that I hoped would come.

Sitting in a large, open ballroom surrounded by hundreds of other eager soul searchers, I gained a piece of wisdom that would change my life forever. Deepak shared with us the three important questions that we should ask ourselves every single day.

The first question was, "Who am I?" *Not my name and what I do, but who am I really, deep down in my soul?* The second question was, "What do I want?" *If I could be totally happy and fulfilled, what would I want my life to look like?*

What would bring me joy? And the final question: "What is my purpose?" *How can I help? How can I serve?*

The questions were so simple, yet I had no idea what the answers were. Deepak said that we discover our purpose by using our greatest passions and gifts to help others. But I had never had the time to consider what my unique brilliance was. He wanted us to name the things that we enjoyed doing so much that we would gratefully do them all day for free, losing track of time. As a sales executive focused on her earning power, it was something I had never explored.

How was it possible that I didn't know who I really was, what I wanted, or what I was meant to do? It occurred to me that no one ever teaches that to us. I certainly didn't learn it in school or from my parents. After being so sure of what I was doing, it was confusing to suddenly feel so out of touch with myself. It blew me away how these prompts had turned my identity on its head. It was unsettling and exciting at the same time as I began to question whether I knew anything at all.

Fortunately, Deepak says that we never know the answers when we first start asking the questions, and that's okay. This was going to become my daily practice, where I close my eyes, take a few centering deep breaths, and then ask myself those powerful questions with an inner longing for the answers. The yearning was real and raw within me, which made the next piece of guidance that much harder to understand. We were told to simply let the questions go, releasing them from our minds with an intention and faith that the answers would start flowing to us in moments of inspiration.

That first night of the retreat, I went back to our gorgeously appointed hotel room, and melted into the comfortable bed, while holding a kyanite-with-fuchsite crystal in my hand; its sparkling green and blue having caught my eye in the gift shop earlier. For whatever reason, I was inspired to hold this crystal on each of my chakras, starting with the root chakra, while I was thinking about my deepest desire to heal my body. I kept saying, "This is not who I am," as I moved that crystal from one chakra to the next. "This is not who I am. This is NOT who I am. THIS IS NOT WHO I AM!!" I screamed it out loud with tears in my eyes, no longer choosing to identify with the illness that had been plaguing me for a year. The moment I brought that crystal up to my heart chakra and shouted, "THIS IS NOT WHO I AM!" a sudden burst of knowing flowed through me, and for the first time in my life, I knew who I was.

It was as if I tapped into a truth that had been hidden from me but was always there, waiting for me to uncover it. In that moment, I transcended the limitations of my body. I knew myself as the spark of the Divine living within my heart: that deepest and highest part of myself that knows everything and is connected to the infinite field of possibilities that exists for us all. It was the purest moment of my life, and I just started laughing and crying tears of joy.

The next morning, I awoke with a feeling of lightness and ease that I had never felt before. It was as if all my burdens had been lifted; a feeling I rejoiced in and was eager to hold onto for as long as possible. After the sessions were over for the day, my dear friend led me through my first *Bhavana*, an ancient practice, to visualize what I truly wanted for my life. That powerful experience gave me the clarity to allow my dreams to come forth. My hand danced across the pages of my journal, filling it with the most beautiful vision of starting a corporate wellness company. I would inspire busy professionals to create balance in their lives so they could thrive.

I believed this was something that everyone needed; the only problem was — I couldn't see how to do it. The idea for the wellness company had been on my mind for several years, but I never seemed to find the time to pursue it with my heart. I was busy traveling the world, winning new business, making money, and having fun partying with my colleagues at conferences in exotic destinations. It's amazing how easy it was to keep putting off my dreams when I was busy with something else. I had a fun job; there was no doubt about it, but the "work hard, party hard" culture didn't have wellness on its radar at that time, which I was suddenly keenly aware of.

The idea of quitting my high-paying job scared me because our family relied on my income. It didn't seem realistic until my friend reminded me that starting a business may require an initial step back financially to ultimately take a leap forward. For the first time, it felt like a possibility to explore, even though the idea of letting go of my salary and status terrified me.

Yet by now, my priorities were starting to shift toward my personal well-being and goals. I left the retreat committed to a daily practice of yoga, journaling, breathwork, and meditating, where I asked myself the three most important questions with a yearning for the answers. By the end of that month, I learned to embrace slowing down, and was even questioning going back to work so quickly, when I wasn't fully healed.

Then I got some terrible news from work. My colleague's beautiful wife, who had been battling ovarian cancer for years, unexpectedly passed away. The reality of it hit me like a ton of bricks as she was the same age as me — thirty-three. *What was I doing going back to work early?* I wouldn't remember this extra time at work when I was old, and taking the full amount of leave would provide me the opportunity to truly heal and change my life. Reflecting on her passing, along with my dad's illness and my own taught me a powerful truth: our health is everything.

I told my boss I needed the three full months off, choosing to be my own best friend and make self-care my greatest priority. I was on a quest to get to know the deepest part of who I am — dive into my spiritual practice, heal my body, and figure out what path I was meant to go down.

In this peaceful space, my vision took a clearer shape. The more I thought about the idea of starting the business, the more excited I got, the better I started to feel, and the more momentum it gained. After several more weeks of truly taking care of myself, I felt the stress finally lift, and the most miraculous thing happened… my symptoms disappeared! Removing a large source of stress from my life and focusing more on my self-care was the catalyst that allowed my body to heal. In that amazing "a-ha" moment, I realized that having a "healthy" lifestyle of exercise and proper nutrition didn't even matter if I simultaneously had so much stress in my life.

My story of stress-related illness wasn't unique. All of my colleagues were suffering but in their own way. Migraines, insomnia, anxiety, depression, auto-immune conditions… the list went on. It occurred to me that busy professionals everywhere were buckling under these issues without even realizing that stress was the underlying culprit. People around me weren't feeling and performing to their greatest potential. There was a stress epidemic happening in our country, and around the world, and I felt called to do something about it.

As I continued asking myself the daily questions, I was amazed how quickly the answers started flowing to me in the form of inspired ideas, conversations where someone said something that resonated with me, meaningful introductions that were being made, and opportunities that started falling into my lap, as if by magic. I was recruited by a smaller national competitor to be their VP of sales, with offers to pay me even more money and allow me to work from home. Suddenly, I had three possibilities to weigh out: go back to my current job, take on this new role, or throw it all to the wind and start a wellness business; a prospect which felt exhilarating but was still shrouded in a blanket of fear and doubt. I didn't know what to do!

I continued evaluating my options, feeling concerned that going back into a stressful work environment would undo all the healing that I had accomplished. My supportive husband shared that same concern, but we both also understood the financial setback that leaving my lucrative job would create in our lives. Many of my friends and family members thought I was crazy to leave what they considered my "dream job." So many thoughts floated through my head: *What if I fail? What if I can't do it? What if we lose everything that we've worked so hard to build? What if I don't try?* My three months were almost up, and there was a lot weighing on my heart.

One sunny day, I decided to go for a walk in my beautiful neighborhood with its tree-lined streets and blooming flowers to clear my mind, and I arrived at my ninety-two-year-old neighbor's house. He was often sitting in front of his home waiting for someone to talk to. He didn't know anything that was going on in my life, or that I was wrestling with a decision about what to do with my future, but the Universe guided him that day to give me the advice that would change the course of my life forever.

As we stood on his porch, he looked me straight in the eyes and said: "You know, in all my years, the one thing that I've learned is that if there's something you want to do, do it now. Don't wait; opportunities won't last forever. And one day, you'll be standing here like an old man, looking back at your life, thinking about the things you did do, and thinking about the things you didn't do. So, if there's something you want to do, do it now."

It took my breath away. As I stood there taking it all in, I got chills everywhere. This was the sign that I had been waiting for! At that moment, I knew what I was destined to do. I wanted to inspire the world and raise the collective vibration, helping people become the best version of themselves that they could be. I turned around on the spot, marched back into my house, and told my husband, "That's it, I'm quitting my job and starting this wellness business!"

And, I never looked back.

I am humbled by the awards and recognitions I have earned while growing my company, Balance by Nature, to become a top player in the employee wellness industry. Global brands trust me to support the well-being of their employees, fulfilling this great purpose that fills me with joy each day. I know that my daddy is smiling down at me from heaven, guiding me along my path as I grow and evolve into the thought leader I was meant to become. I am proud of myself for doing the inner work, overcoming my fears, and standing in my truth to create a positive impact in the world.

There is something so powerful about connecting to who you are, knowing exactly what you want, and being guided into a strong purpose that you know you are meant to fulfill. It's like a magnet drawing you in and pulling you forward. It just feels right. Magic happens when you are willing to break through your fears and say YES!

Ignite Action Steps

- **Start a daily practice** of asking yourself the three most important questions — Who am I? What do I want? What is my purpose? This will be the greatest gift you've ever given to yourself.

- **Consider** one area of your life in which you have been struggling. Write down and plan three ways to nurture yourself in this arena.

- **Take a moment** to visualize what you would love every aspect of your life to look like — your career, relationships, romance, finances, health, mindset, parenting, and hobbies/fun. Paint that picture with as much detail as you can, and then take a moment to imagine that you already have it. Believe it, expect it, and know that this is exactly how to invite magic into your life to achieve your wildest dreams. Write the vision down, and leave it on your bedside table. Make it a practice to read it, see it, and feel it daily.

- **What are you ready to say YES to?** Think of one big or small dream that would light your soul on fire, and brainstorm some steps you can take right now to move the needle forward.

Nicole Mixdorf — United States
Keynote Speaker, Chief Wellness Officer of Balance by Nature
www.balancebynature.com
nicolemixdorf
@nicolemixdorf

Dr. Erin Sepic

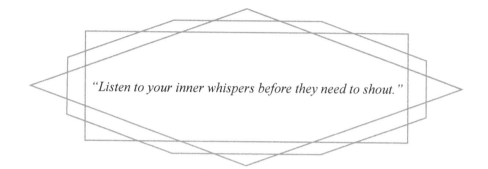

"Listen to your inner whispers before they need to shout."

RECOVERED RESISTOR

BY DR. ERIN SEPIC

If you have ever been humbled by a life event — and been curious if you could have seen it coming — you know that ache of insecurity and the desire for a more fluid communication with your "instincts." Imagine that your intuition is as essential a system as any other in the body and that your ability to connect with it is both innate and trainable. Our awakening to this guidance system can often be brought on by a major or tragic event. Although sometimes the most bitter remedy can bring the greatest healing, suffering is not necessary. Since to suffer is to resist either what you fear or what you wish didn't exist, the good news is that it's optional. Whether you have suffered greatly or not, I want you to know that when you connect with your body, the present moment, and your intuition, you can find everything you need and more.

I was born a pleaser. I remained so for most of my young life, even through grad school. No one ever accused me of being stubborn (except Mom), and I desperately avoided confrontation. I was so "flexible" that my Gemini self often came across as wishy-washy. If not for inheriting my father's physical drive and for playing sports as a youngster, I may have struggled to develop a spine. My resistance energy was not something I was familiar with, so I never expected to embody it, let alone willfully so. Though some tales of spiritual awakenings report serendipitous events, healing miracles, and even transcendence, I assure you, this isn't a story like that.

By my early 30s, I was deeply content, helping others and feeling as much in service as I thought I could. I felt happily married to a wonderful man who I adored. We were living in our sweet country home together, and I was doing work that I loved as a chiropractor in the charming office he and I had purchased. Our lives were vividly mapped out as future parents and vibrant, healthy outdoors-people living in our beautiful state of Vermont, USA. Life was great.

Then somehow, the tectonic foundation of my life abruptly shifted. To be clear, I don't mean that it leaned, gave fair warning, and then gently listed over on its side like a golden retriever. I mean that I heard a single, sharp warning shot, then the ground shook beneath me; the message that our marriage had to come to an end. Instinctually, I knew that my entire life was about to shift on its axis. I had no impression of what that would look like or whether I would ever be happy again. I was only certain that I had no choice but to move forward on my own into the fog.

This all started with a conversation I had with the Universe earlier that year. I was feeling stuck in how I was showing up in my relationship, and I had tried everything that I had learned from books and therapy to clear my block. After three years of focus, I still felt firmly fixed. I knew I was pushing blind against a dead end. I could feel that this wall was broader in scope than my partnership, which made my stomach faintly queasy. Desperate and feeling out of options, I finally asked the Universe for help and promised I would follow instructions if it would only deliver me from my "swamp of stuck."

Shortly after this came the cold call from a psychic in New Jersey, who said — no joke — that God told her to call me and ask if I wanted a free fifteen-minute reading. It was hard not to laugh straight into the phone. This was approaching the deep end for me, but I figured, *What could fifteen minutes hurt?* I ended up doing a few sessions with this lady, and the last one left me puzzled; she'd said that God insisted that I find an intuitive coach and ASAP. I remember chuckling to myself later that day: *What on earth was that? Am I supposed to just open up the trusty yellow pages and look up the nearest listing for an intuitive coach?* I'd never even heard of such a thing, despite living in Vermont, a state that's right up there with Sedona, Arizona, comfortably camped out down the new age rabbit hole. Deciding this coach-finding thing was a dead-end, I shrugged it off and sent the ball back to the Universal server, hoping they'd fix the glitch.

The next morning, my office manager dropped a fresh stack of mail on my desk, and there on the top of the pile was a pamphlet reading, (cue the creepy music) "Gwyneth Flack, Intuitive Coach." Even grudgingly, I had to admit, *Point well played, Universe.*

I booked a session with Gwyneth as soon as possible, and it was a crucial first step toward releasing my resistance and connecting with my intuition. In those early stages, I still felt the need to control my relationship with the Divine, even so far as to how much feedback I allowed in and how much I chose to act on. This response was entirely and understandably based on fear, mostly of the unknown. I needed to be thumped on the head before I would finally let go and allow the full connection in.

Several forces of nature and Spirit converged to cause the mammoth shift that followed. The energy felt like a slow bubbling, a mounting waveform deep inside that I would need to release or get rolled under. I was getting messages more regularly and had some foundational energy tools, so the flood was containable... for the moment.

One morning I woke up sensing a clear message to stay home and rest my body, as it had been a big week and I was processing a lot of energy. That was the first message I ignored that day. My husband and I had been enlisted among a fleet of others to help a couple of our closest friends prepare their house for sale, and we were doing a giant, joyful day of yard work together. I was so excited to support them, and a little tiredness was not going to stop me. Later, we were moving a rack load of lumber to the new house's barn via my husband's truck. He was unloading as I stepped out of the cab, and somehow, a stack of sixteen one-by-four-inch boards landed on my head, right on my crown. I quickly became angry, as we often do when we are either resisting or out of balance. My husband was an incredibly competent man, a professional builder and fine woodworker. He was also safety-conscious and would never have put me at risk intentionally. I looked up to holler something, and I still remember the look on his face; complete shock. He clearly had no idea what had gone wrong. He wholeheartedly apologized, but I was already off in my resistance bubble, petulantly ignoring this more aggressive message; *I needed to be elsewhere.* My higher self was compelling me to be open to my guidance and to gently *be* with my body, but I felt I wouldn't be able to handle what I found in that honest, surrendered space.

I continued to flip off "the powers that be" and walked into the barn, carrying a stack of lumber on one shoulder and stubbornly doing my own cranial work with my other hand, unwinding the impact mid-stride. I was now feeling angry with myself and resentful of the tension between my desire to support my friends and my untimely but clear need for self-care. I was also starting to fear the magnitude of the message coming through, but it was a fear I quickly buried.

Back at the yard again, I hopped on the brush-clearing team, collecting broken or felled brush and saplings, breaking them down further so they could be burned in the firepit. We laid the branches diagonally, then stomped hard over the gap to fracture them, something I'd been doing since I was a child. It helped me in the moment to channel my fear, anger, and resistance into my violent stomping. Experienced branch breakers know to always throw a bent arm up to protect our faces and heads from the uphill end of the stick, lest it pops up and clips you in the face. So when I came across an especially large branch, five feet long and two and a half inches across, I knew to show some respect. It took me three tries, but I gave the third one everything I had and nailed it. The uphill section spun so fast I didn't even see it move. It rotated around my protective arm without even touching it and smashed into my right ear, perfectly end-on. My head rebounded sharply midair as if I'd been struck by a competent but invisible boxer. A reasonable response would have been to crumple, breathe, and assess… but, did I mention I was in a resistance storm? Shamefully, I kept moving, furiously ignoring the event. There must have been a dozen people in the yard that day, but thankfully the only person who saw the blow was my best friend. When I nonchalantly placed the next branch on the block, she rushed over, grabbed my arm, and in an uneasy, intense whisper, said, "Stop. NO. What is going on??"

I couldn't answer. Her witnessing my lunacy had crippled my denial, and my legs wobbled; I suddenly felt lost. I knew the dam was cracking, and though I was terrified by whatever I was avoiding, I refused to detract from this happy and exciting day by having a complete breakdown in my friends' backyard. "I'll be okay, honey. I promise I'll only pick up tiny sticks. Please, let me go." She agreed, but I could feel her watching me like a hawk, alert. I made it a few short minutes, moving slowly, picking up the tiniest twigs and placing them carefully and humbly in the pit. I was in a daze. The grief was coming, and there was nothing I could do about it. The ridiculous thing was that I didn't know what I was mourning yet; I could simply feel in my bones that my life would soon be rendered largely unrecognizable. The fear and frustration of not knowing *how* I knew that didn't lend anything positive to my state of mind.

I could see Grief standing at the edge of the clearing, just watching. I acknowledged her without looking up and finally stopped moving as I bent over to pet my best friend's dog. Sinking my fingers into her long, soft fur, I found that somehow the supple texture gave me permission to surrender. Silent tears began to come. I was still facing away from the group towards the forest, but my hawk knew something had shifted. She came and put her hand on my shoulder wordlessly. I told her that I needed to take a walk alone. "Well, that was a pretty solid blow to the head," she said with a wry smile. "Can you please not go far?" I promised her that I would walk a straight line in the direction I was facing, and she let me go. I was so grateful; it was the support I needed and the space. She had gifted me her trust, which was a huge and timely comfort.

As soon as I turned away from the group and stepped into the woods, grief hit me full in the face, heart, and body. And I let it. I surrendered all my resistance, my need to know what I was resisting, and why I was so devastated; I just *stopped fighting*. At precisely the moment I did, I was shocked to feel, or know, that there were four spirit guides present with me as I walked. The communication I received from them overflowed with warmth, support, wonder, and gentle laughter. Though they were committed to supporting me, they chided my repeated rejection of their messaging and hoped that this "silly" crescendo of schooling would not be necessary again. Somehow, they embodied both purpose *and* lightness. I was grateful for these beings' company, support, and cheerfulness, but I was still in shock. Even so, as I walked, I chuckled to myself; *I now hear voices. Faaantastic.*

I came to a ten-foot-tall vertical rock face with huge, ruddy tree roots tracing down it and was instructed to climb. Distantly, I insisted my body scale the rock and was surprised to find the top as flat as the face. Laid into it was an eighteen-inch deep, seven-foot-long, cradle-like opening in the rock itself, lined with thick moss and fallen leaves. I collapsed into it, fitting like a grown babe in a womb. I felt safe and surrounded, unconditionally supported, beautifully *held*. As such, I was finally able to open that door and let everything I'd been denying in. I wept like I never thought possible. It almost felt like I was somehow laboring in that grief space, perhaps to deliver a part of myself.

I woke as if from a dream and understood clearly that I could either have the path I came here to walk or have my partner and the life we'd dreamed of together. I can still feel the impact of that realization. Almost thankfully, there remained no actual choice for me to make; every cell of my being had already decided. There was only the chilling, distant sense of how heart-wrenching the closing of this chapter would be.

Many changes followed, most significantly the painful but necessary uncoupling of our beautiful fifteen-year partnership. That process illuminated grace, loving kindness, and forgiveness for me. It felt essential to honor the shared time and those many lessons. We had defined ourselves as adults together, and I knew I would feel disoriented for years in his absence. I moved into a backwoods yurt located a mile from the nearest car parking and had to walk home every day. I found this practice fundamental for my healing, as it helped me *bridge* moving from the stability of my husband, our home, and joint life to echo-locating my own methods of grounding. I learned a lot during the months that followed and received essential support from friends old and new. Ironically, I also found my laughter and lightness in the darkest times, and these beautiful gifts remain with me. After living through the unwinding of that life, as well as grieving, processing and integrating my lessons, I emerged from the woods eighteen months later, a different woman. I discovered a new rhythm and a gentleness with myself, which was a very new experience. I continued to engage in self-discovery and training, strengthening and refining my connection to Source. I learned how to lean into courage when I feel afraid, and how to listen to my guidance *long* before the proverbial baseball bat is called for. I'm grateful for my lessons, as they brought me to my*self*, to wholeness, compassion, and to the knowledge that suffering can truly be a doorway to transformation.

I've been supported in building a life that integrates my authentic, evolving self, my passions, gifts, loved ones, and an enduring kinship with the natural world. I am humbled and deeply grateful to be able to move through the world with an open heart and to be able to share what I have learned in support of others.

"Recovered Resistor" is the title of this tale, but I assure you it's 10 percent wishful thinking and 90 percent a commitment to myself. Resistance is something most of us come up against on a daily basis, so I figure that beyond the rare fully-awakened ones, most of us are in a constant state of recover*ing*, not so much fully recovered. We either resist pain and fear, or we simply resist "what is;" something that is what it is, even for just that day, or moment. Once we've judged it to be negative (assigning it a charge if you will), we then push against it. This pattern takes the wind out of our creative sails since we are using our energy to un-make something that already exists, instead of simply focusing on building something new. The only alternative pattern I know of is something called "surrendered action," an idea that was an exasperating vicious circle for me at first. Eventually, I understood that this is still committed and aligned action; just action devoid of resistance to or rejection of what *is*. It is simply "pro"-whatever, and is never "anti"-anything. This surrendered action pattern is one that resonates deeply in my heart, and I hope in yours as well. Whenever we can surrender any "anti" sentiments enough to embody our desired "pro" attributes, we fall infinitely more into flow with the Universe and its ease, as well as our own intentional, creative energy.

It is a beautiful day when you can *decide* to put down your fights, with what and whomever, so you can lean into courage, connection, compassion, and a commitment to a more peaceful and joy-filled world. When you connect with the Universe, get in sync and flow with your vision in mind, there is nothing you cannot do. As you align your dreams and gifts with your intuitive guidance you will receive more support than you can imagine.

IGNITE ACTION STEPS

- Listen to your inner guidance as much as possible, in every situation. Respect and appreciate the taps on the shoulder, and you'll avoid the two-by-fours, as well as hopefully any major injuries or illnesses. This is surprisingly simple; find a rock or a tree you can sit up against, with your feet on the ground. Allow your breath to guide you back into your body and to quiet your mind. Soon, you'll be able to check in and get intuitive, whole-body answers in a single breath.
- High-functioning people who have a lot of ambition or competitive energy, (good thing you're up for a challenge!) refocus on the most challenging goal of all; ask yourself, "How deeply and unconditionally can I love and forgive myself today?" This is the seat of how deeply and truly we can love and forgive others. If you can sink into the discomfort of this practice on a daily basis, you'll watch your fundamental experience of life shift.
- If you are going through an event that is pushing the edges of what you can handle, please reach out for support. Find a great healer or coach to help you completely shift your vibration and support your experience and level of clarity.
- Learn to notice any tension in your breath or body before it turns into a pain or injury. Once you are aware of the tension, pause, give yourself space to be curious, and discern where that might have come from or what it might be a response to. Then you can clear and release that energy before it accumulates and becomes an issue in your body or state of mind. It is a constant practice definitely worth refining for the long haul.
- Sometimes when we are in a place of suffering, it can be a surprisingly huge relief to surrender to the experience for a hot minute. This surrender can reveal strengths and gifts you didn't realize you had and a peace that you never imagined. We can all create much more powerfully from *there*.

Dr. Erin Sepic — United States
Chiropractor, Kinesiologist, Intuitive, Teacher and Speaker
Drerinsepic.com
 Erin Sepic | *@erinsepic*

"If it doesn't bring you joy, don't do it."

CANDIDLY ME

BY ALY INCARDONA

If you take away anything from my story, I want you to know that you can be anything you want to be, on your own terms. If you have the ambition and choose each day to believe in yourself, you can go the distance to achieving your wildly candid dreams.

"Oh! What do you *DO* now?"

I was frozen, grabbing my husband's hand as we were confronted by this simple, small-talk question from a former high school classmate. Our shopping trip was supposed to be a quick in and out, not the moment I had to admit I had just been fired from my current waitressing job. Feeling cornered, I gave the first answer that I could think of and in the process, realized I was speaking from the heart.

"I'm a photographer." I answered quickly and with a rush of nerves.

I remember that day so vividly when I decided I was no longer just a mom or wife. I had made the distinct decision on a new identity that I could be proud of. I had a new purpose. A purpose that was something just for me.

My husband saw the frustration radiating off of me the day I came home after being fired. I walked in with a defeated spirit. He reassured me that everything would be okay and reminded me of the reasons why this job wasn't a right fit for me. He knew my dream was to become a photographer and leave my mark on the world. He encouraged me that this was my turn; this was my golden opportunity. I think back, and it is such a memorable moment in my life because it was the first time I can remember being encouraged. It was the first glimpse of the freedom that comes when you learn: you *can* take a chance on yourself and *your* dreams.

Prior to meeting my husband, I was conditioned throughout my life to accept that things would be hard. Growing up in a one-income household, it was the norm to go without. It always felt as if the things I wanted didn't have value, not because they weren't important, but because they were too expensive. The answer was almost always "no." Because of situations out of my control, the idea of chasing something that truly mattered to me felt like a thought I didn't deserve to have.

The moment I said "photographer" out loud for the first time, felt like I had tapped into my true identity; this was who I was born to be. For years, I had been dabbling in photography as a side hustle. Then, overnight I was a business owner. What had started as a mom taking photos of her kids in the park, turned into a full-time job. I was aiming to reach my full potential as an artist. It was a whirlwind, and I remember the feeling of excitement as business started booming. I hardly had time to hear the little voice inside me saying it wasn't my place, that I wasn't a REAL photographer. I felt like an imposter, but here I was thriving, at a rate so much faster than I felt prepared for.

I was advertising constantly, word of mouth spread, and bookings were rolling in. Maternity, birthday, family, and wedding photoshoots, all started to fill my calendar. No sooner had my doors opened full time, I was overbooked and overloaded.

A big part of me wondered how long somebody can work while feeling so overwhelmed. Especially somebody like me. I was never great at school, had little to no business training, and was trying to learn how to run a business while growing and improving my photography skills. Slowly, I started to figure things out, taking every class I could find: out-of-state photography conventions, online resources, mentorships, and one-on-one courses to learn my camera, posing, and lighting techniques.

As my business and photography skills grew, so did my client base. I was also gaining recognition from other photographers watching my journey. I often felt bombarded by questions from clients and photographers. It seemed as if the only point of my photography gift and talent was to serve everybody around me. I knew there had to be more to life than working crazy hours, being overbooked, and having so much to do. I knew in my heart that I had a bigger calling, but I didn't have the privilege to slow down enough to figure out my true potential.

I was losing control of my daily life. The second I woke up, I hit the ground running on an endless list of tasks between being a mother, being a wife, serving my clients, and taking the responsibility of helping my photography community grow. I lost my Identity in the shuffle of accommodating everybody without serving myself first. I was unprepared and unorganized, confronted all the time with moments where my ideas of business ownership proved to be fantasies. I wasn't collegiately educated and fears, insecurities, and self-doubt started to creep in. I started to become complacent in my work. I began to compare myself to others around me. I watched those around me surpass me in their knowledge and skill sets. I would spend hours getting lost in a mental spiral of comparison and asking myself: "Why them? How did they find these unique niches that set them apart? Why doesn't my work look like that?" I was putting in the work, but I wasn't seeing my growth.

While balancing a full load of clients and never turning down a shoot in any genre or style, the workload and mental stress were too much for me, and I was giving the bare minimum. I was stretched too thin, and my work became shallow, lifeless, and dull.

Then my confidence in my work took an even bigger blow. At an annual photography conference, somebody said, OUT LOUD, that I was uneducated because I hadn't received my degree in photography. The world stopped as every ounce of shame I ever felt came rushing back into my being. Whether one person or a hundred had heard that comment, I felt like it was confirmation of my deepest insecurities. I was nobody. I hadn't reached my potential. Why did I think I could be a photographer? I should have expected things to end up this way. My clients deserve somebody better, somebody who really knew what they were doing.

My past was back, as I began thinking again that somebody who grew up like me, with nothing, could never amount to anything. I felt ashamed, like I was falling short of who I was trying to be. Embarrassed and devastated, I didn't know where to even begin to pick up the pieces. I was an overbooked, disorganized photographer losing control of her business, and now my big secret was exposed. It was tattooed right on my forehead: UNEDUCATED. UNWORTHY. PRETENDER. I wondered if the world I'd attempted to build was about to fall apart.

Then one day, not long after, the world really did stop. COVID-19. Business halted, and I was hit with the crashing wave of cancellations and refunds. I went from a full, chaotic schedule to absolutely nothing. No work. No income. No resources. No dignity and No hope. All that was left was the justification for my self-doubt. I never prepared for emergencies. I never prepared for the possibility I would not be able to provide for my family. What type of mother wouldn't prepare? How naive was I, chasing this dream with no real plan? Were my kids going to grow up like I did: believing there was nothing out there for them? I felt depression consuming me; endless days of tears, fear, and anxiety arose. I questioned if I had ruined my life, chasing a dream I wanted so badly and then making a mess of my blessing. I felt worthless.

I gave up and officially decided to close my business. I lost the war against myself. I couldn't pray, feeling like I forgot how. I felt so detached from God, mad at him for letting me lose myself in this spiral of darkness. I was mad at my husband. Why did he encourage me to do this? Why did I believe him when he told me I could do it? The sadness was overwhelming and overbearing, and the only thing I wanted was to stop crying. That was my rock bottom, the shame like a million pounds on my back. As tension was building in my home over this, I was bombarded with questions from clients and fellow photographers, asking why I closed and when I would be back.

I was struggling, but their focus was on whether or not I would be able to serve *their* needs, and it felt like confirmation of the old, nagging belief that what I needed didn't matter. I was too embarrassed to even answer them. What else could I say besides, *I am a failure*? I felt consumed with darkness and shame.

I needed help *now*. I wanted resources *now*. I had to believe that I could get better. I was determined to use what I knew and tap into that feeling I had when I first started this journey.

Rather than wait for signs or outside support, I chose to take matters into my own hands. I started scouring the internet for resources. I found a video online, and it resonated so deeply with me. A young man was praying, and as he prayed, I spoke the same words with all the meaning in my heart that I could muster. For the first time in what felt like forever, I begged God to forgive me for being so angry with him and to help me find my light, my purpose, and my calling. Most of all, I begged God that night to help me find *myself*. I prayed along with the video for hours on repeat. I gave all of my burdens to him.

I felt the sweetest love fill my soul like a big warm hug. I felt like a child being scooped up and told, "It's okay. Everything is going to be okay." For the first time in so long, I felt secure; He gave me grace, and I was grounded.

That night I slept the deepest sleep of my life, and when I woke up early the next morning, I felt rested. There was a sense of rejuvenation as I saw the sun peeking into the sky. The house was silent, peaceful, and different. I felt my miracle. I felt a beautiful flood of light shining from my heart.

I rolled over in my bed, clung to my sweet, loving husband, and begged him to forgive me. To forgive me for the sadness and self-loathing, but most of all to forgive me for taking his love and encouragement for granted. I needed him to know how deeply sorry I was for being angry with him for pushing me to be the best version of myself. He forgave me without question, and he hugged me tighter than ever. He reassured me that he wouldn't give up on me and he would help me achieve anything.

I also needed to make amends with my three kids. The time away, traveling so much, and consuming myself in my business had made me miss out on so much of them and their lives. The tears they wiped away for me, the stress they saw me under — that is not how I wanted them to think of me. I went to each of them individually; I talked with them and promised that I wasn't going to just get better; I was going to *be* better. I vowed to be more present, more aware of who they are. I was committed to taking the time to enjoy each one of them truly.

I heard a voice in my head saying to hold on to my light, my rebirth. I realized that if I couldn't fill my cup, there was no way I could ever serve others wholeheartedly. I had to learn how to love and respect myself as a human before I could see myself as a wife, mother, artist, or anything else.

I started my journey with positive affirmations, and I remember the first day saying them, I wasn't fully convinced. I felt silly telling myself I was worthy, beautiful, and deserving, but it did make me feel better. And after making this a part of my routine every morning, I started to believe it and convinced myself that it was all true. I started making lists of all of the aspects of myself that made these things accurate and actually believed them. It was a beautiful revelation. I am powerful, worthy, kind, connected, unstoppable, and the world deserves to know who I am. I knew it was time to find my voice in my own way. It was time to be who I was called to be and teach myself that my story of success wasn't defined by what anybody else thought of my work, my education, or me as a person. The only person who had to believe was me. I was ready to get myself back together, my family back on track, and build a business on my own terms.

Through my struggles and rebirth, I learned there are no limits; any dream is possible. You don't have to conform to societal norms to be somebody special. Your past does not define your future unless you grant it the power to. Ambition is enough for you to be whatever it is that you want. There is strength in knowing who you are; you just have to dare to dig beneath the surface. Accepting yourself for your uniqueness and your differences deserves to be celebrated in every way. When you learn to respect yourself and your boundaries, then you are free to reach your true potential.

Now that I had gained this powerful wisdom, I was ready to get back to work. When I reopened my business it was on a solid foundation. My focus points were work-life balance and learning to become a better artist and a stronger business owner.

By prioritizing time to educate myself to learn more about what interested me, I created an artist niche that set me apart. Overall, I was holding my ground as an artist before being a photographer. I found my *why,* and I stayed true to that. I committed to only doing what feels right, and I am growing in my art by leaps and bounds. I feel, for the first time, that I am doing something that will leave a mark on this world. When I reminisce on how this started, was it smooth? No. It was rocky and it was rough. I literally put in blood, sweat, and tears into building something beautiful, and I would never have done it if I hadn't given myself the understanding to do so.

Everyone around me started to see a change in me. The new balance between my work life and family life began to impact my relationships and made me feel closer to those around me. My overall quality of life improved dramatically. I changed how I viewed myself — with confidence and self-awareness. My art started to reflect the "new me," and my talent began to bloom. I was proud and bold *and* unapologetically unique. I like to think that now my home life and work represent the new me. Now every time someone asks, "What do you do?" I strike my power pose and say, "I'm a PHOTOGRAPHER!"

If you need a break to repurpose and reground, take it. It is important to set boundaries and establish yourself as an artist and professional versus stressing yourself over things that don't actually matter. It can feel overwhelming at times to grow your business and yourself simultaneously, but by doing it one-step-at-a-time, you can achieve your dreams and reach your goals. You just have to know that you are capable of it. You have to believe it. You have to know that you deserve it, and you are most definitely worth it.

IGNITE ACTION STEPS

The first step to finding yourself is reflection and honesty. You have to be able to admit and accept your own faults. Realizing what you need to improve on isn't a bad thing. It's realistic. Self-awareness is the only way you're going to be able to make real changes and figure out what areas to work on.

Secondly, take those faults and implement real change. Digging deep to understand your actions and start working towards adjusting them to a comfortable point will give you clarity. Finding balance means prioritizing what needs to get done, accepting that you can't always say "yes," and learning that "no" really is a complete sentence. Taking time for yourself is necessary, but also take the time to appreciate the journey it took to get there. When I reflect on my journey, I see it all had to unfold the way it did, for me to appreciate my future as much as I do now.

Lastly, believe that you can own who you are, and always celebrate being unapologetically unique.

Aly Incardona — United States
CEO of Aly Incardona Photography, Photographer, Author
AlyIncardona.com
f *Mrs.Inc448*
 Alyincardonaphotography

Dr. Kerry A Egan

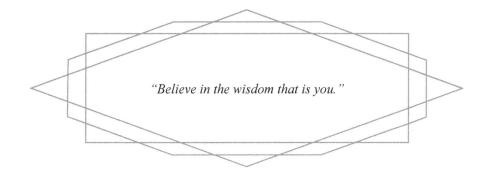

"Believe in the wisdom that is you."

IN THIS SKIN

BY DR. KERRY A. EGAN

My intention for you is to see your life in all of its experiences as the masterpiece of molding that it is. For many, messy is not welcome; unraveled is unacceptable. Take inspiration from the gifts that each moment, loss, challenge, and redirection brings you. When we trust in the ever-evolving process of coming home to ourselves, we connect to the wisdom of our soul, and we heal.

Our eyes glistened above toothy white smiles in the snapshot, taken while walking to the luxurious black-tie event aboard the British luxury liner, the *Queen Mary*. It was a picture-perfect photo, but not picture-perfect for me — a rich, deep irony of mismatched energies against a sparkling beauty and illusion.

There we were aboard this gorgeous vessel, seemingly at a peak moment, returning home to the United States after living and working in Germany. How incongruent to the experience I was having underneath the picture, silently terrified, deeply sad, and feeling totally alone. My marriage was barely functioning, and I was numbed from a series of upheavals, each change filled with an element of loss. I had just left another medical practice to move stateside, a decision that came on the heels of losing my uncle and my mother's diagnosis with metastatic lung cancer. I returned to support her for her treatments over the last year. On that turbulent and final trip to the States, I was returning to my mother, both of us weakened and depleted from all aspects of her chemo and radiation.

We were conditioned to "show well" in our family and inherited the need to be seen as "put together." I never realized how much of an undercurrent it was in my life, what presenting well required. However, I saw the cost and detriment of this programing as my mom unraveled. Her tumors were located all around her heart and lungs. I still remember when they put up the film on the X-ray box in her room. I was struck by the darkened masses enclosing her organs. My mother turned away, glazing over the severity of the image. I heard her lifelong mantra repeated, "I am not going there!" The masses in that X-ray showed her undigested pain, her stored emotions; suffocating. I saw and lived how dense and overpowering that energy is. However painful it was to see her physical deterioration, living and feeling her emotional collapse was the most excruciating part.

When she took her last breath, and her pupils dilated, as I knew they would, the muscular tension from guarding her body against constant, anticipated pain, dissolved. In just a moment, she went from being the physical mother I had all my life to a lifeless vessel that lay before me. There was a complete discharge of energy, or rather a transmission of it. I realized that every cell of my body knew that her energy transferred. My academic brain brought forth Einstein; energy is neither destroyed nor created; it simply changes form. Her essence was still "here," just no longer in the physical realm. In that moment of her last breath, I knew she "continued," but how and in what way, I had no clue.

As I washed and changed my mother for the last time, it was startling to feel the ease with which her body could be moved around. It no longer required the slow and gentle approach you take with a body in constant pain. For months we had to take care moving her painfully contracted body. Now, here lay this pliable vessel devoid of the "is-ness" of her. I felt grateful to somehow be part of this ritual of release.

My mother's crossing had ignited my awakening, quite literally. I started hearing her voice, hearing her talk to me. I was understandably grief-stricken but totally terrified that I was also certifiable. I knew my mother had stayed the last week with us without being able to swallow anything — no water, no food, no liquid morphine — and I wanted to know *why*? Doubting my own "hearing" experience, I called and consulted a medium. Cera, who was tender, gifted, and kind, preferred not to work with loved ones who had very recent losses in order to respect the grieving process.

I was flattened and taken aback. It seemed like the ONLY next step amidst this saturated and foggy moment. She asked me why I wanted to reach my mother, and I replied with a sob, "I want to know why she stayed and if there was anything she was trying to communicate." In a moment, Cera was asking if my mother was a "put together" lady; the exact words that would make me believe her energy was there; I laughingly replied, "Yes!"

Cera said, "She is here and ready; let's set up an appointment." Only half-flattened this time, I took out a calendar to set the date and time together.

The session was very emotional and tender — having that connected space with my mom's energy — and the experience was deeply healing. Cera was so beautifully supportive. The answer that came through Cera from my mother was simply that she had not wanted to go. It was not the wise insight I was holding out for but her truth all the same. My father, brother, sister, and I had spent the last week all together with her in vigil, as you do when supporting a loved one's crossing. Our vigil consisted of ordering take-out, and sitting together by her bed, going through pictures, talking about memories of times long gone; she was alive in the storytelling. She had said, "I didn't want to leave." There was that headstrong energy; denial and resistance were her trademark. I had confirmation of her energetic frequency signature, which validated my own "communications" with her.

I had several other guided meditations and energy sessions after that with Cera to begin to open my otherwise very closed and repressed senses to these unvoyaged horizons. My eyes were opened to the invisible, and not only was I interested, I was permitted to investigate further. I had a deep desire to understand this new and previously taboo realm, to know what was happening to me, and to heal in whatever way Mom was unable to. Partly to cope and partly to be inspired, I promptly pivoted into all things energetic and emotionally directed for healing.

For the months leading up to New Year's Eve, I had spent plenty of time in my mother's closet. My mother was stunning, and she loved clothes. She layered colors, textures, and jewelry; she was fun that way. Often, I would hear her tell me to go try on a certain thing in the closet, at which I would smile, laugh, cry and then go see what she was talking about. Sometimes I would argue as she had different styles for me than I had myself. On New Year's Eve, she was dictating to me and her "other daughter," Robyn, my best friend, what we were going to try on and take home. Those clothes were stunning to behold but a sign of something that was wounded deeper down.

From a young age, we are told to be quiet and not feel what we are feeling. In essence, to distrust our feelings and to hold those energies in order to "show well" and to be "put together." Messy was not welcome in my mother's world; unraveled was unacceptable.

Her mother, who had "made it" to the middle class and to a house out in the suburbs, taught her the importance of how things looked and how to present. Weighed and measured was how she reported to the world, all her value placed on her looks and size. My mother struggled with her weight and being comfortable in her skin for years. An unstable version of self-acceptance was produced by her mother's standards. This limited version of self-identity and acceptance followed her the rest of her life. When she passed, I found a pad where she had continued to record her breast, waist, and hip measurements; she had been taught and done this for years, or until she was too sick to. A lifetime tormented by numbers that are meant to be representative of her beauty, her acceptance, and therefore value. This was my mother's and, hence my conditioning. A line of strong, sensitive, and empathic women without permission to know or have what they wanted outside of mothering and family life. Left feeling alone, criticized, and judged as "not enough," rendered issues with depression and the toggling between binge and restrictive patterns of consumption. That same "thin skin" or sensitive nature that enabled her to read me like a book left her heartbroken and in tears if you did not agree with her. Guilt and shame were weaponized and used to keep within religious and societal lines. Denial and emotional shutdown were the main currency of resistance. I learned that disbelief and disembodiment of self were core agreements to these conditionings.

I began to understand that her, "I don't want to go there," translated to, "I don't want to feel that emotion… yours *or* mine." I see how that served as the only accessible boundary. Unfortunately, through these core agreements the nervous system exists in a perpetual state of freeze. This leads to helplessness, depression, and shut down, in an effort to protect the body creates contraction throughout our connective tissues, turning them into literal "body armor." Unaware of the cost of the armor purchased, suppressed and blocked energy is the source of *dis-ease.*

I had A LOT I was trying to suppress. Beyond the ache of my mother's physical passing, I had also changed continents, was building my own medical practice, and divorcing my husband. As my picture-perfect life dissolved, I realized I had been bound by the same conditioning as my mother. To be "put together" and to "show well" required a focus on all that is "skin deep." Armoring that skin to keep from being hurt equated to survival for my mother, and for me.

I was recognizing the cost of the conditioning of "showing well" and being "put together," the push, the drive, the go and do, so valued and indoctrinated into us. How does one continue to give and do and never learn to replenish or reset? We were never taught that; we learned the opposite, that our worth, value, and place in the world was defined through these patterns of going, giving, holding it all together, and looking good while doing it.

The change my mother's passing, and revisiting, sparked in me helped my armor to evolve. I was no longer "thin skinned," sensitive to criticism, or taking things too personally and to heart. Throughout all that change, I was seen as the strong one; the one that would show up. It was my pattern to shut down and armor up, to get through, to get by, to get on. This armor had kept me safe when I was forced to rebuild my finances, a medical practice, and new life as a single woman. But as the armor set in, got thicker and harder, my ability to feel or flex began to wane.

I remember trying to go to a yoga class and feeling completely rigid. A body that had once been pliable was in total lockdown while attempting a forward fold, sparking the instructor to ask if I was a runner. I remember laughing and somehow knowing my issue was all emotional. For the next three years, I committed and permitted myself to learn, study, grow, and heal by any means or cost: seminars, energy work, and the deep end of the pool with no swimmies on my arms. There were tissues in every pocket of my clothes as I moved through the awakening experience. I was exfoliating the layers of denied and shut down emotions, over-obligations, and grief. I had no idea of what a life cracked open was supposed to look like, but mine felt inflamed, chaotic, and messy.

I had not realized how much I was burning the candle at both ends while providing care to others all day. I was pushing to break out and break down all the armor while staying in a life model that required it. I did not truly understand or make space for the necessity of my OWN self-care, process, and integration. It was a recipe for depletion, breakdown, and drain. After diving deep to shed the layers of conditioning, grief, and pain without support, my system collapsed. My armor, quite literally, broke.

My issues started with my skin. I remember waking every hour to ice it. Then there were hot, itchy phases where I wanted to claw off every inch of it. I remember the dry, cracking, oozing phases, and I remember the peeling, sloughing off phases. Even as I write this now, I am struck by the symbolism. You can't get away from your skin as it pulsates and tightens through the contractions of extrusion and repair. Doctors visits, creams, labs, referral to specialists, more creams, steroids, a twenty pound weight gain, and still miserable. A year and a half into modern treatment, my $2,000 out-of-pocket skin biopsy was sent to Mayo Clinic, diagnosing me with contact dermatitis. Being diagnosed simply as; allergic to something in my environment brought me to a real crossroads. Between my mom's battle during her treatment and now my own, I felt disillusioned and disappointed by the limitations of conventional medicine. I was about to learn that my skin was the key to my complete healing, my path to creating the healthy boundaries that would save me.

The skin is our barrier and so the literal BOUNDARY between ourselves and the world. It is a sensing organ, the largest of our entire body, and is attached to all the nerve endings in the nervous system; the transponder of information inside and out. It holds the memories and stories of pleasure and pain, sensing threats and delight with equal measure. Skin is intimate, it is precious, protective, powerful, and beautiful in all shades and hues. And we can hold so much freeze, contraction, and tension in this miraculous tissue. The skin can breathe, absorb, and extrude life, preserving and affirming information. How we give and receive love through touch is preverbal in our development. Our skin senses whether a touch is safe, its intention before it even meets and depresses the receptor to inform the brain. We feel… before we even think. Our foundational understanding of love is through intention and sensation. Thin and translucent in the womb, your skin grows and heals all your life.

As modern medicine kept me in a holding pattern, I had to find my own way to care for my skin and what it represented. I continued learning and working with different healing modalities. Walking through your own health crisis as a health practitioner is so filled with the wisdom of humility. After three years of extremely painful rashing, autoimmune issues, viral issues, hormone problems, and extreme fatigue, I was brought back to myself. Breathing into the sensation releases the contraction and resistance and allows the molecules of emotion to be dispersed. I did not have this language then, but I have learned how to melt the armor, partner with sensations, and learned that healing is coming home to yourself; loving and accepting yourself and your body, radiating your true light, and reflecting your real inner beauty.

My mother birthed me twice, first in the physical world and then in the metaphysical world when she crossed. I now have the blessing of a parallel experience of what both those situations meant and what I have learned through them. I found the deepest richness in the beauty of self touch and loving self. That was my invitation to Ignite the wisdom within and come home to myself, comfortable in my own skin.

Back in my mother's walk-in closet, I recall going through the jewelry as I had done plenty of times before. Perhaps by fate, I found a crunchy, yellowed, plastic hospital bracelet that I HAD NEVER SEEN. I turned it over, and it was from my birthdate. My mother had worn this bracelet when she had me. Of all the jewelry, the shiny skin-deep pieces of armor she wore, she had guided me to find this faded bracelet, as though it was the most beautiful thing she had ever worn. I could feel all of the love she had for me from that day in that bracelet, and I could feel her all around me in that moment.

When you open your heart to magic, you begin to call it in from the Universe. See yourself in all your beauty despite any of the mess. Trust the parts of you that are coming out, showing up, and wanting to be seen. Look for lessons, teachers, and gifts in every moment of every situation. Love yourself wholly. Accept what you have been given. Know that you are exactly where you need to be and truly love the skin you are in.

Ignite Action Steps

- Know that you have full permission to make any decision in the world not tied to your conditioning. You have the right to change your mind, rethink things and take your time. Whenever you're feeling one thing versus what you have been told to feel, take a moment to stop and pay attention, swallow and take a self-embodied, introspective breath to guide you to the next step.
- Be Messy: Let all the emotions out in whatever way that feels good to you. Use your wiring to your advantage and utilize some aspect of breathwork, movement, and sound to release this stuck energy. Allow the process to go all the way to its completion, thereby transforming any remaining charge in the body and nervous system.
- Trust in the unfolding of your life. Allow the sensation and experiences to pass and ease. Be present in those moments of feeling, fight, flight, or freeze. Instead, as you want to contract and hold or attempt to control it, ride the ebb and flow. Breathe deep and take a long slow exhale. Repeat three times. Trust your breathing as it will bring you through the armor, back to the present, and into your all-knowing skin.

Dr. Kerry A. Egan — United States
Speaker, Healer, Teacher & Doctor of Chiropractic,
www.integrativesoulhealing.com

Mika Heinonen

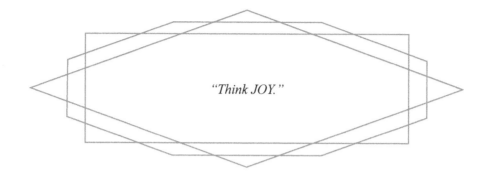

"Think JOY."

THE SOURCE OF SIGNIFICANCE

BY MIKA HEINONEN

This is for you, lightbringer. I know that you are seeking to deliver your light and love to and for the world. I know there have been hard times — maybe you are just going through one, but the light within you will show you the path through anything and everything. You are so much more than you dare to believe. I encourage you to use your light to make a difference in other people's lives. And, I want you to know that you are not alone. There are many of us.

Finally! Finally, I thought…

It had been throbbing somewhere in the back of my head for a few years, but I didn't have a clue how to do it! Or actually, what it even was.

Some people seem to know what they want and where they are heading. I had none of that. I had no clue what I should've been pursuing. I was just bobbing around without a sense of direction or having a thought for any worthwhile goal or meaning. But I felt like I had a dream. Or at least *something*. Yeah, I felt I had *something*. I did have flashbacks from my childhood where I'd had this same feeling, like *something* was touching my field or space. *Something* was trying to come to me, and it touched *something* inside of me.

My adult life history was in the corporate world. I used to work a lot around sales, marketing, and business development. And I loved my job! I had been in a rapidly changing technology field and was lucky enough to be with front-running companies that had world class knowledge about future possibilities. We were doing on-demand media streaming before anyone knew what it was; creating the advances that would shape the future of entertainment consumption.

But this industry had one thing that not everyone could take: change after change after change. I loved change. So it felt like home; not a problem at all. I got to work in a way that made me feel "significant" as I helped new sales people understand how to market our complex technologies to a wide audience. I felt like I was part of something, as I helped them accomplish their goals. It was a very enjoyable time in my life.

Yet, still, I did feel this inner urgency and what I had built my life around just seemed meaningless and the source was a deep subconscious survival program of not being worthy enough. My emotions swirled upward; a vortex of anticipation and anxiety and confused frustration. Even though my life seemed to be just perfect, I was struggling inside, sensing that there was something building, but having no idea if it was outside of me or within me.

Then, *finally*. It was late September in 2011, and I was sitting at a restaurant. On the other side of the table were the two men I had a business meeting with. The man who invited me was an officer in the Finnish Army, and the other one I was meeting for the first time. I had high respect for this officer, since I had seen him in front of his troops, displaying huge leadership charisma. But the other guy connected with me in a way I'd never experienced before. Beneath his traditionally Finnish exterior — so calm, composed, and expressionless — I could feel intense enthusiasm just bubbling. He was polite, a good listener, and genuine. He knew how to communicate, how to put the right words into the right order. And he had something more. Something that I didn't really understand, but I just felt. He spoke with conviction and confidence as he showed me his business plan; a way to take charge of my own future and earn extra money, and maybe even create a full income stream that would exceed anything that I could have ever dreamt of!

Such a business proposition regarding the monetary possibility would have been exciting for most people. But I wasn't like most people. I got excited about the energy they exuded. Who they were; what qualities they possessed. *Finally,* I felt this was it, this was what I had been looking for. A way to grow more, and more importantly, to be more and eventually give more. This really touched my inner wisdom, and the ignition had started. I understood that I could change my life by changing myself. So, I joined the business.

I found myself on weekly training sessions where I was able to meet like-minded people: people who had an entrepreneurial spirit, and were look-ing for something more. I found myself in large training events, where people shared inspirational stories about how their life had changed. They were normal people with extraordinary results and lifestyles. I got to go to big international training events, where the most successful people in the direct sales industry shared their insights and secrets. I myself was fortunate to be on stage several times in front of more than a thousand people. And I made hundreds of new friends who shared the vision of creating life-changing possibilities for anyone who was looking (because surprisingly, not everyone is looking).

Before I experienced this fellowship, I didn't even know an environment could provide so much support and encouragement. I used to just drift from day to day, thinking I must be going somewhere, but with no real direction. But the power of a vision that was created together — through sharing the same values, dreams, and passions — truly hit my heart and gave deep belonging and mean-ing. In that new community I was swapping given goals into unborn dreams. Colleagues into friends. Rationalizing into enthusiasm. Quarterly economy into lifestyle. Even though consciously I didn't understand what I was looking for, my heart certainly had taken the lead and created that possibility for me.

On top of finding a great community, I had some financial success also! There were moments I saw my income expand, as what I produced was being rewarded. The seed of entrepreneurial spirit grew to a tree that had such roots which could not be disregarded. I had learned much about attitude, how to produce, leadership, and how to grow and develop continually. And I knew how to help others do the same.

But then I got a higher perspective.

In 2014, I found myself in a training session where I learned about the capacity of our subconscious mind. In a room with ten other students of intui-tive healing, I came to understand things about energy, the universe, and even beyond; the true meaning of our existence and why we are here. It was a smaller community than I had previously shared, but no less close and connected. While my business training had shown how to generate new possibilities and opportunities, I was also gaining the wisdom to create the mindset that makes it possible. I was ignited by a new kind of flame. I understood that what I *am*, how I *think* and *feel*, is what I *create* around *me*. And, I had the power to change the definition of what *is* possible and impossible.

While that new perspective gave me amazing excitement and joy, I was also feeling very inadequate. I understood that we all had these gifts of intuition and healing, but my psychic abilities were just short of anything I wanted. To magnify the unease of this, my wife had the gift of clear clairvoyance and could see more intuitively with her eyes closed than open. I wanted to have the same abilities; to see things the way she could. But I had my own abilities to discover, a deeper knowing and sensing over seeing. I had to understand what might be possible for me with effort, training, and patience.

My soul seemed to have decided that it was time for me to begin a new path; the new path that felt and sounded perfect. I was journeying toward spiritual entrepreneurship; the *something* that had been waiting to take full shape for so long. I had started to see people differently. I saw beauty in them, in ways they themselves did not know. I felt a deep desire in my heart to help people find the light within them; to help them understand the greatness they possess. I guided them toward realizing they had the possibility to change and direct their life, they could achieve miraculous things, perfect health in every perspective, and lead a prosperous life.

It was amazing! I got to meet the most beautiful people who were ready to start their spiritual development journey. It was their divine timing to find out who they were and why they chose this life's path. And I was honored to witness it: the moment they found out that they had this light within; the true essence of their *Being*. The best part was that these people were the tribe I had been looking for. Many call these people your *soul family*, the people who will share your path and mission on this earth with you.

I also understood the deeper insight of my relationship with my wife, how deep our connection truly is. The depth of our souls' contract was made clearer, and we realized how many lifetimes we had shared in love. Things seemed to be just perfect.

It may have appeared I was actualized, but life is a struggle after a struggle after a struggle; something I learned in very real ways. But I also didn't know that it was a choice. Struggle and suffering was a choice and I had made my choice.

Once I started to focus on spiritual and mental growth, my finances were impacted because I was no longer earning the abundant salary I once did; before I started this new journey. Of course I knew that all there is, is just Love. It's the beginning and the end of everything, everything is a form of *Unconditional Love*. Within my soul there was such satisfaction and a sense of significance that made me feel whole. But without the money to prevent very real suffering, the subconscious survival programming of threat of starvation or homelessness crept in. I was unsure if I could remain tethered to my spiritual strength. If I could not provide security for my family, could I truly say I was expressing my love for them in this existence? These two sides of the same coin, that were expressions of Unconditional Love, seemed to be unattainable for me at the same time. *Was it true that there was only room for one or the other?* Of course not. But did it take some time to change their frequency to a more compatible form? Absolutely, though I wish I could have done it easier. I had to understand deep in my awareness that *they are both made from the same energy, and there is no controversy between them.* But to truly know and understand this in my heart just wasn't possible at that time.

I found myself questioning my faith and trust. I even questioned my existence and was asking myself *why* I chose to come to Earth and experience this suffering. I was struggling to distance my self worth from financial attributes. I found out that I believed that money would corrupt my energy. That somehow, money was not pure and dirty. That I had to choose between money or happiness and I believed I would then possess the energy that my decision would incorporate. I certainly didn't want to identify with the energy of dirt. But I couldn't be happy either. So for me it was neither, not money nor happiness.

I was at the point in my life where I needed to start using the virtues and abilities that were put into me, that I had learned during my eternal journey through infinite time and unlimited space. Little by little, I started to move forward. I began to find actionable ways to implement my awareness. I reached out to more people, teaching them and helping them change their life's trajectory. I understood that I needed to be more to accomplish what I felt in my heart was my mission.

When I asked, I got opportunities to learn and improve my virtues. The best teachers had already come into my life in the form of family and friends, and others arrived. It wasn't always easy, because lessons presented as hardships before there was development. I had doubts and I had to practice faith to know how to start moving. I asked for trust and took one step. I asked for guidance and took another step. I asked for forgiveness, grace, peace, understanding, acceptance, and love. And nothing was denied to me. I understood that I was the one who needed to accept that I was worthy of receiving all of this. When I was ready to do that, the doors for abundance in all the areas of my life were opened. I could see myself creating whatever I had dreamt of. *Finally,* I knew how to create a life of pure joy.

Yet, not much changed. Things seemed to be stagnant and I felt that I was unable to propel forward. I was able to help others in many ways, and they seemed to be permanent changes that benefited their lives. So what was it that was keeping me frozen and unable to move? It seemed that there was still a missing ingredient that I was unable to add to my recipe. Even though I tried lots of things and was serving many people in many different ways, I couldn't feel my soul being satisfied. My intuition and ability to help others transform their beliefs, feelings, emotions, and overall energy — and therefore their lives — had reached a point where I believed that anything *is* possible. It just wasn't possible for me. Or so I had chosen to believe.

I was laying in my bed in the middle of deep thought, feeling the energy swirling through my body. It felt like the vibration and frequency was getting higher and it helped me to have a grander perspective on my life. I could see in my mind's eye that the pieces of the puzzle — all that I had learned in the past — started to come together. I understood that instead of trying to push forward with force, I had deeply misunderstood the law of sacrifice. I used to affiliate sacrifice with suffering, lack, loss, and death and had manifested that into my life along the way. Not huge events of tragedy, but the feelings of inadequacy or absence while there was an abundance of different perspectives of unconditional love around me. Beautiful wife, amazing kids, trustworthy friends, it all was there, but my own perception of my life made me project this false reality. I realized the truth: that the highest perspective of sacrifice is the ability to let go of things that are no longer serving you or not meant for you anymore. And when I understood this, everything changed. When I let go, I was able to receive.

I was shown that my widened perspective offered me the secret ingredient, focus. When I started to focus my thoughts, feelings, and actions and allowed God to magnify all that I was, there was no impossible. I could feel the unity and seamless connection to everything and just knew what was my part of this Divine game we all are playing. While being conscious and aware, I could let my Divine part take charge and let go of the need to control. That brought the feeling of complete focus and alignment.

I decided to extend my reach by helping and supporting others in expanding their growth and purpose. I understood that this had happened to me with every author, teacher, coach, mentor, leader, and many friends that had touched my life during my journey.

The final touch I needed to have pure bliss and love was *focus*. Now I was *free*. Free to move forward. With *love*, *joy* and *happiness*.

Finally! Now I'm finally there.

On the road, did I have many "how did I get here" moments? Or moments where I lacked trust, faith, self-worth, or even self-love. Oh yes, definitely! You name it, I got it! And I suppose there might be some interesting future experiences too! Because as my mentor says, "Everything will be good in the end. If it's not good, it's not the end."

When I finally witnessed my true moment of pure, focused, purposeful wisdom, I understood that everything I ever did, and will experience, is the greatest gift of all. I saw that I needed and *chose* to experience all of this. It gave me the necessary learnings, perspective, understanding, compassion, and love to help those who have the desire to be more, and go through their darkest moments; to rise from survival to significance. Without my darkest moments, I couldn't have the compassion for all situations, and full loving acceptance for others, and... for me.

Luckily, from now on I feel I can learn from a Higher Source without the need to create drama or trauma or to sacrifice my wellbeing and happiness. Now I know that I'm unconditionally loved by my Creator. I am and have *always* been enough. Just like you. You are the source of significance. You are truly *something*.

IGNITE ACTION STEPS

- Get to know yourself, have a professional to help you find the best within you.
- Find out what qualities, values, and virtues you need to develop and cultivate to be the version of yourself that you need to be.
- Decide what you want to do. Who to help? What to share? Focus on that thing.
- Take soul-led and Divinely aligned action. Never stop.
- Let God help you.

Mika Heinonen — Finland
Coach, Mentor, Teacher, Speaker, CEO of Ole Vapaa Oy
www.mikaheinonen.com
www.olevapaa.fi
🟦 *mika.h.heinonen*
🟦 *heinonen_mika*

Katie Smetherman

"Keep moving forward as grace in motion."

ALL THINGS ARE POSSIBLE THROUGH STRENGTH AND GRACE

BY KATIE SMETHERMAN

As you read my story, I want you to know that even if you are a hardwork-ing spirit, you must remember to allow yourself grace. It's okay to take the time *you* need when you are struggling. Low seasons don't have a time limit. It isn't about getting over them but through them. I encourage you to find the help you need from your family, friends, and professionals to get back up and achieve all the dreams you set out for.

"You can do anything you set your mind to."

Mom drove that phrase into my brother's and my heads since the day we were born. My parents were dedicated and supportive while still being very strong and career-driven. They made sure that we knew the power of hard work and commitment — be it toward your job and your coworkers, or your friends and your family. As I grew up, I learned that what Mom meant was: anything is possible as long as you have the heart and courage to keep moving forward in your goals. If my brother or I were ever "slacking off," my mother would give us a laundry list of to-do tasks to get done around the house. This hardworking spirit drove me to excel in my academic studies and my personal hobbies. I never 'half-assed' anything; I always used my whole ass.

When I got my whole ass to the University of Houston, I was unsure of what I wanted to do with my life and career. Two years in, I switched majors and decided to pursue graphic communications. I knew then that I wanted to be in the creative field of fine arts because aside from the power of hard work, Mom also taught me softer things in life. She loved sewing for her family, painting, and being in the garden. She created so many wonderful things with the simplest of ingredients, and because of that, I have found joy in being creative. I love the thrill of making something from nothing, the endless possibilities of what hard work and commitment can make. Mom and I frequently traveled to the Houston Museum of Fine Arts to look at all the exhibits, from sculptures to paintings, abstract to realism. We devoured it all and spent hours captivated and mesmerized by the different artists. I found myself drawn to the more graphical pieces, and it inspired me to dive deeper into my studies.

I surprised my parents by graduating summa cum laude, then moved into the working class, changing jobs only once in six years. I was with a great company but felt it was time to spread my wings elsewhere. I began to think about my next big move and milestone. My parents, always my biggest cheerleaders, sensed a big change was on the horizon and made sure that I knew I had their support in whatever I chose to do.

My dream was to have my own design company; a dream I frequently discussed with anyone who would lend an ear. I knew I would have to further my education and skill set with more business strategy to make this dream a reality. I wanted to complete my master's degree, but it meant moving away from my hometown of Houston, Texas. Mom had been a big inspiration for my love of traveling and exploring new places. After graduating college, she backpacked through Europe with only a camera bag as her suitcase! I listened intently to her stories, excitedly anticipating the day when I would have my own travel adventures.

I achieved both goals at once when I was accepted into the Instituto Europeo di Design (IED) in Milan, Italy. To share that exciting news, I purchased the movie *Roman Holiday* — a favorite of mine and Mom's. I told my parents, "I'm about to have my own Roman holiday!" They were ecstatic and decided to travel to Italy with me and help me move to my new apartment while having a two-week Italian vacation of their own.

Those two weeks with them were pure bliss. It was the first time my dad traveled overseas on a non-military trip. Mom had never been to Milan and was so excited to try all the different foods. As we walked around the city, taking photographs and stuffing our bellies, I felt more like a parent than a daughter. I guided them through the streets, teaching them how to use public transportation, while making sure that we hit the city's tourist spots and its hidden gems. I loved every minute they were there and was so sad to see them leave. But it was time to get to work on my masters in brand management and communications. I was committed to pushing hard in this concentrated program and completing it with high honors.

One month in, everything changed. COVID-19 arrived and Milan shut down. Everything stopped. My classmates and I were devastated and lost. This international program boasted students from all over the world. Milan was in the strictest lockdown in history outside of Wuhan City, China. My classmates and I were stuck, thousands of miles away from our family and friends.

Over the next six weeks, my mental health began to plummet. I missed everyone back home. Most of my classmates found ways to return to their loved ones until the university was open again in the fall. I was one of the remaining six (out of twenty) still in Milan. By the end of April, I arranged to return home for the summer and continue my studies online. I quarantined with my boyfriend at his family's lake house since Mom had a heart condition, and the doctor said it wouldn't be safe for me to see her yet. But that didn't stop Mom. She drove to the lakehouse to visit us and drop off supplies, keeping our six-foot distance and wearing masks while talking on the big porch. I was able to go back to *my* home on Mother's Day, and gave my parents the biggest hug of my life.

Summer flew by, and I was working hard on my program in Italian time, so my sleep schedule was all sorts of wacky. I woke up around 2:30 AM and would be in classes until 9 AM… I napped in the middle of the day, then woke up to continue working in the afternoon while my classmates slept. When fall arrived, I was back in Milan, determined to finish the last four months of the program strong. My classmates and I worked together day and night on our thesis project. I slept at my friend Christina's house to cut down on travel time and honor the curfew that was in effect.

A week before the presentation, I called home and was told my mother was in the hospital due to her heart condition, and she was getting ready for surgery. I was terrified, but my parents assured me that she was with the best cardiologist in Houston. I said I should come home. She said she would be fine: "Just continue working hard for your dreams."

My team absolutely crushed our first presentation. The program director was beyond proud of us. We planned to go out and celebrate completing the first half of our thesis dissertation. Only one more presentation to go before we graduate! I grabbed the phone, eager to tell my parents. I always texted before calling to make sure they were available to talk. I feverishly texted on the group message I had with my parents. Dad replied, *"Katie, please call me."*

In that instant, I knew. I knew what my heart was trying so hard not to feel — my biggest nightmare was coming to reality. I picked up the phone and sat down at Christina's long, white kitchen table. I heard Dad pick up. "What happened?" I asked. His voice was one I had never heard before; I barely recognized it. This strong, stoic man only broke character when he was truly comfortable with someone or if he heard a joke that sent him into a silent laughing fit, wheezing until he caught his breath. This man on the phone was not that man. This man was frail, trembling as he said the words out loud: "Mom died."

My world screeched to a halt. Every emotion vanished from my body, filled with only ache; a pain that I had never felt before in my whole life. Someone had physically removed my stomach, twisting it into knots before replacing it in my body. My chest tightened, and I couldn't breathe. A herd of elephants was sitting on me. *This can't be true. Please don't be true. I'm not ready for this. I'm only 30. I'm not ready. I'm not ready.*

I immediately started crying but tried my best to keep my composure enough to listen to Dad tell me what happened. Listening to the pain and sadness in his voice as he broke down shook me to my very core. His best friend, my mom, had just passed away, and he was trying his best to be there for his daughter but just couldn't. Even my brother, who had always been similar in personality to Dad, was having difficulty talking as Dad passed him the phone. His voice was distant, shaky, and barely audible.

It then struck me. *This is it. It's just the three of us now.* I didn't want to accept that Mom could just suddenly not be here anymore. Thoughts raced through my head, with each second getting heavier and heavier. *How? She was fine the day before. We talked on the phone less than twenty-four hours ago. Why was I in Italy, a million miles away? I said I'd come home. She said she'd be fine!*

Connection issues forced us to hang up. Christina had sat next to me while I was on the phone, patiently waiting to hear the news. She knew it wasn't good, but didn't know the extent. I had told her a lot about my life since moving to Italy. Studying in the same program, we'd become fast friends, with similar mindsets and a shared love of adventure. When I had told her earlier that week about Mom going into surgery, she immediately started praying for me and my family. She had a way of grounding me and prayed with me when I would get stressed or nervous. She always supported me in any way she could.

I looked at her and choked out, "Mom died." As the words left my mouth,

I crumbled onto her wooden table. My head hit my hands as I folded in on myself, crying out and screaming, unable to get control of my shaking body. I couldn't breathe. It was as if the world stopped turning, and I was alone.

Christina was in shock but immediately consoled and comforted me. She held my hand until the phone rang again. I took a deep breath and tried to hold back what I could as I answered for a second time. Dad proceeded to tell me about the complications in surgery that morning. "I'm so sorry for not telling you sooner, but I knew that you wouldn't have been able to stand if I told you before your big presentation."

And he was right. I couldn't stand anymore. I felt as though I was disconnected from my body. Nothing in this world made sense. I couldn't stop shaking, frozen to my very core, the cold emanating from inside me, permeating my bones out to my muscles. Everything around me was foggy and blurry. I was unable to process the room in front of me… unable to think about anything else. I was numb. Lost. Cold.

My cries were so powerful and excruciating that I felt like a shell being tossed in the waves, caught in the undertow. I hung up the phone and looked over to see Christina silently crying with me. She carried me to the couch, with every movement being gentle, comforting, and motherly. I was taking the smallest steps, but she was patient, making sure that each of her steps matched mine.

I texted my boyfriend, Colby, instantly after the phone call. I didn't know how he would take the news. All I could muster to write was "*I need to call you now. It's an emergency.*" He was still working, but called me almost instantly after I sent him the message, which was reassuring. I could barely get the words out of my mouth, and as they left my lips, I thought. *Why am I in Italy right now?* Out loud, I asked Colby questions I knew he couldn't answer. But he responded as best he could. Even though his voice was different, I could still recognize it compared to my dad and brother. He was still my supportive, caring Colby, except this time, there was a new level of softness to him that I had not seen before. He was in shock but there for me, giving me space to cry and vent while being present in the devastating moment. I wanted to be with him in that instant, hating the long distance we had between us, as he was still in Houston.

The only words I kept repeating like a broken record were, "I need to go home… I need to go home." Christina jumped into action. While still wiping away her own silent tears, she got onto my computer and started looking for the next available flight out of Italy. She took the phone as I collapsed on the couch to finish answering questions Colby had.

That whole night became a weird blur. I kept finding myself in various rooms because I would space out as if sleepwalking, and Christina had to come to get me every time. I started to pack, dazed and robotic. Suddenly, I felt a gentle hand on my shoulder,

"Katie?" It was Christina checking on me again.

"I need to pack," I said feebly, with barely any oxygen.

"You don't have to do that right now. We have time. Let's sit down back in the living room."

"Okay," I responded, almost as if I was programmed.

Christina stayed by my side that entire night until my plane took off. She went back to my apartment and helped pack my entire room into two suitcases and a backpack. We made it to the airport at 2 AM, waited in line, and tearfully parted ways as I started the hard, long, nineteen-hour journey home. During the flight, I had to stifle my tears, my sniffles, any sign I wasn't okay for fear the international flight attendants and police would suspect I had COVID-19 and keep me from flying. Every minute was excruciating. *Just make it to the airport, then Colby will be there to take you home,* was all I could focus on.

As Colby's red truck came around the corner, I knew the long, arduous journey was finally over, and I was home. I feebly stood up, grabbed my suitcases, and walked to him. I collapsed in his arms, suddenly losing the ability to stand and unable to stop my body from violently shaking. He softly scooped me into the car and drove towards my parents' house.

I walked through the door, half expecting Mom to be there. Somewhere. Anywhere. But, I knew in my heart that wasn't the case. I saw Dad first and rushed to his arms. I heard him repeating, "I'm so sorry. I'm so sorry," and I knew what he meant. Sorry about Mom's death. Sorry for keeping me out of the loop during her hospital stay. Sorry I had to find out in the worst way that Mom passed. Sorry I couldn't be there when she left this physical world. And sorry that he couldn't do anything about it.

The next couple of weeks became another strange blur. I couldn't focus or pay attention to simple things and would find myself lost within my own home. Between the heavy sobs that left me helpless, weak, and confused, I tried to help Dad the best I could with all the funeral preparations, connecting with family members, and being there for my brother and Dad. I made it through the funeral and wake with all our family and Mom's friends in attendance. I was able to navigate the multitude of people asking me, "What happened?" and having to relive and reshare my mother's death with each question asked.

I took time off from my master's program. I had two months to go until graduation. I didn't know how much time I needed or if I would continue. I was feeling unraveled; *She was supposed to be there for my graduation. We had plans. How was I supposed to continue without her?*

Mom was a strong, devoted Catholic, on top of her being a hard worker, empathetic leader, and inspiration to her colleagues. She knew God's grace, faith, and love and shared it with everyone she met. There were days that I would stress about missing school, but I didn't know how I was supposed to keep going. I found myself leaning on her faith and wisdom; knowing that she would want me to persevere, push forward, and continue pursuing my dreams. She had taught me patience and timing and understood that hard work requires balance and rest. I needed to rest, heal, and find my footing, but I also knew from her fortitude that if she were standing beside me, she would encourage me to carry on.

Amidst all my pain, confusion, and exhaustion, I felt Mom's hand on my shoulder from Heaven, saying, "You need to give yourself grace and space to grieve."

I understood her message. I was relieved. Her sharing permitted me to take care of myself. But how?

I was raised to work hard and put my all into what I do. How was I supposed to come to a screeching halt? Mom's death had swept the ground from underneath me, and I felt useless in my immobilization. Yet, I knew to be able to keep moving forward, I had to find the strength to rest.

A week after the funeral, I was sitting in my room, staring at my computer. I heard Mom's words, "You can do anything you set your mind to." I knew in my heart that Mom would want me to continue my education and complete my dream of having my master's. She wouldn't want my life to completely stop just because God had different plans for her. This guided me back on my feet, and I found the strength to grit my teeth and carry on with my studies for the final month of the program. I knew that if I could finish this month up and reach this lifelong goal, then after I graduated, I would be able to have all the time and space I needed to grieve and heal fully.

Our thesis dissertation and graduation day arrived. The events combined into one Zoom™ call. It was the strangest graduation of my life. I set aside my mixed emotions and locked them in a box buried deep within my soul — for me to emotionally and mentally give a presentation, it was the only solution. My classmates and I knocked the presentation out of the park and couldn't contain our smiles. Even though the entire thesis dissertation was online, you could feel the energy, joy, and happiness through the screens. Then the pivotal moment:

graduation and reading of our scores in the program. "Catherine Smetherman with a cum laude final score of 106." I had exceeded the program's 100 point grade and received additional bonus points, meaning I had successfully graduated with honors. I saw my director give me a proud, special smile as she read my score. I could feel joy radiating from within me and all around me. *I did it. Check it out, Mom. I really did it. I did what I said I was going to do. I got my master's, and I did it with honors!*

I walked downstairs to my living room, which was decorated with "Happy Graduation" signs and my family's smiling faces. I hugged everyone. Dad had visible tears; his eyes filled with a look of pride and happiness. We both wished Mom was there at that moment and knew she was, in her own special way. I was joyous, but deep down, also very sad.

Now that school had finished, I continued to give myself grace. I paused working in my freelancing business for three months before connecting with my clients again. I knew that Mom would want me to keep going and achieve all the dreams I had set out for before she died, but I also knew that I couldn't do it alone. I sought out grief therapy from a reference given to me by one of my clients. This helped me to find some grounding and peace. I took breaks between getting back to the workflow and allowed myself to grieve still. Mom would have wanted me to be kinder, gentler, and give myself more grace than I had ever seen.

After the year was over, I came to terms that just because Mom isn't here physically, it does not mean that I do not have a relationship with her. I also learned that hard work isn't just tactile things. It is being committed to the softer things in life, like your emotions, your relationship with family and friends, and how you give time and care to yourself. I still miss Mom terribly, but I know that we both love each other, and she is with me in all that I do. When I am being creative, she is beside me, cheering me on. When I design things, I hear her voice in my head, feel her love in my heart, and gain wisdom and guidance from her.

Seven months after Mom's passing, I opened up my dream business, Brand Studio Creative™, a fully operating branding and design studio. Every day, I keep Mom with me. She watches over me as I conduct my business and grow. She continues to love me, and I continue to love her with every step I take. She gives me comfort through the waves of grief that still come from time to time, as she reminds me, "You can do anything you set your mind to."

I want you to know; *YOU* can do anything you set your mind to. Life struggles are just seasons, and they are meant to come and go. Nothing is set in stone. If you are in a period of struggle, know that it will pass. As you exercise self-care, grace, and your own personal wisdom, you will discover that you *can* accomplish those things you set out to do. You can feel everything from joy, to pain, to grief, to success. The many emotions you feel are a part of living. They are what allows us to feel alive. Mom wanted so much for me, and I want the same for you. Live your greatest passion, create your life, design your world to be exactly as you envision it, and know that you deserve to *honor* you.

IGNITE ACTION STEPS

Give yourself grace, especially in the hardest times, because that's when you need it most. For those with a strong, hardworking personality, it can be really easy to be hard on yourself. But here's the thing, you can not work at 110 percent all the time; that is the fastest way for you to burn out and become bitter toward life's greatest treasures. Allowing yourself space to process, understand, and mentally work through trauma experiences unlocks your new knowledge and underlying strength. When you sense a hard time coming, first recognize that the season you are in is about to change. Then start writing positive lists about you and your life. This can be what you are proud of about yourself that day or week. It could be things you are grateful for in your life. Or even things that you are excited about for the future. Whatever it may be, make sure that it is positive and encouraging for you. These lists help serve as a reminder of all the good things in your life and that the season you are in is simply a period of time.

Dark seasons are only that — seasons — meant to come and go, as you keep moving forward in life. Know that you will still have time to reach your dreams. When those struggle seasons come, first remind yourself that it is just a season. "This too shall pass." This is the time when you need to be more in tune with your body and practice self-care. Take eight deep breaths in and out as you count down, helping to relax and reset your nervous system. If you are in the middle of work or a project, move to another location, whether it's to another room, to your backyard, or even go for a walk around the block. Changing your physical location will help to encourage your brain to switch moods.

Seek out help when you need it and are ready to accept it, through counseling, doctors, or friends. It's okay to feel emotions, whether it's happiness, fear, anger, or sadness. Humans are complex creatures, and we were given this gift of being able to feel strongly about our surroundings. Remind yourself that it's okay to cry when times are hard. When Mom passed, I leaned on my family and friends, crying and screaming, trying to navigate through the shock of her sudden passing, and I'm so glad that I did. Seeking out help is a strength, not a weakness. Humans were created to live on this earth together, not live in a vacuum alone. Helping others is how we adapt, change, and grow. When I was ready to talk about Mom to a professional, I reached out to my friends for a grief therapist, and it was the best decision. I'm so grateful for the relationships that have gotten deeper and stronger simply because I asked for help.

Baby steps mean that you are moving forward, even if they feel small and insignificant. It's easy to lose sight of your progress and accomplishments in life. And when you are in a period where you feel like you are not making any progress or headway in your life, be it your job, your relationships, or personal development, remember that you are not a tree and are capable of moving and changing. Whether your steps are small or grandiose, steps mean that you are moving forward. Write down actionable things that you have done that you are proud of yourself for doing. Then write down other goals that you wish to achieve. Remember to write down both big and small goals so that you don't get overwhelmed by only the big goals. Small goals can be something as simple as getting a new client, reaching that next level in your video game, or cleaning that part of your house you have neglected. Big goals can be as big and ambitious as you want! Go skydiving, learn how to scuba dive, plan a big trip to a new city, start the company you have been dreaming about. If you want to take it one step further, after you have your small and big goals written down, go in and write some goals that are in between. That way you are always seeing the fruits of your labor and keeping your mental spirits high.

You were placed on this earth to do incredible things. Don't ever forget that or lose sight of your uniqueness. Each person is different, possessing qualities and talents that only they can do. You are here to bring something new to this world and your community around you. Do you need help finding out what makes you unique? Think back to all the times you were helpful to your community and friends. What did you do that someone was thankful for your help in those moments? Next, think about the skills and talents you have that others may have mentioned to you they wished they had. And then finally, think about what hobbies or personal activities you enjoy, just because they bring you happiness and joy. All of these things are just a taste of what makes you, you!

If more people embrace who they are; the world will become a more interesting place to be.

Katie Smetherman — United States
Master of Brand Management and Communication; Brand Coach, Strategist,
& Designer; Founder & CEO of Brand Studio Creative™
brandstudiocreative.com
 @Katie.Smetherman
 @brandstudiocreative
 KatieSmetherman

BOOKS AND RESOURCES MEANINGFUL TO THE AUTHORS OF IGNITE YOUR WISDOM

Dr. Erin Sepic
- *"Courage is telling the story of who you are with your whole heart."* Brene Brown.
- *You Are the Answer* by Michael Tamura. This is a beautiful guide for spiritual beginners and seasoned seekers alike.
- www.intuitiveawarenesscenter.com for Gwyneth and Dr. Gayle's stories

Jane Kilpatrick
- *The Road Less Traveled* by Dr. Scott Peck

Jenna Haji
- *It's Ok That You're Not OK: Meeting Grief and Loss in a Culture That Doesn't Understand* by Megan Devine
- *The Hot Young Widows Club* by Nora McInerny
- *Grief Resource Guide:* https://sunrise-studio-wellness.square.site/grief-resources
- *Soaring Spirits International*: https://soaringspirits.org/

Jo Dee Baer
- Resource KPMedia TV: Life's Milkshake Moments: https://Watch.KpMedia.TV
- *Resource Syndicated Radio*: Building Fortunes Radio www.building-fortunesradio.com/jodee
- www.healthcoachjodee.com
- *"Ignite the Hunger in You"* https://www.amazon.ca/Ignite-Hunger-You-Greatness-Humanity/dp/1792341768

Katherine Davidson
- *The Narcissistic Abuse Recovery Program* by Melanie Tonia Evans
- *Healing the Shame That Binds You* by John Bradshaw
- *Women Who Love Too Much* by Norwood Robin
- *Treating Trauma from Sexual Betrayal: The Essential Tools for Healing* by Dr. Kevin Skinner, LMFT, CSAT-S

- *Stop Sex Addiction: Real Hope, True Freedom for Sex Addicts and Partners* by Milton Magness
- *Hardwiring Happiness The New Brain Science of Contentment, Calm, and Confidence* by Rick Hansen, Ph.D
- *Self Compassion: The Proven Power of Being Kind to Yourself* by Kristen Neff Ph.D
- *Your Sexually Addicted Spouse: How Partners Can Cope and Heal* by Barbara Steffens, Ph.D, LPCC, and Marsha Means, MA
- *Braving Hope 12-Week Program* by Michelle Mays
- *Move Beyond Betrayal Step into Clarity, Power, & Connection*
- https://vickitidwellpalmer.com/

Loree Kim
- *The Power of Now: A Guide To Spiritual Enlightenment* by Eckhart Tolle

Marla Ballard
- www.jumpoffpoint.net

Mary A Swan
- Christian Pankhurst - founder of HeartIQ™ www.heartiq.org
- Tej Steiner - Heart Circle founder and author of "Waking Up with Everyone Around Us" www.tejsteiner.com
- Rachael Jayne Groover - creator of The Art of Feminine Presence® www.theawakenedschool.com

Mary Streeter
- *Mindfulness Guided Meditation*
- *R.A.I.N Practise Tara Brach*
- Podcast: *Zen Mama and Everyday Gurus*

Melanie Summers
- www.confidencetones.com
- www.promotethetruth.com

Michelle Norlin
- Resource Book, *Letting Go* by David R Hawkins,MD.,PH.D.
- Resource Book, *Power of Vision* by Dr. Myles Munroe

Nicole Mixdorf
- *'Blueprint for a Balanced Life'* - https://balancebynature.com
- Nicole's Interview on the Good Day Show - https://tinyurl.com/gooddayshow

Sarah Cross
- *Unstoppable* by Nick Vujicic. Published by Crown Publishing Group, 2013
- https://www.charitywater.org/about/scott-harrison-story
- https://www.mercyships.org

PHOTOGRAPHY CREDITS

Alyssa Incardona - *Aly Incardona Photography*
Barb Lilley - *Charity Swords Photography*
Cindy Tank-Murphy - *Jody Kmetz Photography*
Alessandra Pasut - *Michael Spratt-Johnson*
David Small - *Skyline Video Pros*
Diana Lockett - *Ian Coll Media*
Erin Sepic - *Homer Horowitz Photography*
Jameece Pinckney - *Morgan Morrison, ThirtyWonPhotography*
Jane Kilpatrick - *Mike Gaudaur, Quinte Studios*
Janine Marek -*Chelsie Graham Photography*
JB Owen - *April Stead*
Jenna Haji - *Aimee Marsh, Willow and Thyme Photography*
Jo Dee Baer - *Laz and Andrea Photography, Orlando, FL*
Katherine Davidson - *Anja Shafer*
Katie Smetherman - *Greg Jackson*
Kerry Egan - *Kimberli Nelson*
Loree Kim - *Melika Lynd Photography*
Malissia Woodall - *Karen Jackson Photography*
Marla Ford Ballard - *Your Journey Studios - Tom and Carol Davis*
Mary A Swan - *Trish Beesley*
Mary Streeter - *Bob Streeter*
Melanie Summers - *Malika Hobeheidar*

Michelle Norlin - *Leah Rees Photography*
Mika Heinonen - *Paula Heinonen*
Nicole Mixdorf - *Mily Cooper Photography*
Peter Giesin - *Kersti Niglas*
Rosemary French - *Ten West Photography*
Sarah Cross - *Unscripted Love - Photography by Aimée*
Sharon Eistetter - *Ellen Nguyen Photography*
Stacie Shifflett - *Arianna Fallacaro, Arianna J Photography, Sarasota, FL*
Steph Elliott - *Herring Photography*
Stephanie Fabela - *Dan O'Neil*
Tish Meehan - *Pam Crichton, Ten West Photography*
Victoria Rader - *Jane Mikhailenko*

THANK YOU

A tremendous thank you goes to all those on the IGNITE team who have been working tirelessly in the background teaching, editing, supporting, and encouraging the authors. They are some of the most genuine and heart-centered people I know. Their dedication to the vision of IGNITE, along with their integrity and the message they convey, is of the highest caliber possible. They each want you to find your IGNITE moment and flourish. They all believe in you, and that's what makes them so outstanding. Their dream is for your dreams to come true.

Production Team: JB Owen, Dania Zafar, Peter Giesin, Katie Smetherman, Liana Khabibullina, Carolina Gold, and Frich Dy

Editing Team: Alex Blake, Michiko Couchman, Mimi Safiyah, and Sarah Clark

Project Manager: Diana Lockett

Project Leaders: Sarah Cross, Steph Elliott, Jo Dee Baer

A special thanks and gratitude to the entire team for their support behind the scenes and for going 'above and beyond' to make this a wonderful experience. Their dedication made sure that everything ran smoothly and with elegance.

A deep appreciation also goes to each and every author who made *Ignite Your Wisdom* possible. It is your powerful and inspiring stories, along with your passion and desire to help others that will Ignite the wisdom within each and every one of us.

To all our readers, we thank you for reading and cherishing our stories; for opening your hearts and minds to the idea of Igniting your own lives. We welcome you to share your story and become a new author in one of our upcoming books. Your message and your Ignite Moment may be exactly what someone else needs to read. Readers become authors and we want to be that for you.

Thank you for being a part of the magical journey of Ignite!

WRITE YOUR STORY
IN AN IGN*I*TE BOOK!!

**THE ROAD TO SHARING YOUR MESSAGE AND BECOMING
A BEST-SELLING AUTHOR BEGINS RIGHT HERE.**

We make YOU a best-selling author in just four months!

If you have a story of perseverance, determination, growth, awakening, and change...
and you've felt the power of your Ignite Moment, we'd love to hear from you.

We are always looking for motivating stories that will make a difference in someone's life. Our fun,
enjoyable, four-month writing process is like no other — and the best thing about IGNITE is the
community of outstanding, like-minded individuals dedicated to helping others.

With over 700 amazing individuals to date writing their stories and sharing their Ignite moments,
we are positively impacting the planet and raising the vibration of HUMANITY. Our stories inspire
and empower others and we want to add your story to one of our upcoming books!

Go to our website, click How To Get Started, and share a bit of your Ignite transformation.

JOIN US TO IGNITE A BILLION LIVES WITH A BILLION WORDS.

Apply at: www.igniteyou.life/apply   **Find out more at: www.igniteyou.life**

CPSIA information can be obtained
at www.ICGtesting.com
Printed in the USA
LVHW071539250522
719695LV00010B/263